THE
FIVE NATIONS
STORY

THE
FIVE NATIONS
STORY

David Hands

TEMPUS

First published 2000

Published by:
Tempus Publishing Limited
The Mill, Brimscombe Port
Stroud, Gloucestershire, GL5 2QG

Typesetting and origination by Tempus Publishing Ltd.
Printed and bound in Great Britain

British Library Cataloguing in Publication Data.
A catalogue record for this book is available from the British Library

ISBN 07524 1851 3

CONTENTS

ACKNOWLEDGEMENTS

The first Five Nations Championship match I saw in the flesh was a 0-0 draw between England and Wales at Twickenham in 1962. The absence of any scores did not matter. The excitement, the frosty breath of thousands on a cold January day, the fact that I had a seat (whereas on my first visit to Twickenham I had to stand behind the tallest man in the ground), the bird's-eye view from the back of the old West Stand and the peripheral knowledge of sharing in an honoured tradition all served to make a youngster's day.

That tradition is part of rugby, professional or amateur, part of the game's soul. It has been a delight to sample it so many times and, on particular occasions, a privilege when the sport has transcended the mere winning and losing of a game. The first acknowledgement should go, therefore, to the players, those who have made the tradition what it was and is; in particular to the players of recent seasons whose efforts have done so much to sustain the game when all around them seemed to be administrative chaos.

A second acknowledgement goes to those whose company has been shared in press boxes up and down Britain, Ireland, France and farther abroad. The media are a convenient scapegoat, and sometimes deserve to be, but there has always been a genuine pleasure in each other's company among the rugby-writing and broadcasting fraternity. That company does not change so much as do players but, young or old, there is a mutual appreciation of the game's best qualities and, by and large, a desire to sustain those qualities.

For both reasons it has been a pleasure to attempt to set down a history of the championship, to reflect idly on the merits of this player or that, whether Wavell Wakefield or Wilson Shaw were as great, or greater, players in their time as their modern equivalents. My thanks, therefore, to Chris Harte of London Sports Reporting for suggesting that such a work might be undertaken, and to James Howarth of Tempus Publishing for taking up the suggestion. I am grateful also to John Griffiths, whose work as a statistician and historian of the game has earned him worldwide recognition alongside his invaluable books, and to my son, Robert, for checking the text and the grammar.

Rugby is on the verge of an exciting future. The first faltering professional steps are still being taken but the core values are already embodied in the Five Nations. Those values will pass to the Six Nations Championship in February 2000 only if those who play, and those who organise the players, recognise that they are part of a rich tradition which draws in spectators, broadcasters, sponsors, the whole paraphernalia of modern sport. I'm sure they will do so.

David Hands
Rugby Correspondent, *The Times*
Fordingbridge
September 1999

INTRODUCTION

Sunday 11 April 1999 was a wonderful day for sport. This is not a statement of the obvious, that the sun shone, the ground held firm underfoot and that talented, well-coached players came together to play international rugby. It was wonderful because, within the twenty-four hours that embraced the conclusion of one match in Paris and another at Wembley Stadium, the philosophy which draws generation after generation to sport, to kick or pass or strike a ball, was thrillingly affirmed and at the same time the uncertainty of Rugby Union's oldest international championship was emphasised yet again and for the final time before the Five Nations Championship became, with the addition of Italy, the Six Nations Championship.

What's in a name, you may say? Sport is nothing without its traditions and passionate arguments between one generation and another. Is the presence of one more name on the log so revolutionary a step? In this instance, it is. Rugby Union is at once a world sport and a relict of colonialism, a sport bounded by conservatism but, potentially, a major player in the greedy television market, a game brought so recently to the teeming population of China but played well – that is to say, competitively at the highest international standard – by little more than a dozen countries.

So, when change is broached in what has been, for nearly a century, the market-leader for the game, then it has a significance of its own. The Five Nations Championship was born in the days of the British Empire, before the First World War, though few if any acknowledged it then by such a title. The championship, if such a thing existed, lay between the four home unions of England, Scotland, Ireland and Wales. The addition of France during the first decade of the twentieth century was not taken very seriously, even though it is, in all probability, the French who must be credited with the invention of the Five Nations – their sporting press referred in the early 1920s to the *Tournoi des Cinq Nations* (doubtless as a Gallic way of breaching the insularity of the home quartet) and the name stuck.

But, because international rugby was played in relatively few countries, the tournament assumed a stature beyond normal proportions and not always directly linked to playing standards. It could not be compared with football's Home Championship because, for all the traditional England-Scotland rivalries engendered by that series, football was always the genuine world game whose own world championship is now some seventy years old. Football has its World Cup, then its regional championships – such as the European – then its local rivalries alongside a throbbing club game which has, at times, threatened to assume an importance beyond that of international competition.

Rugby, with its different ethics and its essentially middle-class background, could afford to be snooty – and often was – in the twists and turns it took. For most of the twentieth century there was only one universally-acknowledged international championship – the Five Nations. That the better, more successful rugby was being played in the southern hemisphere by New Zealand,

South Africa and, latterly, Australia, was not necessarily a problem until, in 1987, New Zealand and Australia effectively forced a World Cup upon rugby and showed up the poverty of playing standards in the northern hemisphere. It also created a need to grow the game which, for far too long, had not been recognised and thus fostered the circumstances in which Italy could be invited to the Five Nations party. Twenty years ago the same argument could have been made for Romanian participation but the will was not there and the challenge of that sadly-beautiful country declined.

Having so unique a quality, the Five Nations also developed a certain cachet which the British habitually attach to their sports. In this respect the French eagerly followed suit: for many years the French Rugby Federation was accustomed to playing, say, New Zealand or South Africa before Christmas in the certain knowledge that the games would not be sold out, whereas the chic Five Nations – always played in Paris rather than the provinces – would attract capacity crowds. It was part of the social calendar.

Nowadays the tournament is given 'event status' by the corporate world. It was partly this that roused the hackles of the southern hemisphere, who knew their rugby was better but who played it before a smaller population base. Hence the introduction in 1995 of the tri-nations tournament, though comparisons are facile: that competition, played between South Africa, New Zealand and Australia, does not have the same spectator appeal precisely because of the vast distances that separate the contestants. The Five Nations has its delightful annual routine of migration from one capital city to another, from London to Cardiff to Dublin to Edinburgh to Paris. By road, ferry, rail or air each is accessible to the other and each offers a distinctly different atmosphere.

The ambience off the field is matched by the distinct national characteristics of the contending countries. Each stadium is different: Twickenham, deemed by its original detractors to be too far from the centre of London to become popular, proved a massive investment for the Rugby Football Union, who had played games at the Oval, Crystal Palace, Richmond and Blackheath as well as provincial centres in Leicester, Manchester, Gloucester, Leeds, Dewsbury and Birkenhead. Billy Williams' cabbage patch, as the ground was fondly known, became a place of pilgrimage, defined by the French over the years as the Cathedral of Rugby. As the motor car became the preferred method of transport, Twickenham's West Car Park has become almost as well known for its pre- and post-match parties as the main pitch itself.

Cardiff Arms Park has a unique city centre quality which allows patrons to pour out of the central bus or train station and into the pubs, knowing the ground is no more than 300 yards away. For many years it incorporated a greyhound track and enjoyed a reputation for having a distinctly heavy surface which was, in 1960, overwhelmed by floodwater when the nearby River Taff burst its banks. Whereas Twickenham was a home for the moneyed middle and upper classes, the Arms Park was a working man's ground. With a new stadium for the 1999 World Cup, Cardiff must establish a new identity for itself. Until 1954, the Welsh Rugby Union also used Swansea's St Helen's ground, which had the considerable merit of having a sandier base than the capital and drained far better.

Scotland's home at Murrayfield was opened in 1925 with a grand slam secured by victory over England. Most of their previous games had been played at Raeburn Place or Inverleith, with the occasional excursion to Glasgow or Powderhall Gardens. Murrayfield, too, is a place of pilgrimage in that it is little more than a short walk or bus ride from Princes Street in the centre of Edinburgh and, set amidst open gardens, allows rugby followers to converge as though it is the hub of a spoked wheel. So many of them did in 1975, when Wales were the visitors and Murrayfield still possessed its huge standing area, that an unofficial world record of 104,000 was claimed – unofficial because many are known to have watched without tickets and several thousand more were locked out. During 1999, Australia claimed the attendance record when 108,000 watched them retain the Bledisloe Cup against New Zealand at the new Stadium Australia, built in the Sydney suburb of Homebush for the 2000 Olympic Games.

Lansdowne Road in Dublin has aspects of all the others, save that the suburban railway runs directly underneath the stand. In no other city is it quite so simple to organise a pub crawl before and after the match – assuming, that is, that one actually arrives for the match in the first place. The Irish Rugby Football Union has pondered for years about upgrading the ground, where they first played in 1878, or removal to another centre and when they reach their decision there will be a large body of opinion to tell them they are wrong. Coincidentally, it was in 1954 that the IRFU also discontinued games at Belfast's Ravenhill ground, so recently reclaiming some of its former glories during Ulster's unexpected and acclaimed gallop to the European Cup in 1999.

France have never held a championship match outside Paris, but have moved around that delightful city: from Parc des Princes to Stade Colombes via Stade Pershing and then back to Parc des Princes near the Porte St Cloud. The great bowl of the Parc – distinct from the somewhat ramshackle Colombes (which hosted the 1924 Olympic Games and where France won Olympic silver, losing to the United States of America) – became beloved of visiting teams for its fiery atmosphere and splendid playing surface. In 1998, the new Stade de France was opened in the northern suburb of Saint Denis, capable of holding 80,000 – more than any other ground in the northern hemisphere – but lacking the suburban splendours (and restaurants) of the Parc.

Simplistic as we tend to be, we have also attached labels to each nation. That fashions come and go, that the laws change, that a team strong in the backs may have a powerful pack of forwards twenty years later, does not concern us: thus the English become strong up front, dogged, unimaginative and over-reliant on the boot. The Scots, renowned once as dribblers of the ball (formerly one of the game's art forms, now scarcely ever seen), work on an axis provided by the middle five of half backs and back row and offer a more fluid game than any other British team save the Welsh who, down the years, have displayed as pure a form of back play as any, allied to a native wit which seems made for the rugby ball.

Ireland's characteristic is organised (and sometimes disorganised) chaos which, on its day, will bring them the most notable of scalps but which is hard to sustain over the course of four distinct matches, which may explain their minimal return of only one grand slam. That their playing base is small is another explanation, far smaller indeed than that of France who have become all things to all men. They have traditionally purveyed a sometimes classical, sometimes mercurial form of back play and all-round mobility, yet they have won grand slams off the back of giant packs and kicking fly halves. In Britain, we always expect the French to run the ball and, when they do not, we sulk; so do the French themselves, because it is in that way this most expressive of nations can best parade themselves on a rugby field.

This 'knowledge' of what to expect does not diminish over the years but becomes more like an old friend. The charm of the Five Nations is the biennial return, the check that one's favourite pub in St Stephen's Green or café in the Place Concord is still there. Even Englishmen will have been put out by forgoing the visit to Cardiff while the Arms Park was being converted into the Millennium Stadium during 1998 and 1999; the 'away' game with Wales, at Wembley, was not quite the same. For Englishmen, particularly, there has always been that sense of uncertainty crossing the border since they were never entirely aware how restless the natives were – history makes sure of that.

Indeed, history is invariably bound up with international sport. With England having been so dominant in its subjugation of various parts of the globe, sport has often become the battlefield upon which old slights, real or perceived, can be repaid. There have been times when observers at Murrayfield, watching the demolition of yet another over-comfortable England XV, could close their eyes and dream of wild, cattle-raiding parties by claymore-wielding Scottish reivers over the border; in Wales, the game itself, translated from England's public schools into close-knit, working-class communities, became an expression of national identity like no other.

All this is part of the fabric of the Five Nations, but the essential ingredients of any sport are the games and the players themselves. This book aims to celebrate a great tradition which, in the most technical sense, was recognised only in 1993 when, with the presentation for the first time of a trophy, rules had to be drawn to establish the criteria for winning. Until that time you would have looked in vain for regulations relating to the championship; all you had was custom and practice, most of it established by commentators in newspapers rather than by the game's administrators.

The championship is littered with quaint anachronisms, by triple crowns and wooden spoons, by such outrageous possibilities as a five-way tie – which did occur in 1973, when each country won its home games and lost away. The title was deemed to be shared – one of those situations where you might as well say that everyone lost rather than everyone won. Such a scenario was treated very firmly by Terry Godwin in *The International Rugby Championship 1883-1983*, who adopted the sound principle that the country scoring the most points was entitled to believe it had done better than its rivals. Thus for Godwin the winner of the 1973 championship was Scotland (though Wales possessed the better difference between points scored and points conceded).

But such detail is the very stuff of rugby, a game of myth and legend, whose origin on Rugby School's Big Side is clouded by the uncertainty of what William Webb Ellis did or did not do when he infringed the regulations of the version of football played at his school by picking up the ball and running with it. There is no 'triple crown', beyond the expression adopted by journalists around the turn of the century, while the 'grand slam', which is the northern hemisphere's ultimate achievement, has been plucked from a card game: to achieve a grand slam in bridge it is necessary to win all thirteen tricks so it is merely the principle that has been stolen – that of winning all four matches in any given season.

Even in this, rugby is inconsistent. Wales won the very first grand slam during their first golden era in 1908, but there was no regular pattern of fixtures in which each of the five nations met the other until 1910. The Welsh did the same again in 1909, so there is a certain irony that when Scotland finally came to the party by playing France in 1910 (the year in which the Five Nations Championship as we have recognised it was established) it was England who took the honours. In the year when Twickenham was inaugurated as the national ground, England's clean sweep by a side led initially by Adrian Stoop and then by Edgar Mobbs and John Birkett – names revered in English rugby history – was foiled only by a scoreless draw with Ireland.

But that again is typical of the Five Nations. Every so often there have been periods when one country has apparently dominated the rest and critics have talked blandly of 'two divisions' within the five, yet the reality is that grand slams and, more frequently, triple crowns have been habitually denied countries whose expectations have been justifiably high. The championship has a mesh of trip wires set for the unwary over long periods – England in Cardiff for thirty years, Ireland and Scotland in Paris for a similar period, Wales at Twickenham for twenty years – certain countries have seemed unable to win at certain venues.

Frequently one individual player will claim a place in lore. The most vivid instance of this occurred at Twickenham in 1965 when Scotland, poised to win there for the first time since 1938 and assuage an otherwise dismal season, were denied by Andy Hancock. The Northampton wing ran ninety metres for a try which earned England a 3-3 draw and himself immortality which, for a player who was picked only three times and was on this occasion playing in a completely unmemorable match, is no mean achievement.

That, too, is the ephemeral nature of sport – that a player should claim a place in history beyond his individual merits. Here, however, the context is sound in that the championship is so highly regarded. The first international rugby match, between Scotland and England in Edinburgh's Raeburn Place, was contested in 1871, so there had been nearly forty years of competition to assist the development of the game before the Five Nations became accepted. Britain's proliferation of newspapers, both national and provincial, breathed life into the leading matches for a mass audience and the visits from overseas of such exotic teams as the 1888/89 Maoris from New Zealand and their more illustrious successors of 1905 (the first All Blacks) as well as the touring team from South Africa a year later proved how swiftly the game had put down roots abroad.

For four years there was no more than the England-Scotland series to arouse national passions (how fitting that the series should have so distinct – and real – a trophy as the Calcutta Cup as its prize, after the presentation of the finely-wrought silver cup to the Rugby Football Union by the failing club in India in 1879). Ireland bowed onto the stage in 1875, losing to England at

Kennington Oval with a side drawn from the Irish Football Union (established a year earlier) and the Northern Football Union of Ireland (1875); those two unions co-existed until 1880, when the Irish Rugby Football Union was inaugurated and served, thereafter, as a benchmark for co-operation between north and south, even in the dark days of the 1970s when terrorist activity in Ireland was such that Wales and Scotland chose, in 1972, not to fulfil their fixtures at Lansdowne Road. The silver lining of that clouded season was proffered by John Pullin, England's captain, the next year: 'We may not be much good', the Bristol hooker told the gathering at the official dinner which followed Ireland's 18-9 victory, 'but at least we turn up'.

Wales made a hesitant debut in 1881, conceding seven goals, six tries and a dropped goal to England at Blackheath. So complete a victory was seldom to lighten England's way in the years that followed, but Wales branched out to play Scotland and, intermittently, Ireland, though the Irish had no great opinion of Welsh play in those early years. Jacques McCarthy, the leading Irish critic, held vehemently to the view that Ireland had been 'swindled' out of victory in the first game, in 1882, and that the Welsh were inclined to try 'every other trick and dodge that the rules have not provided against, as a prostitution of a noble, fair and chivalrous game'.

The confidence of the other countries had advanced sufficiently to support the formation of an International Board in the mid-1880s, as a body to sort out such disputes as arose from the 1884 England-Scotland game when the Scots disputed the try from which England kicked the goal and won the match. England, founders of the game with the oldest governing body, disputed the arrangements for the new body and, for two seasons, played only one international fixture, which was against the touring New Zealand native team, the Maoris.

By the time mutual relationships were restored, an even greater menace threatened English rugby, whose traditional power had always been in the north of the country, allied to the swift minds of the students from the two universities of Oxford and Cambridge. The dispute over broken-time payments led to the formation of the Northern Union (later the Rugby League) in 1895 and it is worth noting that, of the next 50 matches played after that date, England – hitherto the strongest country – won 15 and lost 31. The balance of power had been irretrievably shaken and it took a world war before England assumed a position of playing authority once more.

During the dog days of the nineteenth century there were other, fundamental changes in the game. In 1871, the first international had been played with twenty players on each side. Not until 1877 did teams of fifteen compete and then with nine forwards and back divisions which tended to include two half backs, two three-quarters and two full backs. Frank Hancock introduced four three-quarters to the Cardiff club in the mid-1880s, a system adopted briefly by Wales in 1886 and continuously after 1889, though the other three unions did not follow suit until 1894.

As Queen Victoria's reign drew to a close and a new century dawned, Wales assumed a supremacy over the game in Britain and Ireland. Central to their game, as much for the organisation brought to his team as his flaring play in the centre, was Gwyn Nicholls, who appeared on 24 occasions for his country and toured overseas to Australia in 1899. He perceived the possibilities of the system introduced by Hancock and thought them through in a manner typical of New Zealand but not of the development of the British game.

Ireland earned an unbeaten triple crown in 1899 but, during the next ten seasons, Wales won five such crowns and in each year lost no home games in the championship. The names of the backs of that era still twinkle like jewels and the only consistent threat came from Scotland. Rhys Gabe, Jack Bancroft, Willie Llewellyn and Dickie Owen were to their time what Gareth Edwards, Barry John, Gerald Davies and J.P.R. Williams became to theirs seventy years later. Scotland, leaning heavily on the students of Edinburgh University, gleaned three crowns with the assistance – which will have a familiar ring to followers of the modern game – of Alfred Fell, a New Zealander who played with style and grace on the wing. They were led for much of that time by Mark Morrison, who performed the same role for the British touring side of 1903 in South Africa.

Perhaps it was appropriate, therefore, that a Scot, Cyril Rutherford, should have had so much to do with the rise of French rugby during this first decade of the new century. Rutherford worked in France and played for Racing Club of Paris: he even led France in an unofficial international against Canada in 1902 and later became secretary to the French Rugby Federation. He and his colleagues aimed high and the first official international undertaken by the French fledglings was against Dave Gallaher's New Zealanders on 1 January 1906, though eleven weeks later they played England. However, France had played only eight official games before, on 1 January 1910, they began their first full championship season against Wales in Swansea.

Their path was by no means smooth. In 28 internationals before the outbreak of war in 1914, France won only once, by a point against Scotland in 1911 (which was doubtless hard to live down in Edinburgh). They did not win their first outright championship title until 1959 and during the intervening years had suffered the indignity of being thrown out of the championship in 1931 by the home unions, who believed that semi-professionalism and foul play were rife in the French club championship. They did not return until after the Second World War, in 1947, but it could be argued that they have made up for their absence, their achievements including an appearance in the inaugural World Cup final in 1987 and in that of 1999.

France were among the actors in the final twenty-four hours of the Five Nations Championship. Having, for the first time in their history, won back-to-back grand slams in 1997 and 1998, their decline from grace was spectacular. Haunted by injuries they struggled to beat Ireland by a point in their defence of the title in February 1999 and then lost to Wales and England. There was an inexorability in England's step towards the grand slam and, on the last weekend of the championship, they had merely to draw with Wales at Wembley to win the championship. Victory would give them the slam and the triple crown.

In the event, they received nothing. On Saturday 10 April Scotland went to the Stade de France and played compelling rugby against a France side completely lacking in confidence. By doing so they gave themselves three victories from four and an outside chance of the title; by the evening of Sunday 11 April, the Scottish Rugby Union was making plans for the official presentation of the trophy at Murrayfield because Wales, with a late conversion by the nerveless Neil Jenkins, had denied England victory by a single point.

It was sport at its kindest and cruellest. It contained all those patronising characteristics critics have seen fit to attach to each country but also the unique variety which is so much part of the Five Nations Championship. It contained skill and drama, the quick wit of Glenn Metcalfe – a Scot made and moulded in New Zealand – and the dead-eyed discipline of Jenkins. It was the perfect precursor to a new millennium.

1
OFF THE MARK
1910-1924

The first match of the first championship involving the four home unions and France was played on the first day of January 1910 at St Helen's in Swansea, where the chilly charms of Mumbles Bay may have been lost on the eager French. Having been knocking so regularly at the door – which was opened most reluctantly by Scotland, who were first approached for a fixture by France in 1907 but granted it only three years later – France found themselves pinioned by a ten-try hiding.

That it may have been the end of a wonderful Welsh era of back play and the beginning of the 'Terrible Eight' forwards led by that muscular Christian, the Reverend Alban Davies, was neither here nor there to the French. They lost 49-14 (by today's values it would have been 69-18 but this was the age of the three-point try and the four-point dropped goal) and appeared to have problems filling their quota, plucking Joe Anduran from (possibly well-merited) obscurity as an assistant in a picture gallery to play in the forwards.

Anduran was one of six newcomers to international rugby and never featured again. Yet it was a start, albeit three years after the prescient comment of the rugby correspondent of *The Times*, who wrote that 'within the space of a very few years an international championship, organised on even broader lines than is now the case, will be an accomplished thing. Pure amateurism will, of course, be the essence of that competition, and professional football is never likely to be able to boast so desirable a development. In such a competition France in a short time is likely to play an honourable part.'

At times the French may have despaired of acceptance. After all, two of the home unions had been at each other's throats a year earlier, Scotland levelling charges of professionalism at the Rugby Football Union because of England's support for an agreed level of expenses paid to the touring Australians of the previous season. It was, indeed, a period in which the taint of professionalism was perceived round every corner – it was little more than ten years since the northern breakaway and leading clubs in England and Wales were not averse to accusing their rivals of illicit payments.

This was, in many ways, the final knockings of the nineteenth century – before the Great War destroyed a generation – when heavy betting was prevalent in all sports. Regional cup competitions were fought out with great intensity, successful sides were watched by thousands and (literally) borne home in triumph if they won. There are regular accounts of club teams returning from a cup victory by train, being met by cheering supporters at the station and carried in open carts to the team hotel or the ground – today's open-top bus tours of city centres seem tame by comparison.

Yet it was to be England's season, aptly enough perhaps, since the Rugby Football Union finally opened the ground at Twickenham for which they had paid £5,573 two years earlier. There were eight newcomers, one of them the black-haired marauder from Blackheath, 'Cherry' Pillman, whose disruptive play from the back row became a feature of his international career. But, more to the point, England possessed a pair of half backs whose accomplishments were as great as many of their successors: Dai Gent, the Gloucester scrum half who went on to become a leading rugby writer, partnered Adrian Stoop, the Harlequin who was among the foremost thinkers on the game of his time.

Stoop captained a team which also included Ronnie Poulton on the wing. Genius is an easily-employed description, but those who saw Poulton (he later changed his name to Poulton-

The England team that defeated Wales by 11 points to 6 in the first international at Twickenham, 15 January 1910.

Palmer) play are happy to accord it to him. 'There was a magic in Ronald Poulton's play that was, I think, unique', W.J. Carey wrote in 1921, six years after Poulton's death from sniper fire, aged twenty-five, at Ploegsteert Wood in Belgium. 'For witchery of style and individual attractiveness he stood alone.' Poulton ran with a distinctive grace but was blessed with the ability to see space. He also had a trick of crossing his feet in full flight, which allowed him to swerve past opponents who believed him to be running straight, a particular gift when he was playing centre.

Wales had played eleven international matches without defeat before the inauguration of Twickenham. Given that internationals are now ten-a-penny, it should be remembered that those games covered a period of nearly three years at a time when players – particularly in England – did not always choose to be available and when the vagaries of selection were legend. However, from the start of a miserably wet January day, fortune favoured the English. They had not beaten Wales since 1898, but here they scored a try within the first minute after Wales had kicked off, when Stoop, running the ball left, created what would now be called a ruck before the backs made space for Frederick Chapman on the wing.

Bert Solomon, the Cornish centre who decided afterwards that it was too far to travel for any future internationals, scored another try, but on a muddy day it was the steadfast play of William Johnston at full back that caught the eye. A product of a famous Bristol rugby institution, Colston's College, Johnston played 16 times for England and, like the other twenty-nine players, looked as though he had been involved in mud-wrestling by the end. 'The selection committee must be well pleased, as they ought to be, with the choice of the fifteen; and after so brilliant a victory over such formidable opponents, they are not likely to make many alterations', *The Times* enthused, before going on to comment on the 'nasty crush' of people leaving the ground in their carriages and cars – not much change there.

England won 11-6 and it was to be twenty-three years before Wales recorded a victory at the new ground. The match was refereed by John Dallas, the Scot who had gained unwanted notoriety five years earlier when he chose not to award the 'try' by Bob Deans which would have earned New Zealand at least a 3-3 draw in their controversial, highly-charged game with Wales in Cardiff. Deans' claims to have scored, embellished in the *Daily Mail*, are now the stuff of legend, but it is not often recalled that Dallas had played in Scotland's pack only two years earlier: these were the days when young men filled many roles, not only as players but as match officials and administrators.

A week later, France took themselves to Edinburgh and discovered how highly they were rated by the Scottish Rugby Union. Possibly recalling the events of a decade earlier, when the union had disproved the accounts of a visit made to Paris by an Edinburgh XV who then received a French XV for matches played in Edinburgh and Glasgow, the SRU chose not to award caps for the match and probably believed themselves wise after winning 27-0. Such attitudes remained current into the 1980s, when the home unions – Wales were most frequently the exception – chose to field representative XVs rather than a full international side against opponents they believed were not of the first water.

Two youngsters from Dublin University emerged to help Ireland thwart England on their first visit to the new Twickenham ground, where nearly 20,000 expected fresh heroics after the defeat of Wales. Dicky Lloyd and Harry Read set a new benchmark for half-back play; Lloyd made a speciality of playing fly half at a time when each could work the scrum. Had his dropped goal been successful (and he kicked seven such goals in internationals), Ireland might well have won the scoreless game, in which England were reduced to fourteen men for much of the second half by the absence of the injured wing, Edgar Mobbs. Lloyd might be described as Ireland's answer to Adrian Stoop, a master tactician and able leader who gave added structure to Ireland's approach.

This was to be England's only decline from grace. Although there were eight newcomers to the side, France were beaten 11-3 at Parc des Princes in front of some 8,000, yet took considerable credit from a tight defensive effort marshalled (as has always seemed the case in France down the years) by their scrum half, Guy Latterade, from the Tarbes club. Thus England went to Inverleith looking to clinch their first outright championship since 1892 and duly did so after a second half in which Scotland were run ragged before the largest crowd (30,000) to have watched an international in Edinburgh up to that time.

It had been a successful first season for the reshaped championship, even if the addition of France led to a glut of tries when they played outside Paris. Wales returned an aggregate of 88 points, a record which stood until 1976, and scored 21 tries, although the other four countries scored only 28 between them. As has so often been the case with England, however, the sleeping giant promptly returned to its slumbers and left Wales in 1911 to claim what may be regarded as the first 'genuine' grand slam – that is to say, a clean sweep in a season when all five countries had the opportunity to do the same.

This was to be the last ray of glory before a long period of Welsh decline. The championship saw 55 tries scored in its ten matches, England managing 13 to Wales's 18, and 247 points were scored. Even now, when the regulations have been changed so frequently to encourage try-scoring, it was a level of achievement equalled only once, in 1998. Of those tries, two went to Douglas Lambert, the substantial Harlequins wing who also kicked five conversions and two penalty goals to record 22 points in the 37-0 win over France. The French may have been entitled to think Lambert their nemesis: he played against them on their first international against a British or Irish side, at Richmond in 1907, and scored five tries to establish a mark yet to be surpassed by an Englishman (though Rory Underwood equalled the feat against Fiji in 1989).

While Wales worked their way towards the title, Scotland nose-dived to their first whitewash and provided France, en route, with their first championship win. It came at Stade Colombes in the first match of the season and was a deserved reward for the work of Marcel Communeau, the hard-working forward from Stade Français who led France in 13 matches between 1907 and 1912. The margin of success was narrow enough in all conscience, at 16-15, but French glee was unconfined as their backs ran in four tries, two of them to winger Pierre Failliot, who was also a talented sprinter on the athletics track.

The season marked the end of George Hamlet's international career, the Ireland forward leading his country throughout the season before his thirtieth and last game, against France in Cork. He had played since 1902, winning a reputation as a scrummager of quality and a good dribbler of the ball. Now, though, his country, like all the others, had to play second fiddle to England, who not only took three championships in succession but included back-to-back grand slams in 1913 and 1914. Still more importantly, the careers of three players who helped significantly towards their recovery in the post-war period were established.

There is no doubt that the naval officer, W.J.A. 'Dave' Davies, was one of the great players to appear for England at fly half. In 22 appearances, spanning the war, from January 1913 to April 1923, he was only once on the losing side and that in his first match, against South Africa. James Baxter, chairman of the England selectors when Davies was captain, wrote without equivocation that Davies was 'the greatest matchwinner who ever put on a football boot … Idolized by the men under him, trusted to the full by the Rugby Union and all its officers, his lovable personality and intense enthusiasm for the game marked him out as the ideal captain.' There are very few players, of any era, who have won such a paean. Even allowing for a degree of hyperbole which the mannerisms of the age allowed, Davies, twenty-one years old when he was first capped, was clearly a wonderful performer. He would have been the first to observe that much of his representative career was played alongside two accomplished scrum halves, F.E. Oakeley before the war and C.A. Kershaw after it, but respect for his gifts was universal.

The England team that faced Scotland in 1914. Standing: A. Maynard, A. Dingle, J. Watson, C. Lowe, S. Smart, G. Ward, J. Brunton, J. Greenwood. Seated: W. Johnston, C. Pillman, H. Harrison, R. Poulton-Palmer (captain), L. Brown, F. Oakeley, W. Davies.

Above all, Davies valued attack as the best form of defence. He followed in the iconoclastic boots of Stoop but possessed more weapons in his armoury – all of which were the results of self-imposed training in the individual skills. Critics described him as inscrutable; that is to say, a player whose opponents could never determine what he would do next. Every golden age has to have its goldsmith and that was Davies' role. During his six seasons, England played twenty-five games and, of the four they did not win, one was drawn and two lost when Davies was not playing. Even Wales could reluctantly take pride in his achievements, since he was born in Pembroke Dock and played for England at a time when Welsh clubs provided England with enough players to cause serious debate between the respective unions about player eligibility.

England also introduced Cyril Lowe and J.E. 'Jenny' Greenwood to their side, Lowe on the wing and the goal-kicking Greenwood in the back row. Lowe has claims to rank among the best England wings of all time, his ten-year career earning him 18 tries in 25 matches, including hat-tricks against France and Scotland in 1914. Greenwood's judgement was sound enough to win him the captaincy when international rugby resumed in 1920, and he thus provided the continuity from the days of Pillman to those of his equally-skilful successors, Wavell Wakefield and Tom Voyce.

Lowe was also one of the few rugby players to be immortalised in verse, in this case by P.G. Wodehouse, who lamented the poor service he received from his colleagues ('There he stood, poor little chappie, looking lonely and unhappy, while the other players frolicked with the ball…', the inventor of Jeeves and Bertie Wooster wrote as he gently reminded the selectors of the talent in their midst). Typical of the player was the friendly bet he took on with George Will, his opposite number in the 1914 Calcutta Cup match but also a friend from Cambridge University. 'We had a bet that the other one wouldn't score a try,' Lowe said. 'We were a bit better at scoring than we were at defending or predicting.' Lowe's hat-trick was nearly matched by Will, who scored two tries in Scotland's 15-16 defeat, during which Pillman broke his leg and did not play again.

While England were building their side, elsewhere it was a struggle. The French offered an omen of the shadow under which their rugby was later to fall when crowd trouble erupted during and after the 1913 meeting with Scotland in Paris. That the match was played at all was remarkable since Stade Colombes was rendered unplayable by flooding and, at twenty-four hours' notice, the match was switched to Parc des Princes. During the match the crowd took exception to the refereeing of John Baxter, the English official, who required a police escort from the field. Walter Dickson, the Scotland full back who was stone deaf, commented to a colleague on the enthusiastic reception given Scotland, misinterpreting the gestures of the crowd. The consequence of this misrule was a magisterial rebuke from the International Rugby Football Board, who threatened France with a cessation of fixtures, but the enraged Scots went further and refused to play the French in Inverleith the following season. Maybe it was here that the Anglo-Saxon conspiracy myth began (and which generations of Frenchmen have come to believe) – that when it comes to the application of the laws, there is one for the rest and another which is used to flog France.

With what may be regarded as a typical display of English sang-froid, when John Miles refereed France's next home game, against Wales, he stopped the game near the end until the additional police reinforcements who had filed onto the pitch surrounds removed themselves – and was applauded for so doing. The game also marked the twenty-ninth, and last, appearance for Wales of Billy Trew, the influential Swansea player whose adaptability over a remarkable fourteen seasons brought him international honours at fly half, centre and wing.

That Trew was an unselfish player can be seen in his action, when Wales' captain, of standing down in 1907 at a perceived error in selection and also in remaining to try and nurture a refurbished XV as, one by one, the stars of the century's first decade departed. When Wales lost to England in Cardiff in 1913, it was the first time since 1899 that another home country had won in Wales. Perhaps this contributed towards the eruption, just before the war, of the Terrible Eight as Wales began to look inward. Alban Davies, a clergyman who excused the occasional outburst of ripe language by saying that he never heard it under his scrum cap, came into the Wales pack in 1913 and was given the captaincy in 1914.

But for a one-point defeat at Twickenham in the opening match, Wales would have won a grand slam and few could work out how England had achieved enough possession for 'Bruno' Brown and Pillman to score tries in the 10-9 win. After Wales had played Scotland, the visiting captain, David Bain, an Oxford University man, commented that the dirtier team won, but the Terrible Eight's apotheosis came in a battle in muddy Belfast against Ireland which veteran critics consider to have been the dirtiest match they had ever seen. Maybe Dickie Lloyd, Ireland's captain, knew what was coming: he took his place for the team photograph but then withdrew after damaging a tendon during the warm-up.

The presence on the Continent of service units from New Zealand helped France to sustain rugby during the First World War. When international competition resumed in 1920, their rude health was apparent in all four matches: two were lost by five points, one by a single point and, for the first time, an away victory was claimed when they beat Ireland 15-7 in Dublin. It was, quite apart from the blessings of peace, a notable year for France in that the newly-formed Fédération Française de Rugby (FFR) took over the administration of the game from the Union des Sociétés Françaises des Sports Athlétiques.

To mark the resumption of relationships with Scotland, the new governing body presented the match referee, Frank Potter-Irwin (another Englishman), with a medal. They did not do so when Colonel W.S.D. Craven awarded France a try against Wales, then reversed his decision after consulting the Welsh touch judge (at this time the competing countries supplied their own touch judge). At one stage the referee was so dissatisfied with the scrums that he fed the ball in himself – no doubt straight as a die. France lost 6-5, which probably gave a certain intransigence to their mood when they completed the season in Dublin with a five-try rout, Raoul Got from Perpignan scoring two tries in his debut on the wing. The season marked the entry to French rugby of two legendary figures, Adolphe Jauréguy – who also scored twice against Ireland – and René Crabos. Both were outstanding players, but are remembered as shrewd administrators, while Jauréguy also instituted a prize awarded for those who have helped significantly to improve relationships between France and the rest of the rugby world. However, the main contest for the championship was between Wales and England, Wales winning at Swansea before England retrieved their season with a notable fightback against Ireland and then denying Scotland a triple crown at Twickenham: a game in which Lowe scored a try that will have a very strong resonance for modern players, in that he gathered it direct from a cross-kick from Davies – a move now popularised by Australian players.

Despite defeat by England, this was the start of a slow revival for Scottish rugby, presaging their assault on England's supremacy in 1925. In 1921 there were debuts for two outstanding servants, John Bannerman and Leslie Gracie, while in 1922 that remarkable Olympian, Eric Liddell, came into the side on the wing. Bannerman set a lasting record for longevity by making 37 appearances in the Scotland pack and Gracie – like Liddell, born overseas and educated at a missionary school in Eltham – won fame for his unorthodox running at centre, his finest hour coming when he scored the match-winning try against Wales in Cardiff in 1923 and was carried from the field by the Welsh crowd, so appreciative were they of his efforts.

Most of the on-field arguments, however, went England's way. With Davies and Kershaw controlling matters at half back, they were also building a substantial and mobile pack around the multi-talented Wavell Wakefield. It was a mixture of aggressive West Country play, as exemplified by Tom Voyce from Gloucester, with the discipline and thought of such Service and university representatives as Ronnie Cove-Smith and Wakefield himself. Wakefield was another remarkable player and individual, who went on to be a Member of Parliament and was ennobled as Lord Wakefield of Kendal. He could play in any position in the back five and frequently played club rugby in the centre. When he was introduced to the game at Sedbergh, Wakefield played with boys older and bigger than himself and did not enjoy it; however, he made a point of studying the laws and thinking about the game and became, as a consequence, a leading tactician and captain of England in 13 of his 31 appearances. As though some kind of

The England side that faced Ireland at Leicester in the only home international played away from Twickenham between its inauguration in 1910 and Wembley in 1992. Standing: E. Gardner, G. Conway, A. Smallwood, L. Corbett, L. Price, R. Cove-Smith, F. Sanders. Sitting: W. Luddington, E. Myers, A. Voyce, C. Lowe, Mr T. Vile (referee), W. Davies (captain), W. Wakefield, C. Kershaw, F. Gilbert.

magnet was at work, England found Wakefield the hub of a stream of outstanding forwards, Arthur (later Sir Arthur) Blakiston, Leo Price, Geoffrey Conway, 'Bruno' Brown and Sam Tucker among them.

Wakefield and Price were instrumental in the remarkable start to the 1923 match with Wales at Twickenham when, if Wakefield is to be believed, the fastest international try of all time was scored (though Scotland's meeting with Wales in 1999 provided a rival). Wakefield's kick-off was held up in the strong wind, Price caught the ball and tried to drop at goal, the ball rebounded from the upright into Price's arms and he promptly scored a try within ten seconds of the start. The dropped goal had to be left to Alistair Smallwood, the wing who received a pass from Len Corbett between his legs and snapped over the goal which made the difference in a 7-3 win.

Between 1921 and 1924 there were three grand slams for England, despite the retirement for the last of them of Davies and Kershaw. In what appeared at the time to be a seamless transition, Edward Myers, born in New York to Yorkshire parents, moved from centre to fly half and Arthur Young emerged from Cambridge University to play scrum half. In addition, England uncovered Carston Catcheside from Percy Park to play right wing after Lowe's retirement and the youngster rewarded the selectors by scoring a try in every game, a feat which has eluded every other Englishman.

The only break in England's transmission came in 1922 when Wales showed that some bark remained in the old dog. But for a drawn match with Scotland in Inverleith, they would have won the grand slam and the memories of victory over England no doubt warmed them during the lean years to come. During the match Wales scored eight tries on a Cardiff pitch better suited to aquatic activities after a week of teeming rain and the mud probably served to obscure the numbers being worn for the first time in the championship to identify the players. Wales had plucked Dai Hiddlestone from Neath's back row to make his debut at the age of thirty-one and the disruption of England's half backs went a long way towards the 28-6 victory.

Two great Ireland backs, Ernie Crawford (left) and George Stephenson.

While England paraded their ample skills, Ireland struggled. In sixteen matches immediately following the war they won only three and suffered their first whitewash in 1920 when they began the season with eleven newcomers. These were not easy times in Ireland: the game had been disrupted by suspension of activities during the war, and the Easter Rising of 1916 preceded seven years of civil strife before the Irish Free State was proclaimed. Dickie Lloyd gave his country one final season and will have been comforted with the discovery, as he left, of two players who illuminated the 1920s – Ernie Crawford, the Lansdowne full back capped for the first time at the age of twenty-eight, and George Stephenson, who won the first of 42 caps in the centre in the defeat by France.

Stephenson began the 1919/20 season in the third XV at Queen's University, Belfast. His reputation was made through his sterling defensive qualities and his goal-kicking, though he did score 14 tries during a career remarkable in that he played nine seasons without a break until injury removed him from the 1929 game with Scotland. He was also a member of the family dynasties which seem to crop up in Irish rugby like no other – his brother, Harry, played in the same side while Billy and Dick Collopy joined forces in the Ireland pack, following where their father had led in 1891.

The latest representative of the Clinch family, Jammie, also appeared in the Ireland back row as the country strove to recover ground apparently ceded to England and Wales. If talking could do it, then the Irish could always be relied upon: Clinch played centre in an invitation XV with Ian Smith as his wing, and failed utterly to serve Smith as required. The match having been lost, Clinch claimed that while Smith might be known as the Flying Scotsman, he himself was noted as the Irish Mail and was therefore faster than the Irish female.

2
MARKING TIME
1925-1939

By the mid-1920s, the pipes were skirling for Scotland. Piece by piece the team had come together that was to dominate the second half of the decade, including that glorious back division in which the four three-quarters played together at Oxford University. The quartet played together first against Wales in 1924, when Ian Smith **(colour section, picture 2)** made his debut on the wing and scored three tries to demonstrate that here was one of those special players.

Smith joined Phil Macpherson, already well established as an international centre; George Aitken, capped by New Zealand three years earlier; and A.C. 'Johnny' Wallace, an Australian. They played together only five times for Scotland, but it was enough to ensure the country's first grand slam – a fitting celebration of the opening of the new ground at Murrayfield. The Scottish Rugby Union, aware of and responding to growing interest in the game, bought the old Edinburgh Polo Club ground in 1922, though even they were taken aback when 70,000 sought tickets for the opening game, against England, on 21 March 1925 (two years earlier the corresponding game had drawn a crowd of 30,000).

There was, however, far more to Scotland than their multi-national three-quarters (even Smith had been born in Australia). Dan Drysdale had become a full back respected throughout Britain for his dependability and a new half-back pairing, Jimmy Nelson and Herbert Waddell, came together during the season. While this was happening, the thoroughgoing experience of John Bannerman and John (later Sir John) Buchanan in the pack was augmented by the dash and vigour of Jimmy Ireland at hooker. In passing, it is worth noting that four of the forwards in the opening match against France were based with English clubs: Buchanan at Exeter, MacMyn at Cambridge University, Paterson at Birkenhead Park and Gillies (somewhat nearer home) at Carlisle.

This was the last match to be played at Inverleith and proved a bountiful time for Smith: the wing scored four of Scotland's seven tries in a 25-4 win and then repeated the achievement as Wales conceded six tries at Swansea. He therefore shared with William Stewart (against Ireland in 1913) the individual try-scoring record and put himself on the road to a tally of 24 tries in 32 appearances, a strike rate of which any modern player would be proud. Quite apart from his basic pace, Smith also had a high knee-lift to his running style, which made him difficult to tackle, and was utterly fearless in finishing at the corner. Asked by a Frenchman after the match for his time over 100 yards, Smith, mistaking the question, replied 'Four' – which must have come as a shock to an observer already grasping at shadows after a match played in a partial eclipse of the sun. The wing had to settle for short commons against Ireland, however, when Macpherson was absent and Scotland won only 14-8 against an Ireland XV emerging from the doldrums and including that outstanding scrum half, Mark Sugden.

The ultimate triumph was yet to come. With Macpherson restored to the captaincy, they took their hopes of a first championship since 1907 to their new ground against Wakefield's Englishmen. Scotland had a side confident in its running ability behind the scrum – though Smith had taken the initial credits, Wallace on the other wing had scored seven tries in three games (and his eighth against England earned him entry to the small club of players to have scored in each championship match in the same season). Scotland had reason to respect England's forwards, but their pack played beyond themselves in a game which, by its conclusion, left both sides exhausted. This was attributed to the mossy turf of the new ground, yet to settle and yielding by nature, which took its toll on the heavier Englishmen, while it suited the Scottish foot rushes. Furthermore, the Scotland defence, during the final quarter, played with unremitting bravery and when Wakefield acknowledged that it was 'an exceedingly hard game and I felt the effects of it for several days afterwards', we can believe he was in no way guilty of exaggeration. He also observed that Edward Massey, England's scrum half, played much of the game with a broken collarbone, but nothing could be taken from Scotland's achievement.

Their new ground looked a picture: 'Not even the huge arena of Wembley, crowded with ardent followers of Association Football, looks more impressive than the monster stand of Murrayfield … it must rank as second to none in the world of sporting spectacles', *The Times* reported, before lampooning the Scottish Rugby Union for placing the press box so far away from the action. Luddington opened the scoring with a penalty goal before Macpherson, one of the most deceptive runners of his day, created the opening from which Waddell sent Nelson, with a crunching hand-off, to the line. Drysdale's conversion put Scotland ahead but, before the interval, Hamilton's try restored the advantage to the visitors who scored again when Wakefield latched onto a cross kick from Corbett. Luddington's conversion attempt was charged down, a failure rubbed home when Wallace surged into the corner and Gillies landed the touchline conversion.

With one point between the sides, Scotland threw everything into attack. Four chances came and went, among them a dribble by Aitken which bounced unkindly off a goalpost, but the winning score came from Waddell. Earlier, the fly half had lapsed in defence when Wakefield scored; now he dropped the goal and Scotland mustered for the final English assault. Drysdale brought down Smallwood (in his final game for England – the only defeat he played in), Myers was stopped on the line and Corbett tripped just short. As the seconds ticked away, Holliday's long drop at goal flew wide and Scotland were home 14-11.

It was a marvellous season for the Scots, but their brilliant back line disbanded thereafter. They possessed enough firepower to claim their first win at Twickenham in 1926, Smith scoring two tries, but the challenge was emerging from Ireland, whose growing quality was made plain in a 6-0 defeat against the unbeaten New Zealanders of 1924/25, a season which brought together Sugden and

The Wales team that was soundly beaten by the Scots at Swansea in 1925. The Welsh captain, Steve Morris, is the player third from the right. Clearly little mascots have an honoured place in the game.

England's multi-talented forward Wavell Wakefield in 1926 and a caricature of Dan Drysdale, Scotland's reliable full back.

Eugene Davy at half back. Sugden, an Anglo-Irishman, was a classic scrum half from Trinity College, Dublin, swift on the break and tactically astute, while Davy was out of the brilliant Irish mould of fly halves, as complete a footballer as one could wish.

A splendid back division complemented a pack which was said, for the first time, to be capable of lasting the full eighty minutes and included George Beamish **(1)** and W.F. 'Horsey' Browne. Sadly, Beamish, a wonderful tight-loose forward who led England's East Midlands to victory over the 1931/32 South Africans, missed the 1926 season with a leg injury and, therefore, Ireland's first win over England since 1911. They also became the first team to win at Murrayfield, knocking Scotland's crown askew with a 3-0 win thanks to a try by Jack Gage, the wing who later played for South Africa.

With a grand slam on the table, Ireland fell at the final hurdle, against Wales in Swansea. Over the years these two countries developed a habit of denying each other honours and here Tom Hewitt's dropped goal went wide as Ireland lost 11-8. Indeed, for four successive seasons, Ireland had to be content either to share or be runner-up in the championship and each time one of their home-union rivals denied them a triple crown. Instead they learned to enjoy the fruits of such victories as the 6-5 struggle over England in 1929, their first at Twickenham.

Though there were occasional outbreaks of scoring at this time, the game was developing into a very tight affair with greater science being applied to back-row defence. The scrummage had settled into a 3-2-3 formation, the International Board's heavy hand falling in 1932 on the 2-3-2 formation favoured by New Zealand and the eighth 'roving' forward who for so long was a bone of contention. An era ended in 1927 when Wakefield played his final game for England, which coincided with France's first victory over the English, ending a run of fourteen successive international defeats.

The 1920s were not, it is safe to say, France's most distinguished period. They may have been silver medallists at the 1924 Olympic Games (beaten by the United States in the final) but they made little impact on the championship. Much of the blame was placed on the attention paid to the French

Lucien Serin goes over to score a try for France against England at Twickenham in 1930.

club championship in which some players, such as Roger Ramis, the talented centre, preferred to play. That championship became synonymous with ill-disciplined play and covert payment, nor was the game's cause helped by the deaths of such players as Aimé Cassayet and Yves du Manoir.

Cassayet, the Narbonne lock, played 31 games for France and captained the side 8 times, the last against Wales in February 1927. The most consistent of players, he was only twice on the winning side in the championship and died of illness, aged twenty-eight, three months after his final game. Du Manoir, a brilliant fly half from the Racing Club de France, was a byword for chivalrous play but died in a flying accident shortly before the France-Scotland match of 1928 (for which he had not been selected).

Ironically, as the 1920s neared their end, France had the encouragement of beating Wales for the first time, winning 8-3 at Stade Colombes, even without André Camel, their lock who damaged a shoulder in the first half. That scoreline was reversed in Cardiff a year later, but in 1930 France won two championship matches for the first time since 1921: it was nip and tuck throughout a low-scoring season, in which only 25 tries were registered (the lowest total since the five nations came together in 1910). Eugene Ribère, the back-row forward from Quillan, led France to two January wins over Scotland and Ireland and, despite a reverse at Twickenham, they were in a position to claim their first championship when they played the final game of the season against Wales at Stade Colombes.

It was a brutal affair. So disappointed were French officials, among them the worthy Rutherford, that several players were reprimanded and one was told he would never be selected again. In the event, nine of the team were not chosen for a championship match again, but worse was to come. In January 1931, ten French clubs broke from the federation to form their own union and such rebellion was the last straw for the home unions, already concerned at aspects of foul play and alleged payments rife in French rugby. In February they agreed that relationships with France would be suspended until the federation could satisfactorily control events in their own country and on 6 April 1931, France beat England in the last championship game they would play for sixteen years.

It was a breach from which few benefited, the most productive element being that France, forced to uncover different resources, strengthened their continental links by playing Germany, Romania and Italy and formed the Fédération International de Rugby Amateur (FIRA). The 1930s were generally a lacklustre decade, reflecting the dismal economic conditions of the period and the growing threat of world war as Germany rearmed. Many outstanding British and Irish rugby players passed their careers without the singular pleasure of a grand slam; Scotland (twice) and England (twice) enjoyed unbeaten seasons, Ireland won their first outright championship for thirty-six years in 1935 and the British Isles made two successful tours, to Australasia in 1930 and South Africa in 1938, but domestic business was less than usual.

'If you have never tasted caviar and champagne, you don't know what you're missing,' Bernard Gadney, who led England from scrum half in 8 of his 14 internationals, said. Gadney, a tall, strong runner from the base of the scrum, had hoped for selection against France in 1931, only to be told by the selectors that they felt it unfair to give him a debut against the French – presumably because of their rough play. 'Instead I played in 1932, by which time there was absolutely no contact allowed with the French at any level,' Gadney said. 'The players believed the French to be worthy opponents, pretty adventurous, and it was regarded by us all as a great disappointment. You must remember that we took our rugby very seriously.'

Some critics suggested that the constricting tactics employed by Bennie Osler's South Africans in 1931/32 – Osler was a fly half who kicked like a mule – had an effect on domestic rugby, and it is certainly true that incoming touring sides have taught substantial and in some cases immediate lessons: the 1967 New Zealanders and the 1984 Australians are cases in point. Certainly there were outstanding individual players to lead the way towards a better future. Wales produced that wonderful centre pairing of the gangling Wilf Wooller (3) and the crash-tackling Claude Davey, along with the brilliant Swansea halves, Willie Davies and Haydn Tanner.

Ireland offered fervent leadership from such forwards as Jack Siggins, Victor Pike and Sam Walker and England another distinguished half back pairing in Roger Spong and Wilf Sobey. Since Sobey was succeeded by Gadney, who wrestled with Coventry's little Jimmy Giles for much of his international career, there was no shortage of scrum halves nor, in the redoubtable shapes of Doug Kendrew and Ray Longland, good prop forwards, but England remained inconsistent. Not only that, their fortress at Twickenham finally fell to a Welsh assault in January 1933.

Perhaps overcome by winning, Wales failed in both their other matches that season, but at least the spell was broken. Destroyer-in-chief was Watcyn Thomas, the back-row forward who spent much of his career as a teacher in England. Thomas came into the Wales side just as another wonderful player, Ivor Jones from Llanelli, was leaving it and played in the 1931 game at Twickenham when Wales drew 11-11. For his next visit, two years later, Thomas was captain and a singularly thoughtful one, capable of judging the run of play and influencing events.

Even though Wales conceded a slightly fortuitous first-half try, Thomas shifted the emphasis of his defence at the interval, settled the nerves of the young Wooller on his debut and the Oxford University full back, Vivian Jenkins, also making his debut and afflicted by a bout of influenza. Harry Bowcott, at fly half, kicked for position and Ronnie Boon, the fly half-turned-wing, did the rest; from a missed England clearance, Boon dropped a goal and then scuttled round to the posts after his centres had paved the way from a loose scrum.

This was a decade in which authority still held sway. The programmes produced by the Welsh Rugby Union in the early 1930s leave few in doubt about the importance of the game's administrators: the biggest pictures are of the president, secretary and vice-president of the union; the next biggest, those of the selectors – Welsh rugby's so-called 'Big Five' who, according to one caption, 'captured the popular imagination by choosing an experimental team that laid the Twickenham bogey'. Members of the ground committee had their place as well, leaving room for individual portraits of as many as four of the thirty players. On the other hand, as the decade progressed, each player received a pen portrait and a review of their recent achievements.

Watcyn Thomas, the Wales captain, introduces the Prince of Wales to Maurice Turnbull before their historic victory at Twickenham in 1933.

Wooller's greatest moment came in the Welsh defeat of New Zealand in 1935, opponents against whom Prince Alex Obolensky, the Trent schoolboy who played on England's wing, carved an immortal name. Scotland, meanwhile, introduced Wilson Shaw to international rugby as a wing in 1934. However, it was not a conspicuous season and the next year Scotland moved Shaw to centre, and then to fly half and the captaincy while playing alongside the experienced Ross Logan, who had played in the triple crown season of 1933. Gadney, who partnered Shaw on tour, recalled the wonderful handling of such fly halves as Shaw and Wales' Cliff Jones (4) as their distinctive feature, and this with the heavy leather ball which, in wet weather, became very difficult to hold.

Shaw's moment duly arrived in the triple crown game of 1938, against England at Twickenham. England themselves had won the triple crown at Murrayfield a year earlier, but here they conceded five tries to the Scotland backs while scoring only one themselves. Even so, Graham Parker's kicking kept them in the match but could not save them. Shaw, having made the diagonal kick which brought Bill Renwick the first try, scored himself to give Scotland the half-time lead and then made certain with a second try that crowned a splendid, weaving run to the line.

In 1939, with war looming, the home unions decided that France should receive a second chance. On the eve of that season's Calcutta Cup match, they invited assurances from the French federation that their domestic game was now under control which they duly received two months later – including a suggestion that the French club championship would be abandoned. As if to emphasise the need for *la différence*, the 1939 championship – won by Wales – produced the less-than-grand total of ten tries, the lowest ever. The 1939/40 season would have embraced France, but the outbreak of war in September brought formal matches to an end once more.

3
UNCERTAIN TIMES
1947-1955

From 1910, when the five nations came together, to 1947 the championship in full was contested on only seventeen occasions – war and the suspension of France saw to that – and even then, allowance must be made for Scottish predilections immediately before the First World War. Happily, since then, the championship has unfolded with admirable regularity, prey on occasions to the weather and illness but incomplete only in 1972 when terrorist activity in Ireland persuaded Wales and Scotland not to travel to Dublin.

Indeed, once hostilities had ceased in 1945, the rugby authorities were admirably swift to organise what became known as the Victory Internationals in 1945/46. These were unofficial matches so far as the records are concerned (save in France where caps were awarded) but played with a relaxation typical of the spirit of liberation which existed at the time. Moreover, the touring New Zealand Army side, the Kiwis, joined in to wonderful effect and the path towards formal resumption of the championship and the return of France seemed smooth despite the years of rationing which followed the war.

Those years were dominated initially by Ireland and Wales. It may have been England who shared the 1947 championship with Wales, but that was merely the prologue to the Celtic play. Ireland produced, in Karl Mullen and Jack Kyle, two individuals who dominated the decade following the war; not only were they the outstanding players in their respective positions (hooker and fly half) of their era, they also stood comparison with many before and since. Both were medical students and Mullen also proved to be a natural leader of Ireland and the Lions party which toured Australasia in 1950, while those who saw Kyle play never tired of singing his praises.

Throw in a back row of all the talents and Ireland's assault, leading to their one and only grand slam, was set. Their major challenge for honours came from Wales, who garnered two slams of their own as the 1940s became the 1950s. It would have been apt if that great scrum half, Haydn Tanner, had played long enough to be part of the first slam, but the war had robbed him of his best years and, instead, a new hero in Rex Willis came along in a side shrewdly led by John Gwilliam and including the blazing talents of the two unrelated Jones boys, Ken and Lewis.

There were also hints, for those who cared to note them, that French rugby was on the rise. The post-war years saw the introduction of two outstanding players, Jean Prat and Lucien Mias, and the belief – confirmed by the defeat in 1948 of the touring Australians and in 1954 of Bob Stuart's New Zealanders – that France was now capable of rubbing shoulders with the best. That they had still to wait until 1959 before winning their first outright championship points only to a lack of self-confidence at crucial times and re-emphasises the traditional difficulty of beating four different opponents in any one season.

However, the French did not have to wait that long before finally cracking the nut of victory on Welsh soil which Jack Bancroft, the full back of the pre-First World War era, had said they would never achieve. In 1948 France played out a magnificent 11-3 win at St Helen's, which created the sobriquet for Robert Soro, the Lion of Swansea. Soro formed, with Alban Moga, a hugely physical second row in twenty-one international games. The pair were not tall by today's standards – Soro, from the Romans club, was 6ft 1in and Moga, from Bègles, an inch taller – but they were men of substance at 16st 8lb and 17st 5lb respectively.

France scored three tries against Wales, two of them interceptions, but none doubted that they were worthy winners. Michel Pomathios, the try-scoring wing, was carried off at the end by the crowd, some of whom had caused problems by standing on the touchlines. Five weeks later France casually dismissed England 15-0 at Stade Colombes, Soro crossing for one of their three tries.

Perhaps Ireland had given a hint of what was to come when they beat England 22-0 on a bitterly cold day in Dublin in February 1947. Both Kyle and Mullen had made their debuts a fortnight earlier, against France, and now Ireland discovered they also had a pack capable of outplaying the rest. In particular they unearthed a prop, Jack Daly from London Irish, whose athleticism was sufficient to attract Rugby League scouts. Indeed, hard-pressed in his domestic circumstances after the grand slam had been won, with his mother requiring an expensive operation, Daly turned professional with Huddersfield.

During the following year a breakaway trio came together fit to represent the Lions. Ireland have fielded many talented back-row forwards, though seldom three at the same time. However, against England in 1948, Des O'Brien at No. 8 joined Bill McKay and Jim McCarthy and they played in fourteen internationals together, O'Brien and McCarthy subsequently leading their country. The trio were essentially a complementary unit, the size and footballing skills of O'Brien and McKay allowing McCarthy, the smaller man, to flourish. Together, they proved the ideal support for the brilliant Kyle. A truly modest man, Kyle claimed he would not have been half the player he was had not his back row performed his defensive chores – although perhaps it is the mark of true genius that the rest of the team will happily do the fetching and carrying to provide the context in which a Kyle or a Barry John can succeed. After all, these special players are the matchwinners. Kyle had the priceless ability to read the game and the patience to wait. Opponents often thought they had bottled him up, only to be taken aback when turned

Hugh de Lacy, Ireland's scrum half, gathers the ball in the match at Twickenham in 1948.

Jack Kyle shaking hands with George Stephenson on the occasion of Kyle's 45th cap, at Twickenham in 1958 when he overtook Ken Jones of Wales, the previous record holder. Stephenson won 42 caps between 1920 and 1930.

inside out by Kyle's break. Ireland, aware of the talent in that 5ft 9in frame, eked it out for ten years and he made a total of 46 appearances.

Playfair Rugby Annual, then edited by O.L. Owen, concluded that the factors which made Ireland unbeaten in 1948 (after suffering a 16-3 defeat against Australia) were 'Kyle's clever tactics both as kicker and passer – behind a steadily improving pack; Mullen's expert hooking; and the dash and good hands of the wings, O'Hanlon and Mullan'. Instructively, the annual makes no mention of the grand slam; not only, it said, did Ireland win all four matches but 'the still more prized triple crown as well'. Where that leaves France, who came second, is a moot point.

The Irish scored ten tries in the competition in 1948, more than they had achieved in one championship season for twenty years, and won the slam without a kicker of distinction: converting just three tries and scoring no penalties or dropped goals. They opened against France with a 13-6 victory – which clearly did not keep everyone happy, as Ernie Strathdee, the scrum half and captain, was dropped for the next game, against England. In his stead, a Harlequin, Hugh de Lacy, was promoted and the captaincy passed to Mullen, then only twenty-one years old. This proved to be a case of an old head on young shoulders. Mullen's great gift was that he involved all the players, inviting each to have his say before a match, sharing the responsibility in a way which some of today's professionals appear to believe is peculiar to their time alone. He was also a superb technician at a time when hookers could strike for the ball at will and the best of them might take as many as half a dozen balls against the head. He won

Haydn Tanner, the Wales captain, passes the ball away from the base of the scrum at Twickenham in 1948. Mickey Steele-Bodger is the England flanker with his eyes fixed on Tanner.

The teams for Wales' match against Ireland at Swansea on Saturday 12 March 1949.

respect, therefore, both as a player and tactical leader capable of imposing a game plan on his uninhibited players, but not adhering slavishly to it if different needs arose.

Victory at Twickenham, by 11-10, might have seemed a close-run affair, but Dickie Guest's interception try put an undeserved gloss on an England display played mostly in retreat. Two unconverted tries were enough to account for Scotland, whose forwards were overwhelmed by the mobile Irishmen – Barney Mullan scoring one try and Kyle himself cutting through for the second. That result paved the way for a tense meeting with Wales at Ravenhill on 13 March 1948. This was a Wales XV which, though including such personalities as Ken Jones, Bleddyn Williams, John Gwilliam and Rees Stephens, had yet to reach maturity. Even so, the Welsh had dashed Irish hopes frequently enough in the past and Mullen was acutely aware of the fact.

In his pre-match address to his side, the Ireland hooker stressed that victory would come through the pack and Kyle's tactical direction. He was not wrong: a first-half try by Williams emphasised the potential of the Wales back division and cancelled out Mullan's try, made for him by a long skip pass from Kyle. The winning score fell to Daly, the prop, who dribbled through with O'Brien from a lineout and was first to touch down. 'Jaysus, Brien', he is reputed to have said as the two men ran back to halfway, 'if Wales don't score again I'll be canonised.' As 30,000 bit their fingernails to the quick, Ireland's defence held out and the match was won 6-3. Daly, the shirt stripped from his back, was carried off in triumph.

As if to prove it was no fluke, Ireland nearly did it again the following season. Indeed, the championship and triple crown was theirs, but France, the dark horse sidling up on the rails, denied them a successive slam by winning in Dublin 16-9. This was a remarkable achievement in a season where Ireland had found a goal-kicker in the Bective Rangers full back, George Norton. He scored 26 of their 41 points and might have earned himself a place in rugby legend but for an injury which terminated his playing career in 1951. Ireland's cause was helped by the return to scrum half after the France match of Strathdee and the side grew in confidence throughout the season, McCarthy scoring their three tries in the last two games with Scotland and Wales.

Elsewhere, however, there was a complete absence of consistency. The controversial Scots picked Douglas Keller as their leader, the flanker from Wee Waa in New South Wales having represented Australia the previous season. Now studying at Guy's Hospital, Keller was one of eight Scots in the match against France who were based outside Scotland, among them Douglas Smith, the heavyweight London Scottish wing who became the much-loved manager of the successful Lions in Australasia in 1971. Meanwhile, England unveiled Barry Holmes, who some contend was the best full back the country has ever had. However, his tragically early death in Argentina that same year, at the age of twenty-one (and after appearing for Argentina), leaves him as something of an unknown quantity.

Wales were condemned to the wooden spoon in 1949, which was no way for Tanner to conclude his career. The scrum half won 25 caps, the first in 1935, the last in March 1949 when he was thirty-two. He was a player of all the talents, a superbly accurate pass matched by his decisive ability to break. 'He is,' the manager of the touring 1947 Australians, Arnold Tancred, declared, 'one of the greatest scrum halves of all time.' But, if Tanner's time was not to come, then Wales' certainly was. The conveyor belt formed by the Welsh Secondary Schools organisation was beginning to churn out the likes of Clem Thomas, Bryn Meredith, Lewis Jones and Russell Robins to go with the more mature abilities of Bleddyn Williams, Billy Cleaver and the burly centre, Jack Matthews.

Critics suggested they had taken a leaf (a lucky shamrock leaf?) out of the Irish book and harnessed the tactical ability of Cleaver – far more than 'Billy Kick' as he was so frequently known – at fly half to an effective pack. But it was no coincidence that the 1949/50 season also saw the emergence of Roy John from Neath to become one of the great lineout forwards, that the front row included the intelligent and perceptive John Robins at prop and that John Gwilliam had found his proper role in the back row.

There was also Lewis Jones. Wales have a history of producing brilliant youngsters – teenagers who take centre stage but whose careers have a meteoric feel. In Rugby Union terms, this was

Cliff Davies going over for the crucial try in Wales' victory over England at Twickenham in 1950.

the case with Jones who, at eighteen and doing national service with the Royal Navy at Devonport, played no more than ten games for his country. He then turned professional with Leeds but, considering the sustained brilliance of his Rugby League career, the goals he kicked and the tries he scored, there can be no doubt that Jones was a wonderful player, capable of appearing at full back, wing, centre or indeed fly half without prejudicing his team. He had pace, a stupendous swerve and his own variation of what has become known to later generations as the 'David Campese goosestep', the hitchkick of the feet designed to leave a defender flat-footed.

Even so, the betting on Wales for the championship would have found few takers considering that injury had removed Bleddyn Williams, that prince of centres, the rumbustious lock, Rees Stephens, and that the campaign started at Twickenham. Not that England inspired universal awe, indeed they had evoked feelings of antipathy with their consistent selection of overseas players since the war. Against Wales they turned out with Murray Hofmeyr and Harold Small, both South Africans, and Ian Botting – who had toured South Africa with New Zealand only the year before – in the side; two more South Africans had played in trials, one of them the successful centre of a season earlier, Clive van Ryneveld, and it was no surprise when the gentlemen's agreement regarding eligibility was reviewed at the end of the season.

If England opted for so many Oxford University products (in this case, six), Wales reverted to their strong Cambridge links in naming the authoritarian Gwilliam as captain. A sincere student of the game, as well as a history graduate, Gwilliam brought a keen wit to Welsh tactics and towards motivation. He once chose to demonstrate the art of passing to Williams (of whom there were few better exponents) and Matthews, his experienced centres, as a method of squeezing the very last ounce from his players by getting under their skin – in 1950 and 1952 the itch worked to perfection.

A crowd of 75,532 (Twickenham's largest and still not officially overtaken since the stadium's refurbishment in the 1990s was completed) saw Wales triumph 11-5, Jones establishing the position from which Cliff Davies scored a try to go with another by the predatory Ray Cale. The cast remained substantially the same for the 12-0 victory over Scotland, which earned Wales a visit to Belfast where Ireland had succeeded so historically two years earlier but the Big Five were not happy; they introduced Gerwyn Williams, the London schoolteacher, at full back and moved the mercurial Jones to centre with Malcolm Thomas reverting to the wing.

The proof of the selectorial pudding is in the eating and Wales had their revenge at Ravenhill. Their forwards squeezed the Ireland pack, reducing the effect of their flyaway back row, and though they could not score with the wind at their backs, the stage had been set for their 6-3 win. Matthews collected a loose ball to send Ken Jones, the Olympian sprinter, in for a try and though Norton equalised with a penalty goal, Cleaver and Lewis Jones gave Thomas sight of the corner and the burly wing made it with green-shirted defenders hanging from him. The triple crown had come to Wales for the first time since 1911, though the mood after the weekend was sombre when eighty people died in an Avro Tudor V carrying Welsh supporters home from Belfast, which crashed at Llandow.

The *Last Post* was sounded before Wales' final game, against France in Cardiff, in memory of the dead. Welsh resolve, against a France team in transition, was unimpeachable and the grand slam became theirs with a 21-0 win, Ken Jones scoring two of the four Wales tries. Gwilliam, the match programme noted, 'has played the type of game best suited to beat the opposition and whilst it might not have been as spectacular as that seen in the past, it has paid dividends'. There's no keeping some people happy.

Perhaps the expectation in the valleys became too great because Welsh fortunes promptly declined, the stuffing effectively knocked out of their 1951 season by unremarkable Scotland. More to the point, they supplied fourteen members of the Lions party to Australasia, a twenty-nine-match, five-month epic tour which was the last to travel to the southern hemisphere by sea. If they were somewhat stale, it was no surprise – though England would not have thought so after leaving Swansea beaten 23-5. However, a fortnight later the championship produced one of its classic upsets: Scotland, frankly, had little to write home about in the 1950s but this game at Murrayfield kept the embers glowing. It was the only bright spot in nineteen internationals played between January 1951 and January 1955, a period when the Scotland selectors jumped from pillar to post in their restless search of their limited playing base and never allowed a side to settle together.

Theoretically, there was no way in which Scotland, who had to change full backs on the morning of the game because of illness, could win but, as Gwilliam remarked afterwards: 'The art of rugby football is to be better than the other side at any given moment'. That Scotland were; their results across the season were not poor, in that they lost their other three games by two, one and three points respectively, but here Peter Kininmonth's men rose to the occasion. The young Ian Thomson, just twenty years old, kicked a first-half penalty goal but the goal that broke Wales was dropped by Kininmonth himself, the No. 8 collecting a clearance on touch and finding the posts.

Wales mounted a frantic assault but Scotland never faltered: Rob Gordon ran in two tries from the wing and James Dawson, the loose-head prop, concluded what amounted to a rout with the final try. The only sadness was that Norman Mair, who became so fluent and evocative a writer for *The Scotsman*, was playing in the match at hooker and not bent on painting the picture in words. Just over nine months later Scotland lost 44-0 to South Africa, a result which scarred a nation and blighted the careers of several players of genuine ability.

At the head of the championship table, Ireland and France were in contention. Only one point separated the two when they met in Dublin, Noel Henderson's penalty making the difference when set against Pierre Bertrand's single conversion – Jean Prat, France's regular kicker, had withdrawn that morning with influenza. Defeat by 9-8 cost France their first grand slam and left Ireland clear to achieve their second but they were held by their old enemy, Wales: Ben Edwards, the Newport lock, kicked a penalty to match Kyle's try and Ireland had to acknowledge a 3-3 draw in a season where they could only score 21 points in four matches, conceding 16.

Edwards was making a debut which persuaded the selectors that they should play Roy John at flanker, a move not universally praised. Of greater significance, however, was the fact that this match introduced Cliff Morgan to a wider world: with the premature retirement of Cleaver and the dismissal of Glyn Davies after the Scotland debacle, the Welsh were looking for a new fulcrum and the dark-haired, twinkling Morgan provided it. The rivalry that developed between him and Kyle illuminated the British and Irish scene for the next seven years and Morgan's place in the pantheon of great Welsh fly halves is assured.

Morgan himself has spoken fondly of his childhood days in the Rhondda Valley, when he learned to sidestep while avoiding the coal lorries rumbling up and down the valley streets. A man of great personal charm – hence his huge popularity in Ireland where he played club rugby with Bective Rangers for a couple of seasons – he was also able to translate his love of sport through the media of newspapers and television. He was, too, the popular image of the typical Welsh fly half: short, dark, cheeky, a stabbing sidestep, a flaring burst of speed over the first ten metres coupled with a maturing tactical appreciation which probably reached its height when he nursed the Lions to a 9-6 win over South Africa in 1955.

But Wales' immediate target was to retrieve ground lost in 1951, not only in the championship but in defeat by South Africa in December that year. They opened at Twickenham against an England side led by Nim Hall and containing some intelligent and abrasive forwards in John Kendall-Carpenter, Eric Evans and Don White in what turned out to be their toughest examination of another grand-slam season. They were not assisted by a hamstring injury to Lewis Jones, who was a virtual passenger for much of the game, but the day was carried by Ken Jones, whose two tries matched those scored by Albert Agar and Ted Woodward for England. The crucial difference was that Malcolm Thomas kicked one conversion.

They were the first of four tries that season for Jones, the Newport wing with the high knee lift who set the standard for other great Welsh fliers to follow. Gaunt and whey-faced, his 44 appearances testify to a lasting quality, his balance and that raw pace matched by footballing intelligence. 'Though often neglected by his midfield colleagues,' a pen portrait suggested, 'he is a match-winner.' Players are, of course, of their era but one would love to have seen Jones playing in a more liberated time, when he would surely have scored more than his 17 tries for Wales; he held his form so well that he did not make his last international appearance until he was thirty-five, three years after captaining the British athletics team in the European Championships in Berne.

By comparison the remainder of the season was relatively straightforward for Wales, despite difficulties in their scrummaging play. Bleddyn Williams made a brief appearance against Scotland and it is remarkable that so renowned a player appeared in only one of the eight matches in 1950 and 1952 that brought two grand slams, largely because of injury. The Cardiff man scored 185 tries for his club during a ten-year career which brought fame to his family at Taff's Well, since there were eight brothers, all of whom played rugby. Strong in the hips, Williams could jink, he could kick but above all he could pass the ball. Both he and Ken Jones were highly regarded by New Zealanders when they toured there in 1950 and both should probably have gone with the Lions to South Africa in 1955 where the combination in midfield of Jeff Butterfield and Williams might have gone down in legend.

Against the Scots, Rex Willis played with a broken jaw, and Wales recalled Clem Thomas to their back row for the game with Ireland. Of Thomas, a butcher by profession, it was said that never did a man have a more appropriate job; but his ability was not entirely destructive in a period when flankers were expected to tackle their men out of the game. Yet it marked a certain pragmatic style which reached its height in the final match, against France: Wales were without their first-choice half backs, Morgan having joined Willis in casualty, and found that Lewis Jones had lost his kicking touch. Yet he did enough, in his final game before turning professional, to help Wales to a 9-5 win, kicking two penalties alongside Alun Thomas' dropped goal.

France, the programme noted, came to Swansea after a worrying season. In successive years, 1950 and 1951, they had received tart letters from the presidents of the Rugby Football Union, Eric Watts Moses and Sir Wavell Wakefield, suggesting that unless stern measures were taken against new levels of 'shamateurism', then a second rupture was on the cards. In December 1951, the French federation's management committee sought to make the game 'conform to its statutes and to maintain it in the spirit of amateurism which alone is consistent with the playing of our game'. Fine words, but they meant little when it came to sustaining the French club championship, perceived as the root of all evils by those on the far side of the Channel.

A French delegation met the home unions in Dublin in February and talks lasted for seven hours. A month later, the International Rugby Football Board expressed its perturbation at events in France but agreed to wait for notification that tough reforming measures would take place. And indeed, the French federation agreed in May to terminate the club championship, which predictably created uproar with outright rebellion only being averted by the diplomatic skills of René Crabos, then a selector and later president of the federation. He called upon the clubs to respect the amateur regulations, they gave a binding undertaking and the club championship went on. It seemed at the time to be a surrender and it probably was: 'Fresh crisis in French rugby over alleged abuses in club championship,' *Playfair Rugby Annual* noted briskly but it is testimony to the level of play achieved by the national XV that, this time, the crisis was allowed to pass. Swept under the carpet? The same suspicions rumbled on throughout the 1950s, but the French, who had done so much to establish the FIRA organisation on the Continent, had grown as a playing force too and could not be routinely pushed aside as they once had been.

While England's administrators were fulminating, what were their players doing? Making up for lost time. During 1952 a group of forwards came together capable of competing with all comers – that is usually England's way – but they were limited in midfield. Why it should be that Wales and Ireland can produce talented half backs at the drop of a hat, and Scotland have not been backward in that respect over the last thirty years either, but England struggle to make the best of their possession is one of those mysteries. However, that all changed in 1953 when the selectors moved Nim Hall from fly half to full back, and introduced Martin Regan, the Liverpool fly half. More to the point they unearthed a diamond from Northampton, then the country's most powerful club, in Jeff Butterfield.

Butterfield was not only a centre with soft hands and a telling break, who placed a premium on running straight, but he was a fitness fanatic who recognised the importance of pacing one's way through a game. A Yorkshireman who graduated from Loughborough Colleges, he came into the side against France and promptly found an admirable foil in Phil Davies, the powerful Harlequin; the two played together on only nine occasions but their partnership was sufficient to carry them into the 1955 Lions tour party.

It was intensely encouraging for England that they won their opening match against the champions, Wales, in Cardiff. 'In Wales we regard the annual match with England as the classical game of the season – greater than the Calcutta Cup match, or the Celtic struggle between Wales and Ireland,' the editor of the Welsh Rugby Union match programme wrote. 'It certainly provides the biggest drawing power in rugby football and I do believe that if there was a ground to accommodate 100,000 spectators, the meeting of the two countries would fill it.' However, the Big Five had decided on a new pair of half backs, with Willis injured and Morgan omitted; Roy Burnett and Billy Williams from Newport played, for the only time, as England won 8-3, a result which cost Gwilliam the captaincy.

Though Ireland forced a 9-9 draw at Lansdowne Road, the English machine rolled steadily along with victories over France and Scotland, scoring six tries against the latter. It was their first championship since 1947, won with what was regarded as the biggest pack England had ever fielded. The average height of the forwards was just over 6ft, the average weight just under 14st, which confirms that comparisons between the players of differing eras has only

Jean Prat leads the France side out at Twickenham in 1953.

limited validity, modern packs being around three to four inches taller and some two stone heavier.

Promptly the next season, England handed out new caps like confetti to forwards. There were seven newcomers and, predictably, the England set-piece work suffered as a result. Unlikely though it may seem, England were still able to share the championship with France and Wales through the attacking ability of their backs. In all, England scored ten tries, more than any other country, and four of them fell to 'Tug' Wilson, the Harlequins flanker born in Rhodesia (now Zimbabwe), earning the reward for faithful support. They won the triple crown but they were denied the slam by France who, mercurial as ever, introduced some of their most enduring players this season.

They were not enough to beat Wales in a high-scoring match at Cardiff but the names still resound today: alongside the veterans, Jean Prat and Gérard Dufau, appeared the likes of Pierre Albaladejo (at full back rather than fly half), Andre Boniface, Jackie Bouquet, Amédée Domenech and Michel Celaya. These were players who set new standards of excellence within French rugby, whatever turmoil might have been happening at club level. The true genius of a player such as Boniface, picked initially on the wing after the departure of Pomathios, was at centre and (in eighteen games) alongside his younger brother, Guy, though they did not come together until 1961.

All the usual expressions which came to be attached to French back play – champagne rugby, Gallic wit, verve – started with André Boniface and the careless rapture he showed in his play. Typically, he had to fight his way past the sturdier skills of Bouquet, Roger Martine and the younger Prat, Maurice, but the discipline of such players was a necessary adjunct for France to show the world a reliability which had not previously existed. The emergence, aged twenty, of Domenech foreshadowed the age of highly mobile French forwards, capable of handling and running as well as many backs. The Duke, as he came to be called, was a prop who made a substantial impact in his early days but fell out of favour under the captaincy of Lucien Mias. Yet Domenech returned a new man to play his part in the rise and rise of French rugby in the 1960s, alongside Celaya whose skills were such that he could play anywhere in the back five.

All were, to a greater or lesser extent, influenced by the older Prat who played out his final international season in 1955. The statistics alone tell a tale of a wonderful career which lasted from his debut against the British Army in 1945 to the meeting with Italy in April 1955, when he was thirty-one. There were 51 appearances in the national shirt for the goal-kicking flanker from Lourdes, who garnered 139 points including 9 tries and, remarkably, 5 dropped goals. Players of today believe Zinzan Brooke, the New Zealander, to be well blessed for all-round accomplishments. Prat achieved far more, as a points scorer and as a leader of men who stamped his authority on the French displays of the early 1950s. He was captain in 17 internationals and was known, in France, as 'L'extraordinaire Monsieur Prat'. In England he was merely 'Monsieur Rugby'.

He demanded discipline and received it, and the path he blazed was taken up subsequently by Lucien Mias. It would not have been France, of course, if there had not been a hiccup on the way but that is the beauty of the French game – its unpredictability. At times it has been a trying virtue for the French themselves, who have never been entirely sure whether to foster their own innate feel for the game or to veer towards the more solid Anglo-Saxon virtues of precise forward play. Once more, in his final season, Prat was forced to share a championship: in a season when good form meant selection for the Lions, the French set about their British opponents to rare effect, never more so than at Twickenham when Prat dropped two goals and France won 16-9.

Victory in the final game of the season, at Stade Colombes, would have given France their first grand slam and 62,500 turned out to see their attempt. Alas, Wales had rattled up 11 points before France left the starting blocks; Wales fielded a mighty front row fit to be compared with the Pontypool trio of later vintage. The two unrelated Merediths, Bryn and Courtenay, together with W.O. 'Stoker' Williams, underpinned not only Wales but the Lions in South Africa. The streetwise Welsh hustled the home side into errors and Garfield Owen kicked his goals. Had Michel Vannier, the Racing Club full back, been able to match Owen's kicking then the French might yet have triumphed, but he could not and Haydn Morris seized on a cross-kick from Alun Thomas to ensure a 16-11 win.

Yet perhaps the tale of the season was Scotland's. After plumbing almost unimaginable depths, the Scots won two of their four games, breaking a dreadful run of championship defeats by beating Wales at Murrayfield and following up by beating Ireland after nine successive defeats. This was the season in which Hugh McLeod, the doughty Hawick prop, confirmed his promise, in which Jim Greenwood came of age as a No. 8 and that cultured wing, Arthur Smith, made his debut. The experienced Angus Cameron gave them substance at full back and he and five colleagues were chosen for the Lions, as was a flame-haired youngster from Ireland, Tony O'Reilly.

O'Reilly's youth (he was only nineteen), good looks and charm made him the first pin-up that rugby had produced, largely because he made such a name for himself in rugby-mad South Africa. That he never achieved the try-scoring feats for Ireland that he did on tour was sometimes resented at home, where he moved between centre and wing in the course of a 29-match career which ended with a recall to arms for a solitary match against England in 1970 – when he was thirty-three and patently unfit. But always he was a larger-than-life character with a golden touch in the business world which brought him more global fame than the amateur game ever did.

There could have been no greater contrast in Ireland's midfield than the blooming youth of O'Reilly and the ever-dependable Noel Henderson, Kyle's brother-in-law, who played 40 times for his country. Yet the legends were passing. Not only did Prat conclude his international career (though he played on with Lourdes for another three years), but Bleddyn Williams and Rex Willis bowed out from Wales, Nim Hall from England and Jim McCarthy from Ireland. It was a time for change.

4
VIVE LA FRANCE
1956-1968

It was symptomatic of the influential position occupied by the university match between Oxford and Cambridge – a position eroded only over the last decade – that the 1955 encounter at Twickenham should have served as a pointer for the 1956 Five Nations. The debate after Oxford's 9-5 victory centred around the switch tactics employed by Onllwyn Brace, the Dark Blues scrum half, which enlivened a fixture fast becoming very dull.

A glance at the two team sheets, however, reveals a host of burgeoning talent: Oxford fielded future internationals not only in Brace, but his partner, M.J.K. Smith – better known for his cricketing exploits for Warwickshire and England – Robin Davies, Peter Robbins and John Currie. Cambridge played Jim Hetherington, Arthur Smith, Bryan Richards, Andy Mulligan, David Marques and Roddy Evans. Though there was the usual quota of overseas players, notably South Africans in the Oxford XV, all these were the genuine article, enriching the university and club scene in that Brace and Smith could form an Anglo-Welsh partnership to oppose the Irish-Welsh combination of Mulligan and Richards.

Not all received the call instantly, but England had seen enough to introduce Smith, Currie, Marques and Robbins to the side that played Wales at Twickenham in January 1956. Since they lost 8-3, you would not argue that the move was entirely successful but, in the longer term, the gamble paid off: Currie and Marques proved to be the second row that England had been searching for since the war. Currie, the powerful West Countryman who could also kick goals, complemented the elegant Marques from Tonbridge School who, at 6ft 5in, was a giant in his time. Robbins, at flanker, was everything a modern back-row forward should have been then, and indeed now: intelligent, fast, destructive in the tackle but with the perception to play centre (as he was forced to do against Australia the following year because of mid-match injury). That he was also a *bon viveur* of the highest order, as a player and later as a journalist, marked him down as a distinct character.

But not all of England's nine new caps emerged from the universities: three of the others came, you might say, from the school of life but left an indelible mark on English rugby. Dickie Jeeps had, in fact, played international rugby the year before, for the Lions when he toured as the third scrum half behind Johnny Williams and Trevor Lloyd. The nuggety Northampton scrum half was the complete antithesis to Williams, who was England's choice the year before: Williams, tall and swift, was an individualist seen to best advantage in attack. Jeeps, short and stocky, could not be knocked off his game, however hard opponents tried. A reliable service earned him the role in South Africa as partner to Cliff Morgan and his courageous defence was never in doubt. Nor was his character, which marked him out as that rare animal, a reforming president of the Rugby Football Union, in 1977.

Then there was Peter Jackson, a wing who, at first glance, you might think should never be found anywhere so rough as a rugby field. Far stronger than he looked, Jackson was the kind of player who comes along once in a generation. He might have played international rugby earlier but for a fracture of the skull in 1952, which he overcame to develop his career with Coventry. It was not out-and-out pace which allowed him to score so many tries but balance and the ability to deceive defenders by moving inside and out – frequently baffling his own support runners too. His creativity was seen to greatest advantage with the 1959 Lions in Australasia, where he and O'Reilly vied for try-scoring honours and the Irishman nicknamed his rival 'Houdini', after the great escapologist.

Eric Evans after the match against Wales in 1956.

The Midlands also offered England that strong Northampton farmer, Ron Jacobs. An irreverent later generation of young English players referred to Jacobs and Sandy Sanders, whose playing careers overlapped, as 'bookends' when they toured as RFU administrators but it was no bad description. Jacobs had matured into a powerful scrummager and anchored the scrum, alongside Eric Evans, when England cast aside all opposition the following season to win the grand slam.

Not that the selectors had instant faith in their men. They retained the pack after the Welsh defeat but dropped the half backs, recalling Williams and Regan for the rest of the season. Wales had problems of their own: they had paired two distinct individuals at half back in Brace and Morgan, who was also awarded the captaincy. It is infinitely to their credit that Wales carried off the championship, given that their halves did not necessarily fit and so many of their forwards had given their all in South Africa the previous summer. Indeed, after losing 11-3 to Ireland, which cost them the triple crown and grand slam, the two Lions props, Williams and Meredith, were dropped while Rhys Williams at lock and Clem Thomas at flanker also lost their places. Given such wholesale change, the selectors must have perspired freely before Wales sneaked home 5-3 against France with a try many believed had been touched down by Derek Williams beyond the dead-ball line.

Throughout the season the Irish employed twenty-three different players, among them the witty Mulligan at scrum half, but chopped and changed their pack with the result that they could lose 20-0 to England in Dublin then, a month later, deny Wales the triple crown. But England were the coming force – they may not have been kings of style but at least they knew the players with whom they wanted to play, and how they wanted to play. In four matches they conceded only one try, and eight points in total, confirming the old maxim that success is built on defence.

It was also built, in 1957, on the leadership of Eric Evans, the Sale hooker who had made his debut as a prop nine years earlier. Evans had firm ideas on captaincy and on fitness: an athlete

Michel Vannier demonstrates his classical goal-kicking action for France in 1955.

as a youngster, he was a PE graduate from Loughborough who trained with the football professionals at Manchester United. He tried to instil that approach into his rugby-playing colleagues but above all it was his ability to create a common purpose among them, to follow his own example – as Bill Beaumont did so successfully twenty-three years later – that established him as one of England's best leaders. 'He got more out of more players than any other captain I have known,' a contemporary remarked. Like a lot of players, Evans was not averse to concealing his age. The match programme of 1956 gave his date of birth as 1925, whereas in fact he was thirty-seven when his international career concluded in 1958 after 30 appearances, 13 as captain of which the last 9 saw England unbeaten. Sadly, he and two other England players of his day, Bob Stirling (a prop first capped at the age of thirty-one) and Currie died within two months of each other midway through the 1990/91 season.

The side Evans led possessed what the *Playfair Rugby Annual* described as the most accomplished pack since the England eight of Wakefield's day in the 1920s. Intriguingly, the annual also pondered whether England would have been good enough to beat a southern-hemisphere team; the editor probably had New Zealand and South Africa in mind, but his query was answered eleven months later when a substantially-similar side beat Australia 9-6, despite having only fourteen men on the field for much of the match.

There was no chopping and changing, save for injury to Fenwick Allison at full back and the demotion midway through the season of the veteran St Mary's Hospital centre, Lew Cannell, in favour of Philip Davies. The only newcomer was Ricky Bartlett, the Harlequins fly half, who was duly grateful for the wonderful form of his back row of Robbins, Ashcroft and Reg Higgins, the Liverpool man who had broken a leg during the Lions tour two years earlier but now enjoyed an outstanding season. But Bartlett, at twenty-seven, also had the confidence to run himself, even if the scorelines did not reflect his efforts until the second half of the season.

England opened with a minimalist win in Cardiff: Allison kicking a solitary penalty after Keith Maddocks strayed offside some distance from the play. The Neath wing promptly disappeared from international rugby, though Terry Davies, at full back, did not: the timber merchant from Llanelli played the 1953 season but then suffered a string of injuries which threatened his career. However, his persistence saw him become one of Wales' most accomplished players and a Lion in Australasia in 1959.

England doubled their money in Dublin with a 6-0 victory, Jackson scoring a typical opportunist try and Robin Challis, the new full back from Bristol, kicking a penalty for what was England's first success in Ireland for nineteen years. The international rota therefore left them with two home games – a rota, it must be said, under fire from the Welsh among others who sought to make the championship a moveable feast rather than one in which, for example, England always played Wales in mid-January when the British climate is not always conducive to flowing rugby. At Twickenham, England's back division came into their own: they created two opportunities for Jackson, whose finishing proved too much for the France defence, but the alert Evans still needed a third try to give his side a 9-5 win which condemned France to the wooden spoon for the first time since 1929.

Scotland concluded England's season in more ways than one. This was the tournament in which the Scots unearthed yet another gem at full back in Ken Scotland, the aptly-named Herioteer. Slight of frame but possessed of all the skills, Scotland would have been a sensation three decades later. As it was, he stood out in a more pragmatic age, his innate footballing ability allowing him to play in every position behind the scrum at need – and the 1959 Lions did need. He scored all the points in his country's 6-0 win over France and kicked goals against Wales and Ireland; he did so again at Twickenham but it was not enough.

England's coherent play in front of the Queen, Prince Philip and Prince Charles, forced the Scots to play on retreat and gradually they were worn down. Butterfield dispatched Davies for

Ken Scotland makes a successful kick against England at Twickenham in 1959.

French spectators before the 3-3 draw with England at Twickenham in 1959. Nowadays, health regulations would prevent cockerels taking the field.

the only try of the first half; a breakaway by Higgins paved the way for Peter Thompson, that rangy Yorkshire wing, to score a second and Higgins himself finished off. The match reports in *The Times* and *The Daily Telegraph* the following Monday referred to England winning the grand slam – this is believed to be the first time such an expression was used, though O.L. Owen, rugby correspondent to *The Times* as well as editor of *Playfair*, chose not to use it in his summary of the season for the annual.

It was England's first slam since 1928 and was to be their last for another twenty-three years. Partly this was because of a chronic inability to build consistent form over a number of seasons, poor selection and uncertainty at half back. But also the late 1950s marked the period in which France rose to a level of play never previously attained and which, save for certain well-defined periods, her players have seldom deserted. It is true that England remained unbeaten during the 1958 championship – albeit with draws against Wales and Scotland – and retained a place at the head of the table, but the gauntlet was passing to the far side of the Channel.

It is not as though the French year opened brightly: in January 1958 they lost to Scotland in Edinburgh and then their defence collapsed against England in Paris. The 14-0 defeat was their sixth championship loss in a row and angry spectators called for the resignation of the selectors who, in desperation, turned to Lourdes – not for a pilgrimage but for the club three-quarters and fly half en bloc. Moreover, that winter they brought back Lucien Mias for his first cap since 1954. The nominal captain was Celaya, but everyone within French rugby knew who was running the show.

Mias was a remarkable character. He trained as a schoolmaster but then took time away from the game to qualify as a doctor. He also reflected on the lessons learned in defeat against the 1951 South Africans and the need for greater coherence from the forward pack. He experimented with Mazamet, his club, who promptly roared their way through the club championship and reached the final for the first time. He was, clearly, the man to place dynamite into the France pack – indeed Mias was nicknamed 'Dr Pack' – and he introduced radical change into the France lineout which had just acquired the tall, agile Bernard Momméjat.

He worked on what is known nowadays as the driving maul from the lineout, and the peel where forward after forward, short-passing among each other, rams into midfield. The material to hand on which Mias worked his will was outstanding: there was the balding prop, Alfred Roques (few have been better named for his position), the all-purpose Celaya, and two outstanding flankers in Michel Crauste and François Moncla. France also perfected a tap-penalty routine in which the forwards wedged their way forward, battering the opposition in a physical manner which did not appeal to spectators brought up to admire French back play, but which worked nevertheless.

Such tactics are part and parcel of the modern armoury; in the 1950s, particularly in the northern hemisphere, they caught opponents on the hop, but for France it was significant that they also caught southern-hemisphere opponents on the hop. First to suffer as a result of Dr Mias' experiments were Australia, then Wales were dismissed 16-6 in Cardiff – 'It was a bad day for Wales but a great day for rugby football,' the far-sighted Carwyn James, then playing in the Wales centre, said – and Ireland went down 11-6 in Paris. Three months later, on their first tour to one of the leading southern-hemisphere countries, France drew with South Africa in Cape Town and beat them in Johannesburg.

It was a defining year for French rugby, achieved without several leading players. Mias took over as captain in South Africa when Celaya was injured and continued in the role at home when the Five Nations came round again in 1959. France still required the final confirmation of her right to be judged at the highest level that only outright victory in the championship would bring. This was the year it happened, producing the following tribute from *Playfair Rugby*

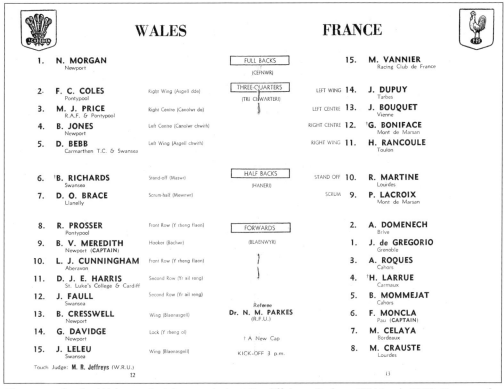

WALES			FRANCE	
		FULL BACKS		
1. **N. MORGAN** Newport		(CEFNWR)	15. **M. VANNIER** Racing Club de France	
		THREE-QUARTERS		
2. **F. C. COLES** Pontypool	Right Wing (Asgell dde)	(TRI CHWARTER)	LEFT WING 14. **J. DUPUY** Tarbes	
3. **M. J. PRICE** R.A.F. & Pontypool	Right Centre (Canolwr de)		LEFT CENTRE 13. **J. BOUQUET** Vienne	
4. **B. JONES** Newport	Left Centre (Canolwr chwith)		RIGHT CENTRE 12. **†G. BONIFACE** Mont de Marsan	
5. **D. BEBB** Carmarthen T.C. & Swansea	Left Wing (Asgell chwith)		RIGHT WING 11. **H. RANCOULE** Toulon	
		HALF BACKS		
6. **†B. RICHARDS** Swansea	Stand-off (Maswr)	(HANERI)	STAND OFF 10. **R. MARTINE** Lourdes	
7. **D. O. BRACE** Llanelly	Scrum-half (Mewnwr)		SCRUM 9. **P. LACROIX** Mont de Marsan	
8. **R. PROSSER** Pontypool	Front Row (Y rhong flaen)	**FORWARDS**	2. **A. DOMENECH** Brive	
9. **B. V. MEREDITH** Newport (CAPTAIN)	Hooker (Bachwr)	(BLAENWYR)	1. **J. de GREGORIO** Grenoble	
10. **L. J. CUNNINGHAM** Aberavon	Front Row (Y rheng flaen)		3. **A. ROQUES** Cahors	
11. **D. J. E. HARRIS** St. Luke's College & Cardiff	Second Row (Yr ail reng)		4. **†H. LARRUE** Carmaux	
12. **J. FAULL** Swansea	Second Row (Yr ail reng)		5. **B. MOMMEJAT** Cahors	
13. **B. CRESSWELL** Newport	Wing (Blaenasgell)	*Referee* Dr. N. M. PARKES (R.F.U.)	6. **F. MONCLA** Pau (CAPTAIN)	
14. **G. DAVIDGE** Newport	Lock (Y rheng ol)		7. **M. CELAYA** Bordeaux	
15. **J. LELEU** Swansea	Wing (Blaenasgell)	KICK-OFF 3 p.m.	8. **M. CRAUSTE** Lourdes	
Touch Judge: **M. R. Jeffreys** (W.R.U.)		† A New Cap		

12   13

The teams for the Wales against France clash at Cardiff Arms Park on 26 March 1960. France, who won the game 16-8, had to make several changes nearer the match day.

The France forward Amédée Domenech gets to grips with Dickie Jeeps in 1961.

Annual which also indicates something of the attitudes of the first half of the twentieth century: 'It was not until 1909/10 that France met all four home unions and so qualified for the role of recognised competitors in what they themselves – with better logic than our own – came to call "the championship of the Five Nations" in preference to "the International Championship". The way in which France were accepted as serious rugby players, tacitly rather than formally, was typical of the rugby game itself which abhors anything like leagues and league points, looks to tradition and goodwill to settle most of its problems and allows those who wish to play each other to do so if possible.' There is both a provocative assumption and an innocence about those remarks, judged by today's standards which are sometimes less than elevated.

The annual went on to refer to France's meteoric rise 'almost to the status of world champions', even while some domestic critics were crying out for some of the French back play of yesteryear. Their *modus operandi* was laid bare as they ground towards the championship title, scoring a modest 28 points (still more than any other country) with only 4 tries, and conceding 15 points. They opened with a 9-0 win over Scotland, the first international match to be refereed by the dapper little Welshman, Gwynne Walters, still regarded by many as the best official they have seen at work for his encouragement of open play and his severity yet good sense in handling violent conduct.

Still, even a Walters cannot force players to fluid rugby if that does not form part of the game plan, and part of the French plan was to win. One critic spoke of France's 'magisterial cohesion, their aggressiveness and their defensive fury', little of which was apparent when they drew 3-3 with England at Twickenham. Perhaps French confidence had been dented by the withdrawal on the eve of the match of Mias himself and they might have won had not Jean Dupuy, the wing, dropped the ball with the line at his mercy, although England's forwards had the whip hand throughout.

Yet it became one of those seasons when no one side could sustain a run of success; the sequence of matches left England losing to Wales, then drawing with Scotland, who in turn beat Wales then lost to Ireland, who had already lost to England. At any event, the championship pushed deep into April and left France involved in the final two matches, victory in either being enough to give them the title. They did not hang around: 'It's only a rugby match,' Mias told his players. 'If Wales beat us, we'll have all the more fun against the Irish in Dublin.' What he told them in private, of course, may be another matter altogether.

France won 11-3, both tries going to the athletic Moncla. Mias was carried from the field by cheering spectators as a nation celebrated fifty years of trying and Paris in the springtime sunshine became a byword in British rugby for a place to be avoided. Had not the Wales defence laboured so hard, they might have been overwhelmed but victory placed France in an unassailable position in the table, though typically Ireland overturned the champions on the final day – deservedly so with a pack of whom Syd Millar, Ronnie Dawson and Noel Murphy have become integral to Irish rugby, as players and administrators, for forty years.

It becomes easy, at this stage, to see the championship as a French domain for a decade. During that period France never finished lower than third: there were four championships in a row, a hiatus and then the build-up to the first grand slam of 1968. In truth, they illuminated the scene in a way that none of the home countries could achieve, even after another Lions tour (to Australasia in 1959) which reflected almost as much credit on British rugby as its predecessor to South Africa of 1955. Perhaps such tours persuaded the British that everything in their garden was reasonably rosy, even as the likes of Cliff Morgan, Jeff Butterfield and Jim Greenwood departed the scene – in the case of Greenwood, the Scotland No. 8, to inspire a generation of young rugby players (mostly English) with his work at Loughborough Colleges and to write two books, *Total Rugby* and *Think Rugby*, that are classics of their kind.

Not only did the French achieve the concrete results they had craved for so long, they did so with a style and a zest the home unions could seldom match. There was, of course, the occasional blip on the radar – the 3-3 draw at Paris in 1960, for example, when that fine full back, Michel Vannier, saved French bacon with a penalty goal. The match contained what one writer described as an 'orgy of scrums and lineouts', which sounds something akin to England's usual way of constricting the French, by tying them into set-piece play. Yet France still enjoyed their first unbeaten season in the championship, that drawn game costing them the grand slam and forcing them to share the title with England, similarly unbeaten. It is no coincidence that the aggregate points total for the season of 187 was the highest since 1931, with France contributing 11 tries – the other four countries together weighed in with only 20. It is as though success had established a new confidence in French rugby. Even though Mias had departed the scene to resume his medical studies, the captaincy passing to Moncla, his methods and his discipline lived on. Moreover, the selectors were prepared to introduce a greater degree of adventure, by recalling Pierre Albaladejo at fly half and introducing Guy Boniface at centre.

Albaladejo, who went on to become a respected television commentator, had been capped once in 1954, as a full back. Now the Dax pivot prompted an end-of-season display against Ireland in Paris that earned him the name of 'Monsieur Drop': in the course of a 23-6 victory, he dropped three goals in an unprecedented display, to go with four tries of which, curiously, only one was converted. The match was described as a 'gift from the gods', in the course of which a Lions front row of Millar, Dawson and Gordon Wood was overwhelmed by Domenech, Roques and the aggressive little Grenoble hooker, Jean de Gregorio.

The tale was almost exactly similar for France in 1961, though now they did not have to share the title with anyone. It was England, once more, against whom they faltered, managing only a 5-5 draw at Twickenham – though they were to take ample revenge in due course. They were armed well enough, fore and aft, to ride over a string of injuries, their goal-kickers, Albaladejo and Vannier, carrying them forward when their try-scoring ability slipped. Buoyed up, too, by a

0-0 draw with Avril Malan's South Africans, who had carried all before them in their four internationals in Britain and Ireland, they were able to depart for their first tour of New Zealand as unbeaten, undisputed champions of the northern hemisphere.

That tour gave France pause for thought. Lacking several leading players, including the indomitable Roques, they lost three internationals to the All Blacks, the final one by the compelling margin of 32-3, which left the selectors casting round for scapegoats. The obvious one was Moncla, the captain, and he was followed two matches later by Celaya, after 50 appearances. The captaincy moved between Crauste and Pierre Lacroix, the little scrum half from Agen, but the New Zealand tour did produce something of lasting benefit – the uniting in the centre of the Boniface brothers, André and Guy. André, the older, had been the *wunderkind* of French rugby at eighteen and was believed not to have matured. In fact, the game in France was probably not quite ready for his insouciance when he first appeared, but now it was.

With their tight five restored to full strength, France shrugged off the All Black effect. They disposed of Scotland at Murrayfield and then tore England to shreds in Paris: the 13-0 scoreline may not sound like a pummelling but that is what it was, all three French tries falling to Crauste. It was a remarkable display by the Lourdes flanker, whose drooping moustache earned him the nicknames 'Attila' or 'The Mongol'. His aggressive play was also somewhat similar in effect to that of an invading horde and England, on an icy afternoon, could have been forgiven for thinking there was more than one Crauste on the field; his first try stemmed from a lineout in the first half, his second from inter-passing among the forwards and his third from a cross-kick by André Boniface.

There seemed little prospect of Wales or Ireland holding the French surge towards the championship but Wales did, in a game remarkable for one incident: Henri Rancoule, the wing, had been liberated in his own half and the mind's eye, admittedly helped by the television

Christian Darrouy hands off Ronnie Thomson, his would-be tackler, in the match against Scotland at Stade Colombes in 1963. France lost the match 6-11. Jim Shackleton and Crauste are to the left.

camera, created the impression that he was entirely alone on the Cardiff turf. But Alun Pask, the Wales No. 8 with seven-league boots, came diagonally across the pitch to catch Rancoule with a wonderful cover tackle and the Welsh hung on to win 3-0.

For four seasons, thereafter, France had to cede first place in the championship, to England (once) and Wales (three times). Their pack was an unsettled area, with Crauste – with 63 appearances before his star finally waned – the only consistent element to be found. There was talent enough in the back division, with the rediscovery of Christian Darrouy, the Mont-de-Marsan wing first capped in 1957, and the inspired selection on the wing of the diminutive (5ft 4in) Jean Gachassin, more accustomed to playing fly half or full back for Lourdes. But the components up front had to be assembled. First to arrive was Benoit Dauga, the rangy second row from Mont-de-Marsan who brought formidable basketball skills to bear and became, according to Jean Prat, the greatest forward ever produced by France. Then there was Arnaldo Gruarin, the Toulon prop, and the formidable Walter Spanghéro, who played with his three brothers at Narbonne and, like Dauga, could play anywhere in the back five of the scrum. The final element was the alert flanker from Toulon, Christian Carrère, who came into the side when Crauste left it and very quickly assumed the captaincy. Having put together another pack of players at once hard and aggressive, but also athletic and fast, the final piece of the jigsaw was to settle on half backs who would use their possession effectively.

Guy Cambérabéro had made his debut at fly half in that 32-3 defeat in New Zealand in 1961; he reappeared briefly a year later when Albaladejo was unavailable and then, two years later, was picked alongside his brother, Lilian, against Romania. The two played together for La Voulte, but over the ensuing seasons it appeared that Lilian, at scrum half, was the more favoured of the fraternal pairing. It was not until 1967, against Australia, that they resumed operations for the national side and Guy gave some indication of what France had missed by kicking 17 points from four penalty goals, a dropped goal and a conversion.

The French lightning flickered on the horizon – against Ireland when they scored six tries in 1964 and Albaladejo called it a day and against Wales, who had won the triple crown and were going for the grand slam in 1965 but who lost 22-13 in Paris (France's highest score ever against the Welsh). A year later a new luminary entered the fray, in the form of curly-haired centre, Jo Maso, soon to be accompanied by Claude Dourthe and Jean-Pierre Lux. These were runners of the highest order but, more importantly, they were inventive and imaginative, with an apparently innate understanding of what the others would do.

It was not instantly apparent that a new era was about to dawn, since Scotland left Paris clutching a precious 9-8 win after Maso suffered a leg injury and forced France to play with a seven-man pack. But that was forgotten in a wonderful French win at Twickenham, their first there since 1955. In a memorable performance, Dourthe crossed after only three minutes and the France backs zigged and zagged their way around the pitch like so many firecrackers. Bernard Duprat scored a second try and Guy Cambérabéro's kicking did the rest in a 16-12 win. Against Wales, Cambérabéro went through the card with a try, a conversion, a penalty goal and two dropped goals in a 20-14 win which overshadowed the introduction to international rugby of that unique scrum half, Gareth Edwards. The championship was secured in Ireland and the stage was set for France to secure that elusive first grand slam.

However, there was the little matter of a four-international series in South Africa to be played first, which closed Darrouy's 40-match career in which he scored 23 tries, and matches against New Zealand and Romania to be cleared out of the way, in which the selectors fiddled around with their half-back combinations before settling once more on the brothers from La Voulte. There was also tragedy to be overcome: Guy Boniface, the younger of the brothers, died in a road accident on New Year's Eve at the age of thirty and, three days later, so did Jean-Michel Capendeguy, twenty-three, the Bègles wing who had been picked to play against Scotland.

Boniface had played 35 international matches and, with his brother, created an attitude which has percolated down through the years to generations of French midfield players. Perhaps it was no surprise that the French were subdued in their opening game with the Scots and were grateful when Stewart Wilson, the home full back, failed to touch down an attempted dropped goal; Duprat steamed up to score the try and though Scotland nosed ahead 6-3, Dauga laid on a second try for André Campaès and Guy Cambérabéro's conversion – on a day so windy that his brother had to hold the ball still – snatched the win at 8-6. Even then, the hapless Wilson had a penalty opportunity in the last minute which flew wide.

There was little sympathy from the France selectors, who tossed out the Cambérabéro brothers for the meeting with Ireland, installed Gachassin and Jean-Henri Mir (an original selection against Scotland but doomed to win only two caps) instead, and brought back the Toulouse full back, Pierre Villepreux – highly-rated but suffering all season from the after-effects of rib injuries sustained against the All Blacks – for the veteran Claude Lacaze. They beat Ireland 16-6, assisted by injuries to Mick Molloy and Ken Kennedy which reduced them to the status of passengers, Campaès and Dauga scoring the tries in an exhibition which was less than free-flowing.

Remarkably in mid-season and with two wins behind them, the French then made nine changes for the game with England in Paris. The Camberaberos returned, and a new front five (only Elié Cester survived) was put together. Many believed that England should have won, but they lost 14-9 after leading 9-3 just after the interval. England's undoing was a gorgeous try with Lacaze chiming in from full back, Campaès kicking ahead and Gachassin (now playing centre) winning the touchdown. Lacaze and Guy Cambérabéro added dropped goals and France were home and dry.

A month later they were home and wet, but they did not care: in the rain and mud of Cardiff Arms Park, the grand slam became theirs fifty-eight years after the Five Nations Championship had begun. There had been change, again, at centre, where Maso and Dourthe came together, and Michel Greffe, the Grenoble No. 8, was called up for his debut after Jean-Pierre Salut was forced to withdraw. If you are going to make only one appearance in the championship, as Greffe did, a grand-slam winning game is a good one to choose. 'Take us as we are or leave us in peace with our club,' Lilian Cambérabéro, the younger of the brothers (and reputed to have the longest pass in Europe) said. On 23 March 1968, their many critics did exactly that. Once again their opponents went out to a 9-3 lead, David Rees kicking two penalties and Keri Jones scoring a try against Guy Cambérabéro's dropped goal. But the France half backs took a tactical grip on the second half, Carrère scored a try, Guy kicked a penalty and converted a try by his brother and the match was won, 14-9.

It was by no means the best XV France had ever put into the field ('The best of a rather poor lot' grizzled the *Playfair Rugby Annual*); they scored only seven tries and the arguments continued about their style of rugby – as they did ten years later when Jacques Fouroux's team achieved the same feat – but the fact remained that they had put together four wins, which none of their predecessors had done. Whether British rugby was at a low ebb at the time is neither here nor there. 'Who would have said in the 1920s that the French would eventually become dominating rugby champions in Europe?' that veteran Welsh critic, J.B.G. Thomas, reflected, attributing much of their success to an ultra-competitive club championship. That was, of course, the same championship that had been anathema to the British a decade and more before.

5
THE HOME NATIONS
1956-1968

So, had British rugby been at a low ebb during the 1960s? Drawing a line through the three tours made by the Lions during the decade, the answer is 'yes', and that period coincided with the mounting enthusiasm for coaches. Hitherto, preparation of the side had depended on the captain, when he and his players gathered during the twenty-four hours preceding the match. Various chairmen of selectors would throw in their ten pennyworth and dark stories have been told of selectors scrumming down against the team to try and sort out technical problems.

Eric Evans would have wanted more from his men, having mingled so much with professional footballers, but custom and practice dictated otherwise. The presence of a physical education specialist such as Jeff Butterfield was always welcome and in every team there would be a quantity of deep thinkers about the game around whom tactical debate would swirl. Take Ireland as an example: any pack containing the likes of Syd Millar, Ronnie Dawson and Ray McLoughlin, strong-minded characters with a great understanding of the mechanics of the game, would have a shrewd idea of where it was going. Millar went on to coach and manage Lions parties, Dawson captained the Lions and McLoughlin, though injured, contributed significantly towards the success of the 1971 Lions through his intelligent appreciation of forward play.

Yet it was a thoroughly depressing decade for the Irish in terms of results. Only in the final two years did they scramble up from the championship basement to challenge, but they did produce a string of competitive players and two who can truly be described as great – Mike Gibson (8) and Willie John McBride. Scotland, with the dark days of the 1950s behind them, were almost invariably competitive and must have been good fun to be with in the early days of the 1960s. Their back division included that ebullient character, Joe McPartlin, and relied heavily on London Scottish, at that time virtual rulers of seven-a-side rugby, with a particularly cultured pair of halves in Iain Laughland and Tremayne Rodd.

But Wales and England led a yo-yo existence which persuaded frustrated individuals in both countries to believe that more, much more, could be achieved by countries with so strong a tradition in the game behind them and, in the case of England, so strong a playing population. In 1959, the English scored precisely nine points in four games yet lost only once – no wonder Jeff Butterfield, with 28 appearances making him at the time his country's most-capped back, retired. However, matters improved dramatically with the first outing of the new season.

As was rapidly becoming their habit, England threw seven newcomers into the clash with a Wales side littered with Lions. One of the debutants was the blond Oxford University fly half, Richard Sharp, selected only because Bev Risman had to withdraw with injury, and it is worth noting that the selectors, who had casually dispensed with Peter Jackson, one of the sensations of the Lions tour in New Zealand, made no further changes throughout the season. Rarely do the same fifteen players survive in the turbulent world of the Five Nations, but England had found a successful formula and stuck with it, forcing a 3-3 draw in Paris which gave them a share, with France, of the title.

Within the space of forty minutes at Twickenham, England scored more points than they had done in an entire season a year earlier and showed that the British game was far from moribund. Don Rutherford, in the first year of a career as player and administrator that was not terminated until 1999, brought stability both to the full back berth and in terms of goal-kicking, but it was Sharp who produced the game's seminal moment when he broke from halfway to create the

The Wales team that beat England in 1956. Back row: G. Owen, M. Thomas, R. Robbins, R. Williams, W. Williams, L. Jenkins. Seated: C. Meredith, C. Thomas, B. Meredith, C. Morgan (captain), B. Sparks, L. Davies, K. Jones. Front: O. Brace, H. Morgan.

Dewi Bebb takes on the England defence at Cardiff Arms Park, with Peter Jackson on the right.

space for Mike Weston to send Jim Roberts, the Old Millhillian, away for his second try. All England's 14 points came in the first half and though Wales pulled back six, the game had been won and lost in that first period (though modern critics would suggest that here was yet another case of England failing to put an opponent away).

Sharp had a relatively limited career for a player who has left such a legend behind him. The tall, slim Cornishman won no more than 14 caps but, on his day, was capable of running more fluently than any other England fly half since the Second World War. Less gifted in defensive terms, he was fortunate to have Jeeps to nurse him during his first three seasons of international rugby and even so, the selectors were seldom entirely certain whether to go for him or Risman until the latter made their minds up for them by turning professional.

England saved their best for last that year, scoring 21 points against Scotland at Murrayfield, 13 of them in as many minutes with Sharp's dropped goal opening the way. Tries by Ron Syrett and Roberts were both converted from difficult angles by Rutherford, who had missed a none-too-difficult conversion in Paris which might have won that game. Ken Scotland kicked his country back into contention, but John Young, the sprinter preferred to Jackson, raced away for England's third try which prevented any hope of a home rally and ensured the triple crown for England, their first since 1957.

The next year, however, Wales edged and elbowed their way to the front of the queue behind France. Maybe it was fear of being drowned at the Arms Park – the River Taff burst its banks during the night following the December meeting with South Africa – but Wales were never less than competitive during the 1961 championship. They started with an attractive game against England: 6-3 may not strike modern eyes as a romp but, on a boggy surface, there was plenty of open play to admire and two tries by Dewi Bebb on the Wales left wing. Bebb, from Swansea, always seemed to save himself for England, 6 of his 11 international tries were scored against the white jerseys in a nine-year career for Wales.

A North Walian from Bangor, rare enough in all conscience, Bebb joined Swansea when he went to study at Trinity College, Carmarthen. He won 34 caps, scurrying over, rather than

The England team that won the grand slam in 1957. Back row: J. Butterfield, P. Davies, P. Thompson, D. Marques, J. Currie, P. Robbins, R. Jacobs, R. Challis. Seated: P. Jackson, G. Hastings, E. Evans (captain), A. Ashcroft, R. Higgins. Front: R. Bartlett, R. Jeeps.

Arthur Smith attempts to break through Mike Weston's tackle during the 1961 Calcutta Cup match.

through, the mud of the Arms Park to score a try on his debut against England in 1959, and learned to go looking for opportunities on the basis that his midfield colleagues were unlikely to offer him many. Like Onllwyn Brace, whose last season this was (curiously he returned for one match, against Ireland, as captain), Bebb became a television commentator and producer when his playing career ended.

This was also the season in which Wales brought Alun Pask into their back row to join his colleague from Abertillery, Haydn Morgan. Pask was a player who would have revelled in the modern game – he had everything, pace, good hands and size (he was 6ft 3in). Initially picked at blind-side flanker, the position in which he would probably have played today, he was a thoughtful No. 8 with leadership qualities which should have earned him the captaincy of the 1966 Lions. That honour went to Michael Campbell-Lamerton, the Scotland lock, who found it necessary to stand down from the team in New Zealand because of loss of form. 'One of the most accomplished all-round footballers in his position that Wales had then seen,' the WRU's official history claimed, and few would argue. So accomplished was Pask that he played full back against Ireland with the greatest facility in 1965, when injury forced a shuffle of personnel. His imperturbable character made him an excellent foil for the flyaway Morgan. Some of the great portraits of the era are those of Pask diving one-handed to score for Wales and the Lions. Sadly he died, aged fifty-eight, in a house fire in 1995 in his native Blackwood, from where he seldom moved far.

Victory over Ireland confirmed the Welsh in second place that year, then it was Scotland's turn to tilt at France. This was no surprise: Wales, in scoring a miserable nine points in 1962 (no tries) used twenty-six players and Ireland thirty-one, while England tut-tutted after losing

13-0 to the French and promptly recast their back division. In addition, they terminated the international career of John Currie, whose run of twenty-two games in the second row alongside David Marques had ended the season before. Scotland, though, had assembled a useful mixture of youth and age: in the former category fell Ronnie Cowan, the Selkirk wing, and Kenny Ross, the Boroughmuir flanker. The hard heads included a strong front row in Hughie McLeod (in the process of passing John Bannerman's record of 37 appearances for Scotland), Norman Bruce, the Army hooker, and David Rollo, the farmer from Howe of Fife. There was also Ronnie Glasgow, playing his first international season in the back row at the age of thirty-one and proving that he should surely have been selected far earlier.

The Scotland forwards held their French opposites, but they were sadly let down behind the scrum and lost 11-3. 'History favours the Welsh,' proclaimed the match programme when Scotland arrived in Cardiff, mentioning happily that the visitors had not won in the capital since 1927, nor in Wales since 1937. 'Scotland rarely appear to do themselves justice as a team at the Arms Park,' the programme went on, but in the wet and the wind, Stan Coughtrie, the lanky scrum half, directed tactics while Glasgow and Frans ten Bos scored the tries that beat Wales 8-3. Even better, Scotland recorded their highest win in Dublin, beating Ireland 20-6 with a significant contribution from Arthur Smith, who scored two tries.

This was Smith's last international year, which culminated with his captaincy of the Lions to South Africa. In 33 matches on the wing he scored 12 tries, embellishing his scoring record with six penalty goals and a conversion, having made himself into a goal-kicker on the 1955 Lions tour when a broken arm limited his availability for matches but allowed him to train assiduously. An effective finisher, Smith was another player who died far too prematurely at the age of forty-two, through illness, and he deserved a better climax to his career than the somewhat tedious 3-3 draw against England which denied the Scots the triple crown – as did McLeod, who finished with 40 caps, and Gordon Waddell who had followed Herbert, his father, as Scotland's fly half. Remarkably, McLeod, then thirty-one, turned up at Twickenham a year later with the Hawick team guesting in the Middlesex seven-a-side tournament and which reached the final.

The gracenote to the season was provided by Ireland and Wales. Their meeting in Dublin, scheduled for March, had to be postponed because of an outbreak of smallpox in the Rhondda Valley so the season was not technically completed until 17 November when the two countries played out a 3-3 draw which did nothing for their standing in the table. It was the final appearance of that fine Newport hooker, Bryn Meredith, who played in 34 games for Wales. Meredith was an artist in the days when hookers could strike for the opposition ball but he was also a mobile player capable – as he showed playing for the 1959 Lions – of playing in the back row. It was one of the mortifying experiences that a player who should have done so well for the Lions in South Africa in 1955 had to play second fiddle to the tour captain, Ronnie Dawson, in 1959.

Nor was it much assistance to Welsh preparations for the 1963 championship, in which they finished last. They were almost as convinced as England of the need for change and included five newcomers to England's seven, among them Clive Rowlands, the Pontypool scrum half who was also entrusted with the captaincy. But on a bone-hard, frostbound pitch in a winter so severe that nearly all rugby was called off for three months – England had been forced to train on the beach at Porthcawl the day before, the surface was so solid – Wales went down 13-6. They were not to know that it would be twenty-eight years before England won again in Cardiff.

Six of England's debutants were in the pack, leaving only Budge Rogers and Brian Wightman, winning his second cap, to offer a degree of experience. Rogers, the Bedford flanker, announced his appearance with a try against Ireland in 1961 and, pound for pound, was one of the most effective back-row forwards England have produced since the war. His fitness was legendary and kept him playing for his club deep into the 1970s when he was nearer forty than thirty. Rogers' destructive tackling was as distinctive as his trademark scrum cap and his value to the English game was illustrated by his selection on the panel which, chaired by Sir George Mallaby in the early 1970s, composed the report recommending far-reaching changes to the structure of English rugby.

Both sides dipped into the Cambridge University bag, Wales drawing forth Brian Thomas and Roger Michaelson for their pack, England claiming Simon Clarke at scrum half and Nick Drake-Lee in the front row. Amid a clatter of studs and on a ground ringed with straw (no under-soil heating or heavy plastic covering in those days to keep out the frost), England ripped into the home side, worked a splendid back move for Malcolm Phillips to score and then created a second try for John Owen. Dai Hayward's try from a lineout arrived only in injury-time, leaving Wales looking at a 13-6 defeat and a dismal season rescued from oblivion only by a 6-0 win against Scotland when Rowlands kicked the game to death behind a series of lineouts which one observer reckoned at over 100. 'Dai Ding-dong', they called him after that, or 'Clive the Kick', but his favourite nickname was 'Top Cat'. Rowlands, with his broad grin and tactical brain, helped pave the way for the Australian dispensation later in the decade, disallowing kicks direct to touch outside the 22-metre line.

England's progress faltered in a 0-0 draw against Ireland. Such a scoreline is virtually impossible to conceive now, but England had achieved the same a year earlier, against Wales. Also in that previous year, Ireland had introduced to international rugby a raw-boned Ulster lock, Willie John McBride, who shared in a 16-0 defeat with Johnny Quirke, the Blackrock College scrum half who, at seventeen, was Ireland's youngest ever player. 'Since his debut for Ulster in 1960,' the match programme noted, 'McBride has advanced steadily, especially in his lineout technique, and is becoming formidable as well in the open.' He could have had no better mentors in tight forward play than his props that day, Millar and McLoughlin, and Bill Mulcahy, the experienced Bohemians lock who was captain.

Opponents were not to see the back of McBride until 1975 and in between he won all the honours going, including five Lions tours, the last of them as captain of the party that finally won a series in South Africa and proved invincible. At 6ft 3in, McBride began his career at 15st 8lb and concluded it a stone heavier and with 63 caps to his credit. If you include

Bryn Meredith in action against the England team in 1956.

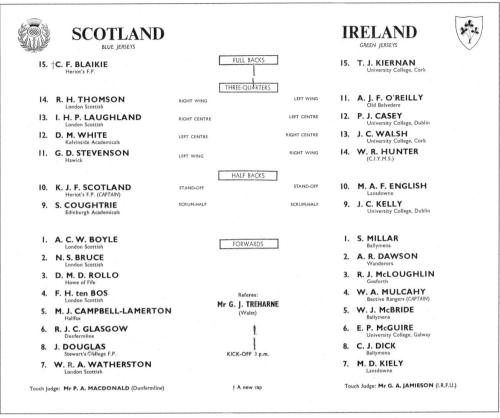

SCOTLAND
BLUE JERSEYS

IRELAND
GREEN JERSEYS

		FULL BACKS		
15. †C. F. BLAIKIE Heriot's F.P.			15.	T. J. KIERNAN University College, Cork

THREE-QUARTERS

14. R. H. THOMSON London Scottish	RIGHT WING	LEFT WING	11.	A. J. F. O'REILLY Old Belvedere
13. I. H. P. LAUGHLAND London Scottish	RIGHT CENTRE	LEFT CENTRE	12.	P. J. CASEY University College, Dublin
12. D. M. WHITE Kelvinside Academicals	LEFT CENTRE	RIGHT CENTRE	13.	J. C. WALSH University College, Cork
11. G. D. STEVENSON Hawick	LEFT WING	RIGHT WING	14.	W. R. HUNTER (C.I.Y.M.S.)

HALF BACKS

10. K. J. F. SCOTLAND Heriot's F.P. (CAPTAIN)	STAND-OFF	STAND-OFF	10.	M. A. F. ENGLISH Lansdowne
9. S. COUGHTRIE Edinburgh Academicals	SCRUM-HALF	SCRUM-HALF	9.	J. C. KELLY University College, Dublin

FORWARDS

1. A. C. W. BOYLE London Scottish		1.	S. MILLAR Ballymena
2. N. S. BRUCE London Scottish		2.	A. R. DAWSON Wanderers
3. D. M. D. ROLLO Howe of Fife		3.	R. J. McLOUGHLIN Gosforth
4. F. H. ten BOS London Scottish	Referee: Mr G. J. TREHARNE (Wales)	4.	W. A. MULCAHY Bective Rangers (CAPTAIN)
5. M. J. CAMPBELL-LAMERTON Halifax		5.	W. J. McBRIDE Ballymena
6. R. J. C. GLASGOW Dunfermline		6.	E. P. McGUIRE University College, Galway
8. J. DOUGLAS Stewart's College F.P.	KICK-OFF 3 p.m.	8.	C. J. DICK Ballymena
7. W. R. A. WATHERSTON London Scottish		7.	M. D. KIELY Lansdowne

Touch Judge: **Mr P. A. MACDONALD** (Dunfermline)	† A new cap	Touch Judge: **Mr G. A. JAMIESON** (I.R.F.U.)

The line-ups for the Scotland versus Ireland clash at Murrayfield in 1963. The home team emerged victorious in a low-scoring contest, 3-0.

17 international appearances for the Lions, McBride's sustained calibre leaves no room for doubt; it was of such players that Colin Meads, the All Blacks lock, was doubtless thinking when he growled after the victorious Lions had left his country in 1971 that the British 'used to believe in fairy stories. Not any more.'

On a wet Dublin day the experience of the Irish blunted the youthful English who were lucky to escape with a draw – had Tom Kiernan been available to kick for goal, they would probably have lost, but he was injured. The full back from Cork was another of those individuals who became a pillar of the Irish rugby community. Kiernan's debut had come against England in 1960 and, after winning 54 caps, he retired in 1973 as his country's leading points scorer with 154, their most-capped player and most experienced captain, leading his country 24 times. He subsequently became a devoted administrator and a member of the panel which created the European Cup tournament in 1995/96.

The use of hot-air blowers – rugby has always had a capacity for hot air – helped make Twickenham playable when France arrived and departed with a flea in their ear, beaten 6-5. Guy Boniface scored the only try but John Willcox, the Ampleforth schoolmaster and one of the bravest players to appear for England at full back, kicked two penalties to carry the day. The result was slim justification for the tinkering with the pack which elevated David Perry to No. 8, but the Bedford player proved an outstanding prospect before his career was blighted by injury. More tinkering followed, to the front row, before the Calcutta Cup match with Scotland which will always be identified with Richard Sharp as much as was his opening international against Wales three years earlier.

Willie John McBride sets the ball up against England in 1964. Ireland won the game 18-5.

Victory for the Scots would have brought them the championship and when they went into an eight-point lead in bright sunshine, their prospects seemed good. Glasgow scored from a lineout and Scotland, playing at fly half, dropped a goal. However, the elusive Jackson, recalled for a final championship season after being inexplicably ignored for three years, found space and Drake-Lee was first to his chip ahead. Willcox converted and Coughtrie missed a penalty, which left England trailing by three points. This deficit was erased by Sharp from a scrum near the Scotland 22. The fly half dummied to Weston in the centre and his audacious run took him clear of three defenders for a superb solo try fit to win a championship title.

Neither Jackson, Sharp nor Jim Roberts appeared in the championship again, though Sharp made a brief and none-too-successful return to international rugby, as captain against Australia, four years later. Yet in their swansong they had provided the antidote to accusations of 'boring England' and provided the platform for the first national side to make a short tour to New Zealand. In the next three seasons, England won only two matches (both against France) and seldom seemed convinced that they knew who their best fly half was: Phil Horrocks-Taylor was followed by the Liverpool crackerjack, Tom Brophy, and Michael Weston had to do duty there before John Finlan brought some measure of continuity. Not only that, the selectors were forever adjusting their back row and then decided that, no, it was scrum half that was the problem: Johnny Williams was recalled for one cap, nine years after his last, the bohemian Harlequin, Jeremy Spencer, received one cap while Clive Ashby and Trevor Wintle traded places before Roger Pickering survived for the 1967 championship.

This left the field clear for Wales for a three-year period. True, they shared the spoils with Scotland in 1964, but the following two seasons provided a cameo of what was to become known as the decade of the dragon from 1969 until 1979. There was a certain dependable quality about the Welsh under Rowlands which was not precisely in accord with the expectancy of the public in Wales – the fervour of the game's followers in that country invariably being a cross for the national side to bear. Rowlands himself encapsulated it neatly enough when, as manager of the side that played in the first World Cup in 1987, he was asked what the future was for Wales after a 40-point demolition by New Zealand in the semi-finals: 'We go back to beating England,' Rowlands said chirpily, which was a neat one-liner but bore a hollow ring when Wales found they could not even do that.

That Wales were unbeaten in the 1964 championship, after losing to Wilson Whineray's All Blacks, offered a limited amount to crow about. They drew twice and won twice while Scotland, in fact, won three of their four matches but lost, of course, to Wales. This was Scotland's best season since 1938, coming off the back of their 0-0 draw with New Zealand, and for the game with France on a greasy pitch they introduced the 6ft 2in Melrose flanker, Jim Telfer. Thirty-six years later, Telfer is still a rock on which Scottish rugby is built, a coach and administrator who has inspired respect the world over. Telfer made his debut alongside the underrated Pringle Fisher and the unorthodox Peter Brown, another goal-kicking lock forward but the only one who turned his back on the ball when he stepped away from it, sniffed at it and then launched it like some deranged missile in the direction of the posts. Curiously, the ball found its target far more frequently than ever seemed likely though, so far as is known, Brown never wrote a book advising young goal-kickers on their technique. If they needed something a shade more conventional, Scotland could turn to the young Oxford University full back, Stewart Wilson, also playing his first match and a competitor who only just fell short of the great tradition of Scotland full backs.

Wilson converted tries by the London Scotsmen, Laughland and Thomson, which gave Scotland their 10-0 victory over France, but they could not sustain their winning form in

Noel Murphy, the long-serving Ireland flanker, scores a try against England at Twickenham in 1964.

Cardiff. They eked out victory over Ireland, keeping their ammunition dry for the Calcutta Cup match in which they ended a sequence of thirteen matches without victory against England. Scotland's back row of Telfer, Fisher and Ron Glasgow dominated the game at Murrayfield. Glasgow picked up the first try, Brown's charge from a lineout led to a second for Norman Bruce and Telfer was credited with the third in a convincing 15-6 win which marked the end of the England careers of John Willcox, Malcolm Phillips and Ron Jacobs.

Wales, meanwhile, stumbled at the last hurdle when an out-of-sorts France team arrived in Cardiff. The Welsh had opened the championship with a draw against England, but victory would have given them the title. Instead they had to thank Stuart Watkins, the gangling Newport wing capped first earlier that season against Scotland, for the try which allowed Keith Bradshaw to kick the conversion and gain an 11-11 draw.

All in all it was not a distinguished season, even though it saw the introduction of Cameron Michael Henderson Gibson to a wider audience. Gibson was the 'most talked-of out-half in Britain so far this season,' the match programme for the England-Ireland game claimed. A product of Campbell College in Belfast, Gibson was studying law at Cambridge and, at twenty, had been a travelling reserve the season before. His dapper, pale looks masked a hugely-competitive spirit and an analytical mind way beyond most of his contemporaries. Gibson was one of those who read the game like a chess master, foreseeing the end play even while the opening moves were unfurled.

His pace and fitness was such that, even playing on the wing in his thirties, he could baffle all but the best, although the debate will always remain whether he was a better fly half or centre. The control he placed on the game seemed made for fly half, but Gibson would seldom settle for the pedestrian – the truly gifted need players of the same ilk if their skills are to be properly appreciated and Ireland could not provide them. The Lions, however, could, and in

The Wales side that won the triple crown n 1965. Back row: N. Gale, D. Williams, B. Thomas, B. Price, R. Waldron, G. Prothero. Seated: J. Uzzell, A. Pask, C. Rowlands (captain), J. Dawes, S. Watkins. Front: D. Bebb, T. Price, D. Watkins, H. Morgan.

1971 Gibson played centre with Barry John and Gareth Edwards as his half backs, and a back row to match. New Zealanders, quite rightly, consider him to be one of the immortals. On that tour he played alongside John Dawes who, coincidentally, also made his debut in this season, though Wales did not require him so frequently as Ireland wanted Gibson in the course of a fifteen-year career embracing 69 Ireland apppearances and 12 for the Lions.

Gibson helped Ireland to a 16-0 win at Twickenham which, though it meant little in terms of the 1964 championship, gave them something on which to build respectability the following year. 'The only consistent factor, it seems, year after year, in the International Championship, is the inconsistency which attends its destiny,' the *Playfair Rugby Annual* observed. Scotland declined, Ray McLoughlin cajoled Ireland to mid-table and Wales discovered another sensational teenaged prospect in Terry Price, who was known both for his exploits with Llanelli Grammar School and as the player who broke Waka Nathan's jaw while playing against the All Blacks on Llanelli's wing.

Price, who died in a road accident in 1993 when he was only forty-seven, was yet another meteor. He played only eight games for Wales before turning professional with Bradford Northern but his career was spoiled by injuries and a certain self-indulgent streak. However, at his best he was a player of startling self-confidence, capable of turning a match with an outrageous break. He was nineteen when he played against England in Cardiff, the first of three matches in each of which Wales scored 14 points and which won them the triple crown. With David Watkins coming to full bloom at fly half, Wales looked certain to claim another grand slam, but they came undone in Paris.

England threw a brand-new threequarter line, plucked largely from Oxbridge, into the Cardiff mud and if they were unrecognisable to the general public before the game they almost became unrecognisable to each other during it. Two tries by Stuart Watkins did the damage in a 14-3 win, and the wing scored another in the 14-12 defeat of Scotland. Ireland, meanwhile, held France to a draw and edged their way past England before setting up a triple crown decider against the Welsh by beating Scotland 16-6 at Murrayfield.

Each side restored an old Lion to its ranks. Wales called up Keith Rowlands, the Cardiff lock who later became secretary to the International Rugby Football Board and co-ordinator of the 1999 World Cup, whilst Ireland invited David Hewitt, that wonderfully-elusive centre and scion of a distinguished rugby family, to play on the wing in what turned out to be his international curtain-call – as it was for the hard-working Mulcahy. Both, perhaps, deserved better than a 14-8 defeat but, on a day when commentators grumbled at the discourteous booing when Kiernan was kicking for goal, Wales proved the more adaptable.

In addition to their better overall play, the Welsh had Price to kick their goals. Peter Brook, the English referee, had to lecture both sides on their behaviour and Wales had to overcome the absence of Dawes for much of the first half, doing so by moving Price to centre while Pask filled in at full back. David Watkins skipped over for a try just before the interval and Price coolly converted. Bebb added another before Kiernan found his kicking boots but Price then punched over a 40-metre dropped goal. A try by Kevin Flynn helped Ireland to within three points of their opponents and their forwards threw everything into a last-gasp effort, but it was Price who had the final word with a penalty.

The last match of the season, the 22-13 defeat in Paris, was also the final word for Rowlands after 14 consecutive games, all as captain. When his playing career ended, he became coach and manager to the national team – and manager of the 1989 Lions – before becoming president of the Welsh Rugby Union. What, he was once asked, was the most important ingredient for a successful team? 'Calon' – the Welsh word for heart – was his reply. Rowlands could forgive technical errors but he could not forgive individuals who did not share his own passion for the game. Perhaps it was that which allowed Wales to fight back from a 22-0 deficit against the French, scoring three tries and 'winning' the second half 13-3.

While Wales were edging their way towards the triple crown, England's motley crew rescued their season by beating France and then provided one of the classic moments in Five Nations history. They had brought Andy Hancock into the side against the French as a late replacement

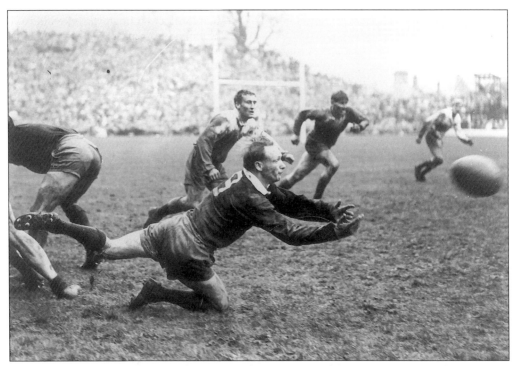

Alex Hastie, the Scotland scrum half, passes out from the base of the scrum against England in 1965.

for the injured Ted Rudd. When Rudd recovered fitness they retained Hancock at the expense of Richmond's Peter Cook for the Calcutta Cup match which was played in gloomy, wet conditions. Then twenty-five, Hancock had played for Cambridge City but had been encouraged by Dickie Jeeps (now an England selector) to move to Northampton. He was not the fastest thing on two legs but he was strong round the hips and thighs which, in muddy conditions, proved a distinct advantage.

The match programme recalled Scotland's dismal record at Twickenham but, with time running out, David Chisholm's dropped goal looked like proving a match-winning score. Chisholm formed, with Alex Hastie, a notable half-back partnership for Melrose and Scotland (they played together in thirteen internationals) and, with Peter Stagg ruling the lineout, there seemed no way back for England. Stagg, from Sale, was a mighty handful: his height varied from 6ft 8in to 6ft 10in, depending on what match programme you were reading at the time, but he was by far and away the tallest player to have played international rugby and remained so until Martin Bayfield came on the England scene in the 1990s.

Hastie had actually crossed the England line but was brought back for an infringement before Steve Richards, the swift-striking England hooker, stole a heel against the head in his own 22. Weston, playing fly half, launched a kick towards touch but found David Whyte lurking on the wing. The Scot veered infield before being engulfed by the England forwards some ten metres from the try-line. Once more the ball came back for Weston, but this time he fed Hancock on the short side and the wing took off, outside the Scotland forwards and towards halfway. Wilson, covering across, should have taken him but did not and Hancock continued his lung-bursting way as Laughland's pursuit proved in vain. The wing collapsed over the line and parsimonious critics said he should have run round towards the posts to make Rutherford's conversion easier but he had done enough to find a permanent place in the history books already.

So inspired were England that they subsided limply to the foot of the 1966 championship, their season notable only for the debut of that outstanding Bristol hooker, John Pullin. Wales sustained their grip on events, though there was particular satisfaction in Dublin when Ireland denied them a triple crown. Allan Lewis, the Abertillery scrum half, replaced Rowlands on the basis that his longer pass would give David Watkins more space, but it was Price's goalkicking that savaged England in the opening encounter. It was, though, the youngster's only appearance that season because of injury and the reliable Grahame Hodgson, from Neath, returned for the 8-3 win over Scotland where, in atrocious conditions, once again Wales scored two cracking tries through Ken Jones, their little centre.

Ireland's game with England was notable more for the referee than anything else. For the first time a Frenchman, Bernard Marie, was appointed to a Five Nations game, an appointment long overdue but the first in a line of officials keen to encourage fluent rugby, sometimes paying only lip service to certain laws. The Irish were braced for a substantial effort, if not for the outpouring of joy at the end as ecstatic supporters invaded the pitch to carry off their heroes. Gibson dropped a goal and kicked a penalty, and Barry Bresnihan scored the try that made the difference in a 9-6 win in which the Ireland forwards played their hearts out.

Thus unbeaten France came to Cardiff with the championship at stake. Knowing their own uncertain weather, Wales named ten forwards and preferred Howard Norris and Bill Morris to Denzil Williams and Brian Thomas on the day. Within ten minutes their plans seemed in ruins, for Bernard Duprat had scored one try then Christian Darrouy another, with Claude Lacaze throwing in a conversion. Two penalty goals by Keith Bradshaw reduced the deficit but the match hung in the balance when Stuart Watkins made an interception just outside his own 22. Three times Lacaze came at him and three times the France full back was fended off, like an irritating fly, as Watkins pounded the sixty metres to score. What he may have felt when Morris

Alun Pask, the Wales back row forward, sets the ball up at Cardiff Arms Park against England in 1965 with support from Denzil Williams, Brian Price and Brian Thomas.

deliberately threw the ball into touch, conceding a potentially match-winning penalty to the French, can only be imagined but Lacaze could not retrieve the situation. His kick at goal, from wide out, was a brave effort but veered away from the posts and Wales had won 9-8.

From champions to wooden-spoon holders: Wales collapsed like a balloon in 1967, though the nucleus of a wonderful side was beginning to come together. You would have had to be a genius to spot this, however, because the five countries handed out first caps to forty-three players in all, with Wales finding fourteen newcomers. England enjoyed a resurgence but ended behind France and, like Scotland and Ireland, with a 50-50 record. Indeed the Scots, having beaten the touring Australians, put their act together swiftly by beating France and Wales in their first two games only to come unstuck when Chisholm missed the meeting with Ireland and Scotland lost 5-3; nor was the fly half available against England, which was just as well since the Scots crashed 27-14.

Ireland, who totalled 17 points in four matches, were hardly the masters of attacking football but enjoyed their 3-0 win in Cardiff thanks to a try by Alan Duggan, the Lansdowne wing. It proved a game too far for Allan Lewis, Alun Pask, Ken Braddock and Grahame Hodgson, none of whom appeared in the red jersey again, but already that season Wales had blooded Gerald Davies, Barry John and Delme Thomas – debutants against Australia – and John Taylor against Scotland. To that quartet they added Gareth Edwards and Dai Morris against France, making up six of the players who were integral to the superb Wales sides of the early 1970s.

Yet still their results on the field failed to improve, France winning 20-14 in Paris on April Fools' Day. Since, a fortnight earlier, Colin McFadyean had led the way with two tries in England's thrashing of Scotland, there were few who expected anything but an England win in Cardiff on 15 April. Remember there was no great hoodoo over the Arms Park for Englishmen at that stage: they had won there in 1963, they had a competitive pack among whom Michael Coulman, the Moseley prop, was a model for mobility and ball-handling, and they had Roger Hosen to kick the goals. Wales were in disarray, threatened with a whitewash for the first time since 1937 – how could they prevent an English triple crown?

Despite the apparently overwhelming odds, Wales won a remarkable match 34-21. Remarkable in the first place that the traditional January date had been moved to sunny April. Remarkable for the fact that England scored more points than they had ever done on Welsh soil and still lost. Remarkable for the debut of the Monmouth schoolboy, Keith Jarrett. In the fortnight since the defeat in Paris, Wales had lost Terry Price to Salford Rugby League Club (he was to be followed there after this match by David Watkins, who became one of Welsh rugby's most illustrious exports to the professional game) and were wildly casting around for a replacement full back.

Why they lit on Jarrett, only the Big Five knew. He had played full back at school between the ages of fourteen and sixteen but, since leaving Monmouth the previous Christmas, he had played in the centre for Newport. He was a strapping lad, 6ft and over 13st, but at eighteen there was no telling whether he had the temperament to play international rugby as the last line of defence, nor, in any of his nine subsequent internationals (before he, too, signed professional forms) did he play there again. However, he adopted the view that attack is the best form of defence and, when the shouting died down, he had scored 19 points and the first try by a Wales full back since Vivian Jenkins in 1934.

The story runs that Jarrett, returning home late after the match, caught the last bus to Newport of which he was the only occupant. The depot inspector, recognising him, instructed the driver to take the single-decker back to the depot and bring out a double-decker 'in case Mr Jarrett wants to go upstairs and smoke.' The Welsh had found themselves yet another hero, even if nothing that Jarrett did during the remainder of his playing career ever came close to his achievements that day. What he did possess in abundance was the natural confidence of youth, helped by the fact that Watkins, his Newport colleague, was leading Wales and spent considerable time talking him through the forthcoming game.

'The most remarkable rugby international of all time,' was how *Playfair Rugby Annual* described it. Jarrett struck within nine minutes, his penalty glancing off an upright and falling

David Watkins kicks past Bristol and England's David Watt at Cardiff Arms Park in 1967.

the right side and thereafter he could do no wrong. He kicked a second penalty and converted a try by Morris while Billy Raybould dropped a goal, giving Wales a 14-6 lead at the interval after John Barton had scored from a lineout and Hosen added a penalty. When the Cornish full back added another penalty, everyone braced themselves for an England rally, only for Gerald Davies to score a second Welsh try after knifing his way through a statuesque defence.

Still England responded with a try by Keith Savage and a third penalty from Hosen, leaving the score at 19-15. McFadyean launched a kick downfield, hoping to catch Jarrett in two minds, but the youngster took the bouncing ball at full tilt down the left-hand touchline, bounced off two would-be tacklers and completed a 60-metre run at the corner. On a soft January surface the ball would not have bounced so high (giving Jarrett the chance to recover from being out of position), on a hard April ground the sporting gods were with him. The Arms Park exploded – there is no other word that could adequately describe it – and then watched Jarrett convert his own try. England, their hopes knocked sideways, conceded another try to Bebb before Davies threaded his way through, Jarrett, of course, converting regardless of the degree of difficulty. No matter that Barton scored his second try and Hosen a fourth penalty (his season's tally of 46 was an England record), Wales were out of sight.

'We were pleased, obviously,' Davies, whose two tries were almost forgotten, said. 'But more than anything, we were relieved, that we had at last won a match. I think that game represented a turning point for us.' This classic encounter served as an indication of what was possible in a game of rugby football. It had everything – the unexpected result, the young hero, the ebb and flow of a well-balanced contest and the new combination throwing off the shackles and playing as if nothing depended on the result.

However, 1968 was no brave new world. It was, in fact, a somewhat lacklustre old one in which France ruled the roost and the rest struggled for some appreciable identity. Scotland were whitewashed, Wales could raise only a solitary win and England could manage no better. Only Ireland stitched something more substantial together and thereby earned the captaincy of the Lions in South Africa for Tom Kiernan, in a party coached by Ronnie Dawson. There were not many applicants from Wales: Norman Gale, that barn-door of a hooker from Llanelli, started the season as captain, then handed over the leadership to Edwards who, at twenty, was the youngest man ever to lead his country and even then John Dawes had a brief incursion before the job returned to Edwards.

Maybe it was the after-effect of Brian Lochore's New Zealanders, whose autumn tour went through four of the five countries like a dose of salts. Only Ireland escaped, and that because an outbreak of foot-and-mouth disease in Britain prevented the All Blacks crossing the Irish Sea. The style of play promulgated by New Zealand left Britain deep in thought, though the England versus Wales game at Twickenham, back in its January slot, contained echoes of the reverberating match of the previous season. England chose that individualist from Bristol, Bill Redwood, at scrum half and gave him a couple of teenagers in the supporting back-row cast, David Gay and Bryan West. Wales paired Edwards and John at half back, but both sides had to be content with an 11-11 draw.

Ireland, weakened by injuries and the absence through illness of Gibson, could not contain the French and left Twickenham shaking their heads after the latest of penalty goals from Bob Hiller forced them to accept a 9-9 draw. Hiller, the Harlequins full back, plagued the Irish throughout his career though here his kicking was far less reliable than that of Kiernan, who landed three penalties from four attempts. England's problems were compounded when Redwood was concussed and Peter Bell, the Blackheath flanker, was chosen to work the scrum, his slowness leaving Brendan Sherry, his opposite number, ample time to disrupt him.

Yet in a sense, Bell had the last laugh when Sherry conceded the penalty that Hiller kicked to draw the game. Ireland then went home to savage the Scots, Kiernan's tactical acumen and points-gathering going alongside Duggan's try-scoring: the wing scored two tries, Bresnihan a third and Scotland slunk home after their sixth successive defeat at Lansdowne Road, beaten 14-6. They then gathered the Welsh scalp, though not before an incident which may be unique in the Five Nations annals. Ireland were leading 6-3 when Edwards dropped for goal, the kick flying just wide of the upright. However, Mike Titcombe, the English referee, awarded the goal and it was fortunate that Mick Doyle scored the try that brought Ireland their 9-6 win. There were claims that Gibson's dropped goal had been touched in flight which, under the law as it then stood, would have invalidated the kick but most felt that justice had been done.

By the season's end, however, it was transparently obvious that standards within British rugby needed elevation. A year earlier the Welsh Rugby Union had appointed Ray Williams as its first coaching organiser and, in 1968, David Nash, the former Ebbw Vale No. 8, was given responsibility for the preparation of the national XV. In due course the other home unions followed suit, England inviting Don White, the former Northampton flanker, whose knowledge of the laws – as a player – was said to be encyclopaedic, and Ireland plumping for Ronnie Dawson. The Scots, preferring to appoint an advisor to the captain, chose Bill Dickinson as their man. Law changes decreed that kicking direct to touch outside the 22-metre line was barred and replacements for injured players were to be permitted. A wind of change was about to sweep through the championship.

6
THE DRAGON'S ROAR
1969-1979

The post-war 'baby boom' threw up a generation in the 1960s and 1970s who became a byword for liberation in all kinds of fields, notably fashion and popular music. But who would have predicted that Wales would be blessed with so many world-class performers on the rugby field at the same time? Allowance should first be made for the inclusion of two forwards whose merits are so often overlooked, Delme Thomas and Dai Morris, both born in 1942.

However good the Wales backs may have been during the 1970s, they always needed forwards to provide the ammunition: Thomas, like Brian Price before him, was an artist at the lineout while Morris was the continuity man on the blind-side flank. They called him 'The Shadow' which perfectly illustrates the support the man from Neath offered his talented three-quarters. But, once the war was over, Welsh maternity hospitals were in full swing – though admittedly Barry John and Gerald Davies were born just months before the war in Europe ended – with John Taylor, Mervyn Davies, Gareth Edwards, J.P.R. Williams and Phil Bennett all being part of the British population explosion in the late 1940s.

The supporting cast was not bad either. It boasted two knowledgeable heads in the front row, John Lloyd and Jeff Young, the wonderful organisation of John Dawes and his production line at London Welsh – which included two stalwart locks, Geoff Evans and Mike Roberts – and John Bevan on the wing, who was followed by another snapper-up of unconsidered trifles, J.J. Williams, and who himself followed the powerful Maurice Richards into the side. One wonders if Richards, who turned professional in 1969, regretted that he left just before the glory years really arrived.

The temptation is to view the period between 1969 and 1979 solely through red-tinted spectacles, which would be wrong because there was a perpetual challenge from France (grand-slam winners in 1977), a championship for Ireland in 1974 and the famous five-way tie of 1973. Yet the fact remains that, during those years, Wales won three grand slams, four other championship titles and shared the spoils twice. Critics talked of a first and second division within the championship, with Wales and France on one plateau and the rest on another, with England invariably lurking in the basement.

Was it merely coincidence, so many great players buying into a rich rugby heritage? It could be said to have been the first fruits of coaching, in which Wales led the way, while the other home unions struggled to keep up. Instructively, for nearly that entire period, Wales did not expose herself to an overseas tour: the 1969 trip to New Zealand proved a salutory experience and was important for the tactical approach taken subsequently, while the 1978 tour to Australia was undertaken without several legendary names as the decade of the dragon waned. Only in concert with the other unions, as the Lions, did Wales provide the axis for success in New Zealand in 1971 and South Africa in 1974. Arguably, that success should have been sustained in New Zealand in 1977 but it was not.

The leading names of this era, who will always fight for inclusion in any rugby hall of fame, are five: Edwards, the scrum half; John, the fly half; Gerald Davies, the wing; Williams, the full back; and Mervyn Davies, the No. 8. Three of these players are from the critical decision-making area of No. 8/half back which ensured that the XVs in which they played made optimum use of the ball. If one makes Edwards *primus inter pares*, it is only because his unique skills came so often into play – athlete, gymnast, rugby player, footballer, Edwards was all these things but his mentor at Pontardawe Technical School, Bill Samuel, made sure that he would be a world-class rugby player.

The debt that rugby in Britain owes to Welsh schoolteachers this century is one that cannot be paid, many of them operating at levels well away from the representative sphere. The dedicated Samuel read the first pages of rugby's book to the boy Edwards and dispatched him to Millfield to hone his skills in the best sporting environment then available. By the age of nineteen he was ready to play for Wales and at twenty he was the national captain and a Lion. Ten years later he had played in 45 consecutive championship games, won 53 caps and scored 20 international tries. Furthermore, because he was a master of all the skills, he had also dropped four international goals and spent one season as Wales' goal-kicker. There was an indestructible quality to Edwards, such that when injury forced him off the field against England in 1970 and for the Lions against New Zealand a year later (on both occasions he was replaced by Maesteg's Ray Hopkins), you felt something unnatural had occurred. Blessed with superb balance and great pace, Edwards also worked hard on his kicking – initially the weakest area of his game. By the time he retired, he had perfected the art of the rolling kick to touch which broke so many opposing hearts (most of them English).

Outside him John, who played first for Llanelli but then joined Edwards at Cardiff, performed with a studied insouciance. He was not judged a success when he first appeared, during the 1966/67 season, but the selectors knew their men and gave the half-back pairing time to settle. No game plan suited John: he made up his mind on the spur of the moment and it was for others to follow him thereafter. Carwyn James, coach to the 1971 Lions, knew that he had to hold John on a loose rein and allowed him to play football while others trained for the next game. James, so imaginative a man himself, saw in John a rugby intellect upon which he could depend and besides, anyone playing alongside Edwards, Dawes and Gibson could scarcely go wrong. 'The dragonfly on the anvil of destruction,' was how he was memorably described in *Fields of Praise*, the Welsh Rugby Union's official history.

There seemed no effort to John's play. A lazy swing of the boot, whether out of hand or off the ground, was all he needed; not for him the flashing dart or the big sidestep, rather the impression of a man floating past opponents at no great speed but sufficient to rip holes in the tightest defence. True, coaches did not look to John to tackle, as was the case with fly halves during the 1980s and 1990s, but if he had to, John could perform those pedestrian chores too. He was named 'King John'

Barry John clears to touch, watched by Gareth Edwards, Mervyn Davies, Barry Llewellyn and the referee, Mike Titcombe, against France in 1972.

when he returned home from New Zealand with the Lions and the popularity he attained embarrassed him. A year later, rather than remain in the goldfish bowl with people gawping at him, he retired, aged twenty-seven.

When the world's best wings are debated, the name of Gerald Davies (6) will always be in the frame. There was not a lot of the dapper little man from Llansaint – 5ft 8in and 11st 8lb – but every inch was packed with dynamite. Ironically, he himself worried when the suggestion was made to him by Clive Rowlands during the Wales tour to New Zealand in 1969, that he should move from the centre to the wing. He had already achieved a fine reputation as a darting, speeding gamebreaker in midfield, at Loughborough Colleges and Cambridge University and, in another era – such as that of Dewi Bebb – he might not have enjoyed the move.

But the liberated 1970s was to be his time. So intelligent a player could not have been left blowing on his hands to keep them warm while others played the game their way. He possessed not only great speed off the mark, but also the athletic strength to sustain his run. Deceptively strong, he had the classic swerve and the not-always-classic weapon of the wing, a sidestep to die for. In one club match, between Cardiff and Pontypool when the Gwent club were at their height, Davies touched the ball four times and scored four tries to win the match virtually single-handed. He was a mesmerising presence in 46 internationals, which brought him 20 tries in an ongoing scoring rivalry with Edwards. There were also three tries for the Lions against New Zealand and there might have been more had not Davies' principles prevented him touring South Africa a second time in 1974. Davies made no song and dance about it but made a private decision – as did John Taylor – that he should not visit a country with so repressive a government. Even when pressed to fly out as a replacement, he would not be moved.

Immoveable was also a quality applicable to John Peter Rhys Williams (5), forever known by his initials (hence also the flying Llanelli wing, John Williams, had to be known as J.J. to distinguish the two). He did not have two of the traditional full back's skills in that he was no great kicker, either out of hand or at goal, but he and Scotland's Andy Irvine brought an entirely new dimension to the game in an attacking role, no matter the depth they came from. There was an elemental force to Williams, who made his debut as a medical student, aged nineteen. He embraced the clattering collisions of the game and revelled in his youthful power and exuberance.

If he was a rock in defence, he relished the opportunity to run, ball in hand. One moment Williams would be there, waiting the arrival of a high ball, the next he would be pounding up field, long hair flowing beneath his distinctive headband, fending off opponents, looking to link with his wings. He was one of those players whose fame, as his career expanded, went before him. His sheer force of personality imposed itself on no nation more than England, against whom he scored five of his six international tries. It was entirely apposite that, on tour in Australia in 1978 with a lengthening casualty list, Wales should have invited him to play in the back row which he did with huge zest.

J.P.R. Williams captained Wales to the 1979 championship before retiring, only to respond to a recall in 1980 and win three more caps to take his tally to 55. Mervyn Davies might have extended his playing career too, but for the injury in 1976 which cut him off in his prime. A product of the great London Welsh side of the early 1970s, Davies was playing in a cup match for Swansea when he suffered a brain haemorrhage and was rushed to hospital. He was twenty-nine and strongly tipped to lead the Lions in 1977, having just led Wales to a grand slam in his 38th international, but he never played again.

A gangling 6ft 4in No. 8, Davies was unknown outside London Welsh when he was thrown into a Wales trial in the 1968/69 season. His father, D.J. Davies, had played in the Victory Internationals, so the pedigree was there, and within weeks of making his debut against Scotland, it was acknowledged that the young Davies had come to stay. He possessed a highly-developed sense for where the ball would go – a virtue replicated by England's Dean Richards who would later pass Davies' international record of appearances at No. 8. Davies was a potent force at the lineout too, as well as a sweeping tackler and an artful ball handler; the back row he formed with Taylor and Morris was truly one of all the talents since Taylor could also kick for goal.

The quintet proved a wonderful nucleus around which Clive Rowlands, now coach instead of

Mervyn Davies, captain of Wales and a No. 8 with all the back row skills.

Nash, could build a successful side. Squad training was introduced on a regular basis, which was something of a strain for the large London Welsh contingent which had to travel to Port Talbot in pre-motorway days, but success soon crowned Rowlands' efforts. The 1969 championship aggregated more points (234) than any season had produced since 1911 and a total of 32 tries, 14 of them to Wales. But for the fact that France, the 1968 champions, held them to an 8-8 draw in Paris, the team led initially by Brian Price and then by Edwards would have swept all before them at the first time of asking though, as is sometimes the case, fortune smiled on them too.

Ireland arrived in Cardiff on 8 March seeking a grand slam. The Arms Park was not much of a venue that year, since redevelopment was under way and the North Stand had been demolished, limiting the capacity to 29,000. There were fears that ticketless spectators would try and storm the gates, recalling scenes before the war when fire hoses had to be used to discourage invaders, but in fact the streets outside the ground were deserted, with all the illegal action taking place within. Only ten minutes had elapsed before Price, in full view of everyone including the Prince of Wales in the stand and the match referee from Scotland, D.C.J. McMahon, laid out Noel Murphy with a blatant punch at a lineout.

'How, in any sport, one player can be seen viciously punching another in the face and knocking him almost senseless to the ground and be merely cautioned as to his future conduct is quite beyond the comprehension of any rational man,' the *Playfair Rugby Annual* fulminated. Murphy, the long-serving Ireland flanker, was a key component of the visiting pack and Price had toured alongside him with the Lions three years earlier. As it happens, it was the 41st and last appearance in a career that had started in 1958 and Murphy continued to be a dominating presence in Irish rugby, as a selector, manager, coach and finally president.

Had Price been sent off – and whatever may have happened in the opening exchanges when the lock claimed his face had been clawed, his offence was so obvious that he should have been – Wales might not have achieved their 24-11 victory. Yet they did, with a mixture of guile and organisation which was typical of Rowlands and became symptomatic of their successful years. The try by Denzil Williams was a fine example of their play: Ireland led 6-3 when Wales received a penalty well within range of the posts but Keith Jarrett, as his opponents retreated under the presumption of a kick at goal, tapped the ball to Williams and the Ebbw Vale prop trundled over the line before anyone could stop him.

Thereafter, everything Wales touched turned to gold. There were tries for Watkins, Morris and Taylor, with Jarrett kicking goals like a metronome, and all Ireland could manufacture was a kick-and-chase try for Gibson. Yet Irish hopes of the title were far from dead when France, during one of their seasons when the selectors plucked players from all parts of the country, held Wales to an 8-0 lead and then levelled matters when Villepreux added a conversion to his earlier penalty goal, leaving time only for Bennett to become his country's first replacement (for the injured Gerald Davies) without once touching the ball.

The absence of Davies meant a recall for John Dawes, who had accumulated ten caps in five years, against an England side which had an interest in the title too. That interest survived for forty minutes in Cardiff but was then swept away. The architect of defeat was Maurice Richards, one of two strapping six-footers on the Wales wings. He scored four tries to equal the achievements of Willie Llewellyn (1899) and Reggie Gibbs (1908), but there was little hint of this before the interval when his first negated Hiller's penalty and left the sides level. A try by John and good goal-kicking by Jarrett helped Wales to a solid 14-3 lead, but, in the final quarter, England were crushed – Richards made their tackling seem paper-thin as he ran in three tries and Wales won 30-9.

Was it merely coincidence that so overwhelming a win had come with Dawes in the side? The centre was then twenty-eight and had played for Newbridge before taking up a teaching post in London and joining London Welsh. His gifts had been noted but clearly Wales thought they could do better. Yet Dawes was the essential oil in the works of any successful back division: his was the thoughtful pass, the unexpected break, the smother tackle, the ingredient that made others look better. He brought to the team a ready appreciation of the modern game but also the steadying influence to complement the more exotic skills of his illustrious colleagues.

He played in eleven of the next twelve internationals, five as captain, and Wales won eight, including the 1971 grand slam which swept Dawes triumphantly to leadership of the Lions. Significantly, however, Wales had first to endure a poorly-organised schedule in New Zealand, where they played the All Blacks within a week of arrival and never recovered from a 19-0 hiding. The second international was lost 33-12, but it marked Gerald Davies' first appearance on the wing instead of the veteran Stuart Watkins. If he had any doubts about the move, they were removed when he scored one try and made another in the 19-16 victory over Australia with which the short tour ended, though he had time for reflection because he withdrew from international rugby the following season so as to concentrate upon his university studies.

The main benefit of the tour was the thought Wales gave to their forward play, and the advent of the young Newport prop, Barry Llewelyn – 6ft 2in and 16st 4lb of player whose star never shone as brightly as it did on his first entry to international rugby – was a source of great encouragement. He was strong and mobile, not that the latter talent was terribly relevant on his debut when Wales drew 6-6 with South Africa in yet another mudbath. Yet the season unfolded happily enough as Wales lowered the colours of both Scotland and England, coming from behind at Twickenham in a manner which characterised their eighty-minute approach in a series of games which were won in the last quarter. England led 13-3 at the interval, only to fall to the first of the super-subs, Ray Hopkins, who made a try for J.P.R. Williams then scored himself, leaving his full back to kick the goal which gave Wales the lead before John's dropped goal gave the visitors their 17-13 success.

Their third match, though, was at Lansdowne Road against an Ireland side itching to avenge the perceived injustice of the previous year. It is tempting to describe it as Kiernan's day, since the Ireland full back and captain was setting a new record with his 47th appearance, passing the mark set by Jack

Kyle. But it was also Ken Goodall's day, the No. 8 from the City of Derry club striding over from halfway for the try that sealed Wales' fate.

The first half was scoreless, but already the Wales half backs could read the tea leaves. They were harried unmercifully by an Ireland back row which included Fergus Slattery, a Dublin student in his first international season. Slattery, with his mop of wild hair, became as identifiable a figure in the 1970s as J.P.R. Williams, whereas Goodall, later that year, became one of the few Irishmen to turn professional. Barry McGann began the rout by dropping a goal and then Alan Duggan changed a wild pass by John into a try for Ireland. Amid growing clamour from the terraces, Kiernan added a penalty and Goodall rubbed salt into Welsh wounds by gathering a kick ahead, chipping over the attackers and running in from fifty metres.

It says much for Wales that they were able to regroup and beat France, thereby earning a share of the championship. The French had already beaten Ireland and Scotland, and would go on to slaughter England, but Wales brought them down 11-6, without John and with four newcomers in the side. They gave Bennett his first chance to play alongside Edwards – the first of twenty-five such pairings – and restored Taylor to the back row, the flanker having been judged to have served his penance after declining to play against South Africa three months earlier. But it was the debutant lock, Stuart Gallacher, who caught the eye, both for his all-round play and the interception which brought a try for Morris.

The groundwork had been laid. Now came the ultimate reward. The 1971 grand slam-winning Wales side used only sixteen players and scored thirteen tries in four matches (the next best was six by Ireland and Scotland who, surprisingly since they ended the championship bottom, came nearest to overturning Welsh ambitions). The core of the side came from London Welsh who, guided by Dawes, could claim to be the outstanding club in Europe: six of their players helped towards the slam and a seventh, Geoff Evans, joined his colleagues on tour with the 1971 Lions.

A sound, experienced front five gave a brilliant back row the chance to dominate play alongside Edwards and John. With Gerald Davies returned from his studies, Wales unveiled another outstanding finisher on the left wing in John Bevan, whose play always revealed traces of the No. 8 he had been as a schoolboy. If the centres, Dawes and the stalwart Arthur Lewis, would not make too many world XVs they nevertheless revealed qualities of unselfishness and dependability which was all that was required to give the back three a sniff of a try.

With so much class, Wales did not need the assistance of the opposition, but they received it from England anyway. There were eight new caps in the side that arrived at Cardiff in January, of whom only one – Tony Neary, the Broughton Park flanker – had the requisite staying power. Wales had sewn up the match by half-time and went on to score three tries on the wing (two for Davies, one for Bevan), demonstrating too that they were prepared to vary their goal-kicker depending on the side of the field the kick was taken. Thus J.P.R. Williams kicked a penalty and John Taylor two conversions, with John apparently in reserve.

Kicking was to have a crucial effect on the championship in Wales' next match. Those who saw Taylor's match-winning conversion at Murrayfield will never forget it – 'The greatest conversion since St Paul' was how one newspaper described it. With less than five minutes to go, Scotland led 18-14 after a great-hearted effort and the clock was winding down as Wales threw everything into a lineout in the Scotland 22. The ball was transferred swiftly to Davies who left his marker and Ian Smith, the Scotland full back, for dead as he hurtled into the corner then back round towards the posts.

The conversion, out to the right, was made for the left-footed Taylor and his round-the-corner style, and though some of his colleagues could not bear to watch, the ball soared between the posts and won the match 19-18. The heart bled for the Scotland forwards, who held the whip hand for much of the match – there were, after all, four Lions in their tight five as well as Alastair McHarg, who should have been one – and exerted an unaccustomed pressure on John. Yet the fly half refused to be fenced in: he scored a try, a conversion and a penalty while Peter Brown, with four successful penalties, kept the Murrayfield scoreboard ticking over.

Three times within eight minutes of the second half the lead changed hands. Sandy Carmichael's try and Brown's third penalty allowed Scotland to nose ahead, John snatched back the lead, then

Benoît Dauga drives into England's John Pullin at Twickenham in 1969.

Brown again and a try by Chris Rea put Scotland four points clear. The conversion was relatively straightforward but Brown's kick hit a post, otherwise the Welsh goose was cooked. In the critical move, J.P.R. Williams made the extra man for Davies and the Scottish fans, to their infinite credit, allowed Taylor to kick at goal in relative silence.

After such a climax, the triple crown game with Ireland was straightforward. The Wales half backs dominated the match, scoring 17 points between them in a 23-9 victory, and there were two tries for Davies which brought his season's tally to five. Yet the slam was by no means certain as France, too, were unbeaten, though their record included draws with Ireland and England. This season they had introduced Roland Bertranne to the centre and paired the Spanghero brothers, Walter and Claude, in the second row, moving Benoît Dauga to No. 8.

It was Dauga who almost made the match for France. Charging forward, ball in hand, he pulled a mighty defensive tackle out of John at the cost of a broken nose to the Welshman, who walked off for repairs. Wales trailed 5-0 at that stage, Dauga having scored a try converted by Villepreux, but John's return to action – there were no blood replacements in 1971 – inspired Edwards to a vital try just before the interval. It was, though, made for him by J.P.R. Williams' brilliant reading of the play: he went for an interception deep in his own half, succeeded and pounded upfield to find, amazingly, Denzil Williams, the veteran prop now thirty-one and in his final season, in the vicinity. His presence checked the defence and gave Edwards, sprinting to join his full back, the chance to score. John added a second-half penalty and then, as though flinging defiance in French faces, scored a delightful solo try which brought Wales their 9-5 victory and their first grand slam since 1952. Critics asked if this was the best Wales side ever and agreed that never before had the red jerseys played with such sustained pride and collective will.

Welsh rugby had been 'radically changed', Ray Williams told that year's annual meeting of the WRU. The preparation of the coach, Clive Rowlands, was first rate, the decision-making and application of the whole team demonstrated an understanding of the game that was unusual in the northern hemisphere and which flowered on behalf of the Lions that summer. Success bred a confidence (some said an arrogance, but all the best sportsmen possess that in their play) that rubbed off on those itching to join the chosen few. It was not the fault of the players of that wonderful era that administrators did not understand the nature of the beast and allowed the national game to decline during the 1980s.

There would, in all probability, have been another slam in 1972, but Wales and Scotland chose not to fulfil their fixtures in Ireland. For once the political and civil strife that had become part of life in Ulster since 1969 had spilled over to Dublin's streets, where there was an attack on the British Embassy. The home unions agreed the matches should be played but first the Scottish Rugby Union, then their Welsh counterparts, decided the safety of their players and supporters came first and declined to travel, despite the emotional overtures made by an Irish delegation in Edinburgh and Cardiff. That Ireland won their two away games made it all the more frustrating for the side led by Tom Kiernan who, during the season, became the first home unions player to reach 50 caps.

However, an unchanged Wales tweaked England's nose (only six newcomers this time) at Twickenham yet again, then destroyed Scotland 35-12. With Dawes now retired, the captaincy had passed to John Lloyd, the Bridgend prop, and Roy Bergiers had come into the centre. The blond Llanelli player scored one of Wales's five tries (now worth four points) despite the departure of the apparently indestructible J.P.R. Williams with a broken jaw, Phil Bennett replacing him at full back, having already appeared in the national side at fly half, wing and centre. The second of the tries scored by Edwards was a classic: from a scrum near his own 22 he broke to the short side, beat the back row and raced up to halfway. Kicking over Arthur Brown, the Scotland full back, he toed the ball ahead and still had the pace to hold off the cover in a dive into the muddiest corner of the ground that left him looking like a monster from the deep as he rose to his feet in triumph.

Wales prepare for another destruction of England in 1972. Back row: J. Young, A. Lewis, R. Bergiers, M. Davies, G. Evans, B. Llewellyn, D. Thomas, D. Morris. Seated: J.P.R. Williams, J. Bevan, J. Taylor, J. Lloyd (captain), B. John, G. Edwards, G. Davies.

The multi-talented Phil Bennett in action for the Lions.

Wales ended an attenuated season by beating France 20-6 in the game made notable by Derek Quinnell's frantic efforts to reach the pitch and win his first cap (having played international rugby for the Lions the previous year) when Mervyn Davies left the field late in the game. Few there realised that they would not see Barry John playing for his country again. The fly half kicked four penalties for a season's tally of 35 points and, six weeks later, announced his retirement. He was no more than twenty-seven and the outstanding player of his day, but in a decade becoming ever more prurient and demanding of its 'stars', John chose to withdraw and would not be tempted back, even by the prospect of playing for the Barbarians against New Zealand the following year in what was, in essence, a recreation of the Lions versus All Blacks series.

Lucky the nation who had so ready-made a replacement in Bennett, the pale-faced, side-stepping impresario from Llanelli. Where John was languid, Bennett darted like a fish, his jagged running lines creating havoc in opposing defences. Would Wales have beaten New Zealand in the autumn of 1972 if John had been there? With Bennett kicking four penalties, they lost 19-16 which served as the prelude to a mediocre season in which each of the five nations won their home matches and lost away. After the ritual defeat of England, Wales tripped up for the first time in ten championship matches at Murrayfield, where Scotland's 10-9 victory suggested that if anyone was to carry off the honours from the 1973 season, it should have been the Scots.

It was a season in which the Wales captaincy switched between Delme Thomas, Arthur Lewis and Gareth Edwards and not one of their battery of goal-kickers could save them in the final match against France, notable for little more than the introduction of John James (J.J. to distinguish him from the full back) Williams, the Llanelli wing, as a replacement for Lewis. Nor was 1974 much better, though the championship itself took on a different aspect since the committee had agreed to the rotation of fixtures with two internationals being played on the same day, reducing the number of Five Nations weekends to five.

Wales examined new combinations in the centre, the second row and the front row where the first of the famed 'Viet Gwent' – as the comedian, Max Boyce, described the Pontypool front row – appeared in the burly shape of Bobby Windsor at hooker. Taylor had gone too, though Pontypool also provided an apt replacement in Terry Cobner, the balding flanker whose leadership qualities were so vital to the 1977 Lions. But it was coming to something when England, after eleven years of waiting, beat Wales 16-12 at Twickenham to deny them a chance of the championship. Wales sulked off into the night in the belief that two valid tries had been disallowed, nor were Dai Morris and Delme Thomas to be seen again, but it was the jolt their system required.

As if confirmation of their quality was needed, Edwards and Bennett were the fulcrum round which the Lions constructed an invincible tour to South Africa, and John Dawes was appointed coach in succession to Rowlands. The Pontypool front row of Graham Price (12), Windsor and Charlie Faulkner came together in all its glory, whilst Mervyn Davies – now with Swansea and at the height of his considerable powers – took over the captaincy. A powerful new combination appeared in the centre in the form of Steve Fenwick, the cool Bridgend goal-kicker, and Ray Gravell from Llanelli, a powerful, bearded runner who lived every moment of his international career on the crest of an emotional wave.

Curiously, though, the Wales selectors were less convinced of Bennett's qualities than had been his Springbok opponents. Maybe the post-Lions anti-climax had set in for the introspective Bennett, but he found himself relegated to the Possibles in the national trial and then overlooked in favour of another John Bevan (the wing had left for Rugby League two years earlier), the Aberavon fly half. At all events, the selection looked accurate enough when Wales scored five tries against France in their opening match, Price demonstrating his speed in the loose by sprinting sixty metres for the final try.

England were dispatched soundly enough, but at Murrayfield, before a world-record crowd of 104,000 (many of whom had swarmed past the barriers without paying), Scotland ruined Welsh dreams of a triple crown by winning 12-10. It did not help that Wales lost Bevan and Fenwick in the first half to injuries, nor that Bennett played poorly when he came on as a replacement; but the Scotland forwards took a grip and squeezed a series of penalties out of Wales, Douglas Morgan kicking three of them to go with a dropped goal by Ian McGeechan. Even so, Wales might have scrambled a draw after Gerald Davies created a try for Trevor Evans but Allan Martin, the Aberavon lock (no Taylor he), could not make the difficult conversion.

Yet Wales showed their mettle a fortnight later, in Cardiff. Both Ireland and Scotland had hopes of the championship but both lost on the same day, Wales posting their highest score against the Irish. Five tries were shared in a 32-4 win, a spectacular victory which hinted that the young Wales forwards had the edge on an ageing Ireland eight of whom McBride, McLoughlin and Kennedy would not be seen again. It was the total rugby to which Dawes aspired, a synthesis of backs and forwards with Bennett back to his best form. If Edwards started the ball rolling, his colleagues were quick to follow and the only crumb to come Ireland's way was Willie Duggan's interception of an Edwards pass which gave him a consolation try.

Wales were back where they felt they belonged, at the top of the heap, and they gave glorious affirmation to the fact in 1976. Never before in championship history had one side scored so many as 102 points in an imperious display of all-round rugby though, for those who had eyes to see, France outscored Wales in the matter of tries by 13 to 11. Yet there was controversy enough with which to start the championship, since Bennett found himself relegated to fourth place in the fly-half list: he had been selected to play against Australia but withdrew with an injury, leaving Bevan to turn in a good display. When the trial came along, Bevan was in the Probables, David Richards from Swansea in the Possibles, and Gareth Davies (Cardiff) later took the field.

In fairness to the selectors, they may have felt they knew their Bennett by now but the public clamour was great. Despite this, it was only injuries to Bevan and Richards that restored Bennett to the team to play England. His response was a championship-best performance of 38 points in the season – effectively a two-and-a-half-match season since the kicking at Twickenham was done by Fenwick and Martin, who also took over after Bennett damaged his leg against France. The try-scoring at headquarters was done largely by J.P.R. Williams, whose reading of the play had seldom been better. He scored two tries alongside one by Edwards that left a brave England beaten 21-9.

The talking point of the game with Scotland in Cardiff was the display by the French referee, André Cluny, who pulled a muscle but declined to leave the field. He limped optimistically after the play in a haphazard match, but the 28-6 scoreline tells its own story. As the season grew longer, Welsh play became better, though for an hour in Dublin it was nip and tuck. Ireland trailed by only a point at the interval, thanks to McGann's three penalty goals, and the home forwards were in rampaging form, but in the final quarter they were blown away. Within six minutes, Wales scored 18 points with Bennett running the show: there was a second try for Gerald Davies, a record 18th for Edwards and then Bennett himself jinked his way to the line, his conversion giving him a match return of 19 (which equalled the Welsh record set by Jack Bancroft and Keith Jarrett).

The slam hung on the meeting in Cardiff with unbeaten France and Wales chose the day to offer their worst display of the season. However, their great resolve saw them through to a 19-13 win, characterised by a slamming shoulder charge made by J.P.R. Williams on Jean-François Gourdon when the France wing was poised to score. Gourdon had opened the scoring after sloppy Welsh play but Edwards pinned the French back with his kicking and the penalties began to stream Wales' way, five in all shared between Bennett, Fenwick and Martin. Fenwick worked an opening for J.J. Williams but 13-9 was a small enough lead at the interval. Two more penalties widened the gap, but Jean-Luc Averous beat J.P.R. Williams to the touch and the final quarter was a procession of French assaults, all of which came to grief on the dam of the Wales defence.

It was a triumph for willpower and organisation, and a fitting tribute to Mervyn Davies in what turned out to be his final international. Moreover, the French had their revenge a year later, beating Wales in Paris en route to their own grand slam. The Welsh had to settle for second place in a season long remembered for the double dismissal of players from each side just before half-time during the Wales versus Ireland game in Cardiff: Geoff Wheel, the Swansea lock, and Willie Duggan, the No. 8 from Blackrock College, were sent off for punching by Norman Sanson, the Scottish referee who was one of the best officials of his day.

The shock wave came as much from the fact that a referee had, in a sense, broken with convention and taken action as the law suggests, as the fact that two had gone at the same time. It should be remembered that, at that time, no more than four players had been sent off in the history of international competition and only one of that quartet – Mike Burton, the England prop against Australia in Brisbane two years earlier – had been British or Irish. What Brian Price's fate might have been in the equivalent match eight years earlier had Sanson been the referee needs little imagination, but the home unions were determined that foul play should be sternly treated with their game coming more and more into the public eye.

The loss was felt more keenly by Ireland, and when Ronnie Hakin, their lock, went off injured, Wales achieved the upper hand and a 25-9 win. However, they were crushed by the French steamroller and had to 'make do' with the triple crown, beating England 14-9 in an unusually tense match and then surviving a torrid time against Scotland to win 18-9. Wales clinched this final match of the season with a wonderful try, started in deep defence by Gerald Davies, sustained by David Burcher and Fenwick, and finished by Bennett, who sidestepped two defenders before completing the eighty-five-metre move. Bennett had taken over the captaincy from Mervyn Davies and, inevitably, became captain of the Lions to New Zealand alongside a great swathe of his fellow countrymen (eighteen Welshmen eventually made the trip in a party swelled to thirty-three by replacements and coached by John Dawes). Some, it is fair to say, should not have been there.

Others, like Edwards, Gerald Davies and J.P.R. Williams, could not go and their absence made a vital difference. Retirement was looming for the scrum half and the wing but one last hurrah remained: Wales became the first country to win three consecutive triple crowns and Edwards left the scene – permanently – and Bennett retired from international rugby clutching a grand slam. It was a fitting end, the more so for Edwards whose control and experience proved utterly vital in four testing games. Dawes, the coach, claimed that this was one of the greatest sides of all time; not everyone agreed but Dawes had achieved the important part in talking Edwards into one last season that would carry him past 50 caps, becoming the first Welshman to reach that figure.

Few players have turned the screw as Edwards did against England at Twickenham. The game was won 9-6 and, if Alastair Hignell had kicked more than two penalties from six attempts, not even Edwards might have made the difference. But, on a dismal day, he tormented England with the precision of his kicking and gave Bennett the territory from which to kick his three goals. There were no tries that day, but four came against Scotland on a bitter February day in Cardiff, including a final trademark score from Edwards: the Scots may have known what the master would do but they could not stop his athletic lunge from a scrum ten metres out, Gravell, Fenwick and Quinnell following him over in a 22-14 win.

The 20-16 success at Lansdowne Road had little to commend it. There were too many memories of the violent encounter of the previous year, too many scores being settled, too many careless boots in rucks and a professional foul by J.P.R. Williams on Gibson which, in another era, would have seen the full back dispatched to the sidelines. Victory hung on the experience dredged up at vital moments by Edwards, Williams and their stout front row from Pontypool. It also hung on the dead-eyed goal-kicking of Fenwick, who kicked four penalties – the first from his own half – and scored the first try thanks to an overhead pass from Edwards. Approving the ploy, Fenwick conjured a similar score for J.J. Williams which made the vital difference.

The team took many minutes to emerge from the changing room. When they did, Gerald Davies was limping, the effect of a damaged hamstring, and he missed the final game with France. The championship, and so many baffled opponents, had seen the last of him, though he played twice on tour in Australia that summer, leading his country in his 46th and last international when his 20th try kept him level with Edwards in the scoring stakes. He was thirty-three and few would dispute the official Welsh history's claim that 'it was as the greatest of many great Welsh wings that he will be remembered'.

As it happened, the old Wales had saved their best for last. France, grand slammers the year before, came to Cardiff and were themselves slammed. Bennett, knowing it to be his final game, ripped them apart for two tries in a 16-7 win after the French had gone seven points up in the opening twenty-five minutes. A try for Jean-Claude Skrela – part of a formidable back row alongside Jean-Pierre Rives and Jean-Pierre Bastiat – went with a dropped goal by Bernard Viviès before Wales offered the perfect response – thirteen points in eight minutes. Bennett scored from a heel against the head and converted, Edwards dropped a goal and J.J. Williams made the running for Bennett to score his second. In the second half the French held firm and it was not until the dying moments that Fenwick added another dropped goal. Bennett concluded with 166 points from his 29 internationals and, adding on his points for the Lions, 210 in his career – which was then a world record ahead of the 207 scored by Don Clarke (New Zealand).

It was an achievement for character and discipline rather than flair and it was, in many ways, the end of the dragon's decade. Yet the beast had one final fiery breath before retiring to its cave: the 1979 championship showed that the seam of talent had not run out, however unreal the expectations may have been for Terry Holmes and Gareth Davies, the Cardiff half backs taking over the mantle worn by Edwards and Bennett, and Elgan Rees, the stocky Neath wing who succeeded the immaculate Davies on the wing.

Holmes and Rees scored tries against Scotland in a match which suggested the ageing Wales pack was beginning to creak too. Another newcomer, the moustachioed Paul Ringer, scored a try against Ireland having taken the place at flanker of Terry Cobner, whose superb organisational and motivational skills as a player eventually carried him to the post of director of rugby for the Welsh Rugby Union. The Irish, defeated by only 24-21, scored more points in this game than they had previously achieved in Wales, helped considerably by the kicking of Tony Ward whose all-round play and build suggested that he came from a not dissimilar production line to Wales' fly halves.

Defeat, when it came, was in Paris where the Welsh crumbled on the rock of Rives' defence. The blond flanker was everywhere and made the difference in a 14-13 scoreline. Had Holmes, who scored his country's try, not been so industrious, the difference might have been greater and it gave France a sniff of the title until they departed from Twickenham, beaten themselves by a point. No-one expected England to be pushed aside, but the margin of Wales' 27-3 victory was crushing: even though injuries forced them to recast the front row and recall the veteran Mike Roberts to lock, their second-half display sank England without trace. It mattered little that they lost J.P.R. Williams, their captain, with a calf injury, Clive Griffiths emerged to win his only cap and watch five tries scored against the hapless English – one of them by Roberts who may have felt it was an unexpected but highly enjoyable climax to his international career. There was one too (his 12th) for J.J. Williams who was also playing his final game. His namesake, J.P.R., thought Wales' fourth triple crown in a row the right moment to retire as well but he was to be lured back for one final throw of the dice.

7
THE BEST OF THE REST
1969-1979

The best of the rest at this time was, quite clearly, France. England showed a prolonged capacity for making a sow's ear out of the silk purse of playing personnel available to them while Scotland and Ireland had only a limited number of core players around whom they could build sustained success. Even so, for five years Ireland were never less than competitive, culminating in their championship success of 1974; Scotland, on the other hand, struggled to get out of first gear, all too frequently contesting the wooden spoon with England.

The Scots had claimed the limited privilege of the championship's first replacement player, in January 1969, when Ian McCrae, the chunky little Gordonians scrum half, took over from Gordon Connell against France and thereby shared in a 6-3 success which would be Scotland's last in Paris until 1995. There were strict regulations relating to replacements, which ensured that change was made on a doctor's decision on the injured player's capacity to continue. As time wore on, that regulation became severely abused, coaches making tactical changes under cover of injury while the size of the replacements' bench grew from four in 1969 to seven in 1999, by which time temporary and tactical substitutions had both become accepted.

Meanwhile, Ireland marched confidently through 1969, scoring 17 points against France and England, and 16 without reply against Scotland before facing their Welsh nemesis in Cardiff. Indeed, they played seven internationals without defeat, a record sequence founded on the strength and leadership of Tom Kiernan at full back, a bouncy and thoroughly competent scrum half in Roger Young and an aggressive, knowledgeable pack which included four players who would go on to coach at national level – Syd Millar, Willie John McBride, Noel Murphy and Jimmy Davidson – and a fifth, Ken Kennedy, who did a splendid job of rejuvenating London Irish ten years later.

It was also the season in which Mike Gibson moved to centre to accommodate Barry McGann, the stalwart Lansdowne fly half with a kick like a mule. Gibson had broken his jaw in the trial and was not available against France, so McGann came in to drop a goal alongside 14 points from Johnny Moroney, the sometime London Irish fly half who played international rugby on the wing. Moroney's return constituted an individual record at the time and Ireland emulated Scotland by introducing Mick Hipwell as their first replacement for the injured Noel Murphy. It was an encouraging start against a France side glum after losing to the Scots and Moroney's try was smartly taken, together with his conversion and three penalties.

England, for their first match of the season, decided yet again to introduce a shoal of newcomers; the opposition may have been Ireland rather than Wales, but a principle is a principle and there were five new caps in Dublin. It was not the worst quintet either: Keith Fielding, the sprinter from Loughborough Colleges, joined a new midfield combination of David Duckham and John Spencer, while Keith Fairbrother and Nigel Horton, both from the Midlands, came into the front and second rows. Had such players been left alone to develop their careers, England's fortunes might have been better during the decade to come.

Duckham and Spencer were one of those splendidly-balanced combinations. Duckham, the powerful blond runner from Coventry complemented the more orthodox steadiness of Spencer, then nearing the end of his Cambridge University days. They played together in nine successive internationals before the selectors decided that Duckham should emulate Gerald Davies and move to the wing: 'This was not something I particularly relished, firstly because I still preferred playing at centre and secondly, because I didn't receive another pass for about two years,'

Tony O'Reilly in action for Ireland against England at Twickenham in 1970.

Duckham wrote later. However, he scored the first of his ten England tries on his debut and Bob Hiller's goal-kicking kept Irish nerves taut before Kiernan, his eight points taking him past 100 for his country, helped settle the issue at 17-15, McGann adding another dropped goal and Bresnihan and Murphy scoring tries.

It was becoming an eventful final season for Murphy, even though the flanker did not feature among the four try-scorers against Scotland. Laid out as he was by Brian Price in the championship's decisive match, at thirty-two he decided it was time to go, having played his part in a notable rugby dynasty – his father, also Noel, was an international flanker and president of the Irish Rugby Football Union, while Kenny, his son, played for his country at full back. The French, meanwhile, subsided to the foot of the table and Duckham scored two tries against the hapless Scots during a game in which Tim Dalton gained his footnote in history, the Coventry fly half winning his only cap as his country's first replacement (for Fielding).

You can never, of course, take the French for granted and they promptly bounced back to win the 1970 championship. They were the only one of the Five Nations not to play the demonstration-haunted South Africa touring party and, drawing a line through the results of that tour, England and Scotland should have had reasonable seasons having beaten the Springboks while Ireland and Wales could only draw with them. As it was, England and Scotland propped up the rest: the best that can be said of Scotland's season was that it introduced a baby-faced lock, Gordon Brown, to international rugby and he proved quite a handy contributor.

'Broon from Troon', as he became known – particularly on the after-dinner speaking circuit – was the younger brother by six years of Peter Brown, with whom he played on ten occasions in Scotland's pack. Indeed, until Gordon's arrival, most of Peter's caps had been won at lock but now he was able to move to No. 8, though not before he had been replaced by his young brother during the meeting with Wales in Cardiff. Brown senior's shift to the back row, where he was better able to exercise his leadership skills, coincided with the end of Jim Telfer's international career and so self-sacrificing a player deserved better than to captain his country to three successive defeats, lose his place and then find his successors beating England, the sacrificial lambs.

At 6ft 5in and 16st, Brown junior proved a handful for opponents around the world. He was a significant component of the 1974 Lions pack, awkward to jump against and a powerful driving force in the loose. In his early Scotland days he played in a tight five with Sandy Carmichael and Ian McLauchlan, both props of considerable stature in the metaphorical sense though not, in McLauchlan's case, the physical sense – the 'Mighty Mouse', as he was nicknamed, stood no higher than 5ft 9in and weighed 14st 6lb at the start of his career, yet he burrowed so effectively under bigger opponents that few could get the better of him. With the cultured Frank Laidlaw at hooker, Scotland possessed an effective tight five but the sum of the parts never amounted to as much as it might have done.

France, for example, could only win 11-9 at Murrayfield in 1970, the season in which they introduced the massive Jean-Pierre Bastiat to their pack. Bastiat, from Dax, stood just below 6ft 8in and had played basketball at representative level. With the formidable Elie Cester as his mentor, Bastiat made his debut at lock but it was as a massive ball-handling presence at No. 8 that he was to make his name. Possessed of a deadpan sense of humour, Bastiat formed a wonderful back row with Jean-Claude Skrela and Jean-Pierre Rives in 18 internationals, including the 1977 grand slam.

An 8-0 triumph against Ireland in Paris, marked by a wonderful try from Jean Sillières, raised hopes in French breasts, promptly squashed when they lost in Cardiff. As if to vent their anger, they took England apart 35-13 at the Stade Colombes, the highest number of points they had

Scotland prop Ian McLauchlan, with Frank Laidlaw in support, causes havoc against England in 1969.

scored against any championship opponent and twice their best ever against England. There were six mesmerising tries, the France backs and forwards weaving wonderful patterns against an England XV including three newcomers (one, inevitably, at fly half) while the rest felt more insecure as the season wore on. Pierre Villepreux, the France full back, offered Duckham the chance to play for Toulouse and the Englishman must have been sorely tempted after such a hiding.

The 1971 season, the Rugby Football Union's centenary, was memorable for Wales but no-one else. England played six internationals and won one, Bob Hiller's three penalties beating Ireland 9-6 in Dublin. France could only draw with Ireland and England and lost to grand-slam Wales, though it was a good season for Villepreux at full back. His brilliance in attack and his examination of all the possibilities foreshadowed his success as a coach and his propagation of total rugby – a concept not always totally understood. Villepreux sought to liberate players but within a disciplined framework. He carried his theories to Italy, to Toulouse and, finally, to France whose committeemen could never come fully to terms with their countryman's philosophy, but who enjoyed the grand slams towards which Villepreux contributed in 1997 and 1998.

If anyone other than Wales had reason for modest celebration, it was the Scots. Since 1938 they had been waiting to win at Twickenham and, on 20 March 1971, they finally did so. To cap everything, the president of the Scottish Rugby Union was Wilson Shaw who had played so memorable a match thirty-three years earlier. England led 9-5 at the interval, Hiller having scored a try on the end of an outstanding move which England could not recreate subsequently. The full back also kicked two penalties while Peter Brown, Scotland's captain, converted his own try. Duncan Paterson, an underrated scrum half, dropped a goal but Neary's try and Hiller's third penalty gave England a comfortable 15-8 advantage. At least, it was comfortable until a slipshod defence allowed Paterson in for his try and Chris Rea gave Scotland the chance to win. Rea's break had created Brown's first-half try and now the Headingley centre, who became a successful journalist and television presenter, slipped smartly over in the dying seconds. The issue rested with Brown's conversion – earlier in the season John Taylor's last-minute conversion had dished Scottish hopes against Wales and now Brown returned the compliment, his kick swerving drunkenly through the posts for a 16-15 win. To prove it was no fluke, Scotland won the second match against England a week later (commemorating the original international played at Raeburn Place in 1871) 26-6, scoring five tries including one each for Rea and Brown. It was clearly too much for the Scotland selectors, who did not pick Rea again.

Nonetheless, Scottish fortunes improved distinctly a year later when they and the Irish were joint second to Wales, despite the fact that Scotland played only three championship matches and Ireland only two because of the political problems in Ulster. Ironically England, who played all four, came stone last, whitewashed for the first time with 88 points conceded. They let in 11 tries, each of them worth four points rather than three, which swelled the debit side.

Kiernan joked at a rugby writers' dinner that it was a long time since Ireland had won all four matches, two by the sweat of their brow and two on a walkover. The first, moreover, was in Paris where Ireland had not won for twenty years and were not to win again for the rest of the century: their 14-9 success came courtesy of a team including five newcomers, among them Johnny Moloney at scrum half and the thickset flanker from Dungannon, Stewart McKinney. There was also a recall for Kevin Flynn in the centre, whose first cap had been in 1959 and who had not played since 1966, which was nearly in the Tony O'Reilly league for comebacks, though in his case the gap between his 28th and 29th caps was seven years.

Moloney and Ray McLoughlin were the try-scorers, the prop's try being a deserved reward for the forwards who effectively won this game for Ireland. They swarmed all over the luckless Richard Astre, the France scrum half, and with Kiernan kicking two penalties, all France had to show for their efforts was a fortunate try conceded when Gibson went for an interception and missed. The same side went to Twickenham for Kiernan's fiftieth appearance and, trailing 12-7, looked likely to return home pointless until a combination of sorry England defence and extended injury-time came to their rescue.

Captain, coach, administrator – the Ireland full back Tom Kiernan.

When Gibson's attempted penalty missed its target, a defender was generous enough to knock on in-goal, conceding a five-metre scrum from which McGann dropped a goal. Still there was time for Flynn to carve an enormous hole through the centre to score the winning try that Kiernan converted for a 16-12 win. It was the last international for Bob Hiller, the Harlequins full back whose goal-kicking had been so valuable to England and the Lions. In five internationals against the Irish he had scored 41 points from a total of 54 and the men in green were not sorry to see him depart.

Having won both their away games, it was entirely frustrating for Ireland that they could not play at home through the refusal of Wales and Scotland to travel, though France generously agreed to play an additional, non-championship match in Dublin. Thus it remained for Scotland to unveil a little, curly-haired centre – though the hairline receded as the years went by – in Jim Renwick (11) from Hawick. In a twelve-year career, Renwick was to win 52 caps and torment many an opponent with his speed and guile. He may have been only 5ft 8in, but in a broken field there were few to match his ability both to create and to score tries.

In fact, Renwick scored one on his debut, the 20-9 defeat of France when Scotland's presentation of the ball was compared favourably with that of New Zealand, with whom they have such strong links. The story against Wales was somewhat different, but a 23-9 win over England was intensely satisfactory, particularly for Peter Brown who scored 13 points from a try and three penalties, dominated the lineout and generally out-thought a sedentary England. Perhaps it was not surprising, as three weeks earlier England had been utterly demolished yet again in the last match to be played at Stade Colombes before France took themselves off to Parc des Princes in the suburb of St Cloud. They conceded six tries again, five of them converted by Villepreux who was enjoying his last year of international rugby.

It was, though, an unsatisfactory season which was followed by another one, since no country could gain an ascendancy in 1973. True, there were elements of promise as each side won its two home games. France christened the Parc, where they had played their first international in 1906 and had now refurbished at a cost of £8m, with a 16-13 win over Scotland, when the

Andy Irvine at a rare standstill against Wales, watched by Bobby Windsor and Terry Cobner.

kicking of Jean-Pierre Romeu was decisive, although the Montferrand fly half was to go on to even greater things four years later.

Tom Kiernan said farewell to international rugby with a try against Scotland to celebrate the end of a marvellous career. Walter Spanghero also reached the end of the road when France lost 6-4 to Ireland. However, the 1973 season saw Scotland introduce two hugely-significant newcomers: Andy Irvine and Ian McGeechan (7). Irvine, the eighth member of Heriot's Former Pupils to be chosen at full back for Scotland, was the only genuine rival during the 1970s to J.P.R. Williams – he lacked Williams' immense physical presence but compensated with riveting attacking skill and speed which brought him first to representative notice as a wing. Irvine had balance and vision and the attitude to bring both together. It was a dreadful irony that when Scotland finally won the grand slam, in 1984, Irvine had to watch it from the replacements bench when no-one would have begrudged him an appearance at the end of his career.

McGeechan was a different kettle of fish: fly half or centre, it made no difference, he was the oil in the works who helped others play well. As he played, so he coached and the Yorkshire-based Scot became one of the world's leading coaches, for Scotland and for the Lions (whom he helped to series victories against Australia in 1989 and South Africa in 1997). Two years later he was appointed to his second stint (though his first as a professional) as Scotland coach. It was a good year for Scotland to light upon these two, being their centenary season which promised more than it delivered: if the Scots could have sustained their ascendancy over England, the triple crown and Calcutta Cup would have been their reward, but England had discovered the makings of an effective XV.

Under the captaincy of John Pullin, the selectors remembered young Fran Cotton (9), whom they had picked two years earlier. They restored the intelligent and athletic Peter Dixon to the back row, alongside Neary and the long-haired Andy Ripley, the unorthodox No. 8 with the speed of a high-hurdler (which he was) and found a rugged lock from the north-east in the shape of Roger Uttley. They even unearthed a scrum half they were prepared to keep for more than a handful of games in Steve Smith, like Cotton a product of Jim Greenwood's coaching at Loughborough, and though they had a glum start they achieved their first championship win for two years against France and then scored four tries against Scotland, two of them by Dixon.

Given that England then beat New Zealand in a one-off international in Auckland (a year earlier they had done the same against South Africa in Johannesburg) and beat the touring Australians at Twickenham, all seemed set fair. Instead, England sank to the foot of the table and Ireland's star soared. The difference may have been the steadiness that such seasoned campaigners as McBride, Gibson, McLoughlin and Kennedy brought to Ireland's games; England had Pullin and Duckham but their side was still growing together and they played hopscotch all season with two scrum halves, Smith and Jan Webster, the Moseley player who had been so influential against the All Blacks.

Even so, Ireland had to chew their nails before learning that the 1974 championship would belong to them. Two wins and a draw left Wales and France both capable of overtaking on the championship's last weekend but, at Twickenham and Murrayfield respectively, both lost and Ireland had their first outright title since 1951. It was a crowning moment for McBride in what was rapidly becoming an *annus mirabilis* – a few weeks earlier he had become the most-capped player in the Home Unions when he won his 56th cap against England, a few months later he had led the invincible Lions to a series win in South Africa.

That England match served to convince Ireland of what was possible. It was not the best of starts to the season, beaten 9-6 in Paris and drawing 9-9 with Wales, but it allowed Maurice Ignatius Keane to find his feet in the international game. Moss Keane, 6ft 4in and 17st, was the first Gaelic footballer to win a rugby cap (for many years, ending in 1970, there were strict rules that prevented such a crossover) and did so in the second row, alongside McBride, after a

The England team that played against Ireland in 1973. Back row: F. Cotton, R. Uttley, C. Ralston, A. Ripley, P. Dixon, A. Jorden, P. Preece, S. Smith, D. Duckham. Seated: A. Neary, M. Cooper, J. Pullin (captain), C. Stephens, G. Evans, P. Squires.

rumbustious season with Munster. There could have been no better place to learn the game he had been playing for less than three seasons.

Ireland also had a bouncy pair of half backs in Moloney and the irrepressible Michael Quinn, with Gibson and the dependable Dick Milliken calling the shots in midfield. Indeed, this was arguably Gibson's match, a day when he scored two tries, kicked three conversions and generally pulled the strings which brought England down. At one stage Ireland led 26-9, having scored three tries in fifteen minutes after turning to take the strong wind – Moloney took advantage of a defensive fumble but Gibson scored his first with a splendid dummy, then supported faithfully after a telling run by Tony Ensor from full back. That Alan Old, with five penalty goals, kept England in touch at 26-21 did not disguise the fact that Ireland had equalled their highest score against any opponent and thoroughly deserved to.

It was shorter commons against Scotland at Lansdowne Road. This time Ireland were hanging on in the face of a second-half wind, helped immeasurably by Gibson's judgement and a storming display from flanker by Slattery. It was probably the season which confirmed the Blackrock player as one of world class: Slattery was always among the fastest of open sides and would have contested a place in the 1971 Lions international side but for injury and illness at the wrong time. As it was he enjoyed himself for the Barbarians in their classic match against New Zealand in Cardiff in 1973 and now showed himself to be a player of great stature – and one of seven Irishmen picked for the 1974 Lions, for whom he played an inspirational part.

The title also teed up the Irish Rugby Union's 1974/75 centenary season but, try as they might, they could not celebrate 100 years with another championship. Perhaps it was the anti-climax after the Lions tour or, more likely, the fact that McBride (thirty-four), McLoughlin (thirty-five) and Kennedy (thirty-two) had little more to give at the coal face of the game. Only the apparently ageless Gibson (thirty-two) seemed to ignore the years but for the three musketeers in the pack, this was their final throw. Against England Gibson was the best back on view, scoring a try which showed he had lost none of his pace, but it took a dropped ball and alert action by the young fly half, Billy McCombe, to secure a 12-9 win.

This was the game which gave Bill Beaumont (9), the Fylde lock, his first cap. Looking back, there is a sense of a torch being handed on, Beaumont playing his first game against the departing McBride whom he succeeded as Lions captain in South Africa in 1980. By massive application and the ability to set a heart-warming example, Beaumont turned himself into a fine international player and one of England's best captains, a player whose career was rudely interrupted by injury just when he was in his prime.

Ireland, too, were bringing in new players: their pack against England included Pat Whelan, the combative Garryowen hooker, and Willie Duggan, the tall Blackrock No. 8 whose attitude to training might best be described as permissive but who proved distinctly difficult to quell on the field of play. However, the Irish could not deny Scotland a 20-13 win, tactically devised by McGeechan, and though their forwards dug deep in a 25-6 win over France – McBride, in his 62nd game for his country, scored his first try to rapturous acclaim – they collapsed against Wales, the new champions.

Two other influential players also took the stage for the first time, both at Twickenham. England decided it was time to give the skilful young Leicester hooker, Peter Wheeler, a run in succession to the long-serving Pullin (though the Bristol man did return) while France introduced a man who was to become their trademark figure, Jean-Pierre Rives. The long-haired blond flanker from Toulouse had the better of the day, sharing in a 27-20 win over an England side uncertain of where it was going. Early scoring chances were missed while France, well-directed by Richard Astre from scrum half, notched up four tries. The side that was to win the 1977 slam was gradually coming together.

Rives was a player of great charisma and there was the physical aspect: the speed over the ground, the flamboyant ball-handling and the flowing locks which so frequently appeared bandaged or bloodied. But that, too, was an example of Rives placing his body on the line in an era when flankers expected to receive harsh treatment when they went to ground. Then there was Rives the philosopher, the bohemian, the sculptor, the chivalrous opponent respected by all because of his attractive personality. He was, of course, fortunate in the way that so many talented players in the number seven shirt are, in that he played much of his career alongside the selfless Jean-Claude Skrela and the imposing Jean-Pierre Bastiat. Later there was Jean-Luc Joinel, Dominique Erbani and others, hard men who allowed the eloquent Rives to flourish in a career of 59 internationals, in 34 of which he was captain.

Coincidentally, Wheeler's career with England also ended in the same year as Rives, in 1984. As a young man Wheeler was not only a developing front-row forward but was also blessed with good hands and mobility, to which he added the ability to kick both out of hand and off the ground. He spent one season as his club's goal-kicker, though he was never called upon in that regard by England, before becoming a hooker respected not only in Europe but in New Zealand and South Africa. Arguably the front row he formed for the Lions in 1977 with Fran Cotton and Wales' Graham Price could have held its own against all comers at all times.

Not that, in 1976, you would have guessed at England's resources. Bottom for the third year running and whitewashed for only the second time in history, conceding 15 tries (six of them, in what was becoming traditional fashion, to France in Paris), argument raged about the reasons for English decline. Many accusations centred around poor selection, but there were also interested glances north where the Scottish club leagues, which started in 1973/74, were now in full swing. It was not that England refused to consider structural change, as the Mallaby Report confirmed, but the clashes of vested interests and agonised debate over the best way forward so frequently seemed to get in the way.

Maybe there was also a glance across the Channel to the structured nature of the French club championship, with memories of past disputes pushed to the back of the mind. France were

Jacques Fouroux launches another French attack against England in 1976. Peter Dixon and Gary Adey can only admire.

building again, not swiftly enough to knock Wales off their perch just yet, but the makings were there: Jacques Fouroux was captain once again after a chequered career covering five years and this time he made it tell. The scrum half from Auch, at 5ft 5in and 10st the smallest man playing international rugby, made every pound count and, more to the point, he was surrounded by the big, formidable pack he felt France needed.

The sight of Fouroux barking orders at his mastodons became a familiar one, but this was no ordinary set of forwards. Quite apart from a talented back row, France possessed an awe-inspiring tight five of whom Robert Paparemborde was an outstanding tight-head prop. 'Papa' possessed sloping shoulders (that seemed, as Fran Cotton said, to go all the way down to his waist) which made him difficult to prop against but he retained the mobility of a man brought up as a three-quarter. He scored tries in each of his first two internationals and retained his place for 55 matches, mainly alongside two hard and talented hookers, Alain Paco and Philippe Dintrans.

Gérard Cholley, on the other side of the front row, had been a successful amateur boxer, a quality he sometimes took with him onto the rugby field. At 6ft 3in and 16st 7lb he was a huge, immoveable force, short on the technique possessed by Paparemborde but very long on physical presence. Cholley was nearly thirty before he won his first cap, having spent most of his career as a lock, and occasionally he alternated with Armand Vaquerin from Béziers. The nature of some of the players of this generation may be illustrated by Vaquerin's death from gun-shot wounds in a bar, seventeen years later, playing Russian roulette.

Behind these formidable men, Jean-François Imbernon and Michel Palmié formed a substantial second row. They were not the tallest of players, but both were well-equipped to look after themselves, their team-mates and, as occasion demanded, the opposition. Furnished with a pair of half backs in Fouroux and Jean-Pierre Romeu who played the percentage game, this was the pack that steamrollered its way to second place in the 1976 championship and to the 1977 grand slam. It was not a greatly-loved team – of the backs, only Roland Bertranne would find a place in the list of all-time French performers – but it was hard to argue with the statistics. France scored 13 tries (two more than Wales) and conceded two (one less than Wales) and their aggregate of 82 points pushed the championship tally past 300 for the first time.

In retrospect, Scotland did well to hold them to a seven-point margin, Ireland (with Phil Orr at the start of a long and distinguished career in the front row) conceded 26 points and drab England, uncertain about the fitness of their hooker and fly half, conceded 30 with the forwards Paparemborde (two) and Bastiat joining the try spree. There would be no more international appearances for Duckham, Ripley and Pullin, all of whom had given England service beyond the call of duty, or for Ireland's McGann and Scotland's Gordon Brown – though the latter did make another Lions tour in 1977 after spending most of the domestic season suspended following a dismissal during an inter-district match. There was plenty of rugby left in Ripley too: one of the most genuine characters in the English game, he kept turning out year after year for Rosslyn Park until he was forty. He was worth his place, not only for his skills but for his remarkable attitude. Such was his sportsmanship and honesty that in a club game he once signalled a dropped goal – which might have cost his side the game – by Wasps, when the referee was unsighted.

In view of what had happened in 1976, and was to happen in 1977, the quality of the Romania team of this time is amply illustrated by the fact that they beat France 15-12 in Bucharest in November 1976. The French, who have suffered some unexpected indignities in Romania, simply shrugged it off and they fielded the same fifteen players throughout the 1977 championship, bringing home their country's second grand slam, nine years after the first, though they could not have complained had they lost at Twickenham.

Their greatest hurdle was the first, that represented by Wales (albeit a Wales team shaken by the dismissal three weeks earlier of Geoff Wheel against Ireland). Moreover, France had the benefit of beginning their campaign in Paris. They dominated possession and only energetic defence kept Wales in the match. Two second-half tries, by Skrela and Dominique Harize, gave France an advantage they were not to lose in a 16-9 victory. Perhaps it was the very fact that they had accounted for Wales which contributed to the banana-skin on which they nearly skidded a fortnight later.

England had picked themselves up, given the captaincy to the craggy Gosforth No. 8, Roger Uttley, and given him his club scrum half, Malcolm Young, to play alongside. The new combination easily accounted for Scotland and sneaked a 4-0 win over Ireland in Dublin, thanks to Martin Cooper's solitary try. Understandably, therefore, England were feeling better about themselves than usual when the French arrived and if they had taken all their scoring chances, would have won by a distance.

Nigel Horton, the Moseley lock, dominated the lineout and twice in the first half England spurned try-scoring chances. Compounding their problems was the fact that Alastair Hignell, their full back, could not find the posts. He missed five penalty attempts from six and since France, through François Sangalli, scored the only try of the match, the visitors won 4-3 and made off into the night rejoicing. The omens were with them and they comfortably dispatched Scotland 23-3, though they were fortunate to complete the match with fifteen men on the field as Cholley flattened Donald Macdonald, Scotland's No. 8, with a punch shortly after the match started and was spoken to twice more by the referee before the home forwards took complete charge.

Ireland, in a season of reconstruction which left them whitewashed, were hardly going to hold the French juggernaut, even in Dublin. They made a gallant fist of it, led by Willie Duggan from the front, and might have fared even better had not John Robbie, their scrum half, broken an ankle five minutes into the game. Gibson and Quinn kicked penalties which gave Ireland their 6-3 interval lead but Jean-Michel Aguirre, that cultured full back, added two penalties to that kicked in the first half by Romeu and France recalled their traditions by scoring a seventy-metre try, started by Jean-Luc Averous, supported by Sangalli and Aguirre and completed by the two forwards, Paco and Bastiat, who loped the final twenty-five metres.

'The most ruthlessly efficient team I have played against' was how Cotton categorised the French vintage of 1977. 'Any realistic appraisal of the French season has to note that they have dominated the championship by rejecting their rugby heritage,' The Times noted with a sad shake of the head. Fouroux did not take such criticism to heart: he had found a winning formula (one to which he returned later as a coach) but the debate raged in France and, by January of the following year, Fouroux had gone. He was replaced by the young Toulon scrum half, Jérôme Gallion, who many regard as the best French occupant of the number-nine jersey in the last thirty years.

It had been a sensational year for France, since they were also admitted to full membership of the International Rugby Football Board but, beaten by a young New Zealand team in Paris at the end of the year, they opted for change at half back and in the three-quarters, giving the captaincy to Bastiat in what proved to be his final international season – as it was for Skrela. For a while it seemed that they might secure another championship, but the margins of victory became ever smaller – nine points against an England XV ravaged by injuries, three points against Scotland, one point against Ireland before Wales, themselves going for the grand slam, laid them low in Cardiff.

England proved the best of the rest under the captaincy of Bill Beaumont. The genial lock was not, at the time, the most obvious man to lead the side, but he grew effectively into the job at a time when the Rugby Football Union were looking hard at ways of improving their fortunes. Their preferred method was the introduction of regional teams, but it is also true that a group of talented players, in or around the national squad, were tired of being regarded as whipping boys. To such knowledgeable forwards as Cotton, Neary, Dixon, Uttley and Wheeler were added John Scott and Maurice Colclough, while this season also uncovered John Horton at fly half and the elegant Leicester youngster, Paul Dodge, at centre.

England lost their opening matches to France and Wales, the first of those games adding to the championship's tales of heroism when Robin Cowling, the England loose-head prop, remained on the field to scrummage against Paparemborde with a dislocated shoulder because England had already used their two replacements. However, they won at Murrayfield for the first

Alastair McHarg launches Wilson Lauder against England.

time in ten years and finished on a high note against an Ireland XV with a gifted newcomer at fly half. Tony Ward made his debut against Scotland and finished the season with a record tally of 38 points, matching the standard set by Roger Hosen (England) and Phil Bennett (Wales).

Controversy was seldom far from Ward and it was Ireland's curse that they should have had, in him and Ollie Campbell, two outstanding claimants to the same position at the same time. Ward, short, dark and with slightly-bowed legs, looked more like the traditional Welsh fly half and he offered the same jinking running skills. Campbell, who had won a solitary cap against Australia in 1976, was a more sinuous player capable of exercising a greater degree of control and whose kicking ability was the equal of Ward. At times the selectors tried to play them together, but it was seldom a happy experiment. Since Ward, in the view of the Irish Rugby Football Union, strayed close to the boundaries of the amateur regulations at times, Campbell's career turned out to be the longer.

This made Ward's international experience one of constant frustration though, as he reeled off nine internationals in a row, he was yet to become aware of it. 'The future of Irish rugby is in the hands of Tony Ward and some others,' Noel Murphy, the new Ireland coach, declared – though a year later there was to be a falling-out between the two on tour in Australia. Ireland also gave a first cap to John O'Driscoll, the London Irish flanker, and yet another medical man to become a stalwart of his country's pack, and decided that at the age of thirty-five, Mike Gibson could do a job for them on the wing – which, of course, he did.

Gibson played in that position against France after the Irish had achieved a narrow victory over Scotland, a match in which Sandy Carmichael became the first Scot to achieve 50 caps in what turned out to be his final game. Ireland might have achieved a similarly narrow win in Paris, on a frost-bound pitch which many deemed unplayable, but instead they lost 10-9 and thereafter could not offer much more than Ward's goal-kicking. That, at least, was more than Scotland achieved in a season when they lost all four games though they, too, discovered a gem in the Hawick hooker, Colin Deans.

If there was a *fin de siècle* feel to 1979, it was probably because Mike Gibson announced his retirement from international rugby. There were others who came to the end of the road at the end of the decade too – Ian McGeechan and, at the end of the year, Ian McLauchlan (both captains of Scotland in their day), their colleague Alastair McHarg (after 44 appearances as one of the most mobile locks of his era) and the substantial Gérard Cholley. But Gibson had been involved with Ireland since 1964 and he was not allowed to go easily: the Ireland selectors, with an injury doubt in the centre, summoned him to training despite having been informed of his intentions and not only gave him another cap against Scotland but took him on tour to Australia in the summer before he was allowed to leave, trailing clouds of glory, with 69 appearances for his country and 12 for the Lions.

During all that time, Gibson only captained Ireland five times – three times in 1971 and twice in 1976 – which may be an illustration of a man determined to do things his way. So perceptive a player, you might have thought, would have made an outstanding leader but there was a certain ascetic quality to him which led the selectors to look elsewhere. Just to confuse the issue, Ireland fielded another Mike Gibson this season, the 6ft 5in No. 8 from Lansdowne who enjoyed a splendid debut season only for a promising career to be disrupted by injury.

It was not, though, a memorable season for the rugby and it could be argued that France's own failings prevented them pipping Wales for the title. There was a desire to recover the free-flowing rugby of yesteryear and the giants, Bastiat and Imbernon, departed. Furthermore, there was a goal-kicking deficiency and France were fortunate to escape from Dublin with a 9-9 draw, though they did give a first cap to the powerful Brive back-row forward, Jean-Luc Joinel. At Twickenham, however, their luck turned and they went down 7-6 to an England side which, yet again, had lost its way.

The confusion in England circles was apparent with the captaincy issue. Roger Uttley replaced the 1978 captain, Beaumont, against Scotland, withdrew from the game with Ireland because of injury and then could recover neither place nor leadership. On the plus side, in the absence of the injured Cotton, England found a tight-head prop from Aylesbury, Gary Pearce, who was to serve them well for twelve years. It is typical that, in an unsuccessful season, England should discover a prop and Scotland – from the wreckage of another season with no victories – a fly half in John Rutherford.

A schoolmaster from Selkirk, Rutherford became one of the most elegant occupants of the Scotland No. 10 shirt. At 6ft 1in, his long-legged stride proved deceptive for would-be tacklers and by dint of application he turned himself into an excellent tactical kicker. He formed, with Roy Laidlaw, one of the best half-back pairings Scotland have ever had though his link with the sturdy little man from Jed-Forest had to wait another year.

8
SHUFFLING THE PACK
1980-1990

The 1980s were a curious decade for British rugby and became what may be called a buffer zone between the amateur tradition and the encroaching professional era. The Rugby Football Union was scandalised by the appearance of 'boot' money (cash from commercial sources such as boot manufacturers) regardless of the fact that the concept was hardly unknown in Wales and France. Players generally were aware of increasing demands being made upon them, in preparation as well as performance, with no suggestion that they should be recompensed for their time and effort.

The 1970s had seen growing interest from the media in the Lions tours and in international rugby generally. Sponsorship had now become accepted, both for domestic competitions and for individual internationals and, in short, the game was creating more money than it had ever done while the leading players tried to juggle the demands of a career, their families and their sport. At the same time the world was growing smaller and tours more frequent: New Zealand turned up in Britain during three successive years between 1978 and 1980, which gave players the chance to learn more about conditions in other parts of the world.

This, too, was the decade when, during the Conservative government of Margaret Thatcher, society at large appeared to become more selfish, less caring. If rugby players started asking 'What's in this for me?' it was no more than professional businessmen were doing. In such a philosophical maelstrom, it was no wonder that no one team dominated the Five Nations Championship: 1980 brought England their first grand slam for twenty-three years, 1990 brought Scotland their third slam in history (at England's expense) while in between France (twice) and Scotland again carried off the ultimate honour, which suggests that if anyone deserves the accolades it is the Scots for making the most of their small playing population.

By the end of the decade, of course, there were even critics who dared to ask what the future of the championship might be, now that the sport had its own World Cup. It was, and is, a remarkably short-sighted question given the standing of the championship and its popularity both for sponsors and spectators and it was also a negative one. Rather than working to make the championship better, critics were content merely to denigrate it, forgetful of the cyclical nature of all sport. Yet there had to be concern over the gradual decline of Welsh rugby. The principality, having occupied so high a mountain, had farther to fall than most, but there seemed a singular lack of vision in the years that followed the Welsh Rugby Union centenary in 1980/81, which reached its nadir ten years later.

England, of course, knew all about nadirs. They had suffered a few during the 1970s but, at long last, the triple crown, championship and grand slam were to be theirs in 1980 for the first time since the team led by Eric Evans in 1957 had achieved the honour. All the pieces fell into place: the experienced pack, the settled half backs, the goal-kicker. That nearly all these components had been available to the selectors for the previous five years only confirms the extent to which English rugby has squandered its resources.

Dusty Hare, for example, won his first cap in 1974 but, playing full back for unfashionable Nottingham, he was quickly forgotten. Not until he moved to Leicester, the Midlands giant at last emerging from the doldrums, did he win genuine consideration again and then he proved a matchwinner and the greatest accumulator of points England had yet possessed. Then there were two contrasting but direct wings in Mike Slemen and John Carleton and, by accident and design, a midfield came together to serve them. John Horton and Steve Smith were allowed to settle at half back but the pivotal element was the pack, possessed not only of physical prowess but footballing intelligence and mobility.

Dusty Hare, who kicked England's crucial goals during the 1980 grand slam season.

The presence of Roger Uttley and John Scott in the back row allowed Tony Neary to play at his best, and that best was considerable. Neary never moved from another unfashionable club, Broughton Park, but now, nine years after the first of his 43 caps (then an England record) he demonstrated the best of open-side flank forward play. Moreover, his tight forwards, including the uncompromising newcomer from Gloucester, Phil Blakeway, gave him a platform from which to operate and England the chance to take their revenge for all the inadequate displays of the previous ten years.

Ireland may have thought this could be their championship, after a successful tour to Australia in which Ollie Campbell and Ciaran Fitzgerald, the Army hooker, stamped their mark but they learned swiftly at Twickenham that it was not to be. They were crushed 24-9 (England had only scored 24 points in four matches in 1979) and the 9-3 lead that Campbell's volley of penalties gave them became merely a fleeting glimpse of victory. Hare's five goals embellished tries from Scott, Slemen and Smith but this was as nothing compared to the joy of victory in Paris. England, slightly fortunate that Cotton remained on the field after kicking an opponent, won 17-13, their first victory in the French capital since 1964, with tries by Carleton and Nick Preston.

A broken leg sustained by Tony Bond against Ireland had introduced Clive Woodward (10) to England's centre. After Paris he was joined by Paul Dodge, his Leicester colleague, because of a further injury to Preston but the two were able to establish a complementary pairing that survived fourteen internationals. Every Woodward needs a Dodge – the steady presence and, above all, the ability to read the game that Dodge offered allowed Woodward to indulge his elusive running to the full and in 1980 Scotland were the primary sufferers.

First, however, England had to negotiate the obstacle of Wales, so often their nemesis. Why there should have been such a brooding atmosphere around this match is hard to say – maybe the upbeat media support for England, even though Wales had beaten France quite comfortably, had

Bill Beaumont in action at the line out in 1980 against Ireland, watched by Nigel Horton and Roger Uttley.

something to do with it but most participants in the match were braced for a battle. So it proved. Paul Ringer, the Llanelli flanker, was sent off only fourteen minutes into the game, a general warning having already been given by David Burnett, the referee. Ringer was the first player to be sent off in the championship at Twickenham but the foul play continued in his absence: 'There seemed little point in going on if rugby had degenerated into this,' Uttley reflected later.

Uttley, his head split open, did not finish the match but Hare finished Wales. Even with fourteen men the visitors scored two tries, through Jeff Squire and Elgan Rees, and seemed at times to be the more likely winners until Hare stepped up to kick his third penalty, from an acute angle, and England won 9-8. Given that four kickers missed seven attempts at goal between them, you could say that Wales had kicked it away. There could have been no greater contrast with the match at Murrayfield when England at last threw off their inhibitions and claimed the slam with a 30-18 win of which the highlight was a treble for Carleton.

The forthright Orrell wing started the ball rolling with his first try which owed much to Woodward's break through the midfield. This match saw the slim Leicester centre at his best – head up and leaning out of tackles with his pace baffling opponents. Sometimes Woodward, who has brought to the role of England coach the same impulsive and generous qualities he showed on the field, played for gaps which were not there, but here he tore the Scots to shreds, creating a path for Slemen on the left wing to score. Smith and his back row did the spadework for Carleton's second and, after an exchange of penalty goals between Hare and Irvine, England led 19-3 at the interval.

This became a classic encounter with Scotland's spirited response in the second half. Smith crowned a long-range attack by his forwards with England's fourth try before Jim Renwick showed that anything Woodward could do in broken play, he could match. The little centre danced through to present Alan Tomes, his lock, with a try and Scotland shrugged off an indifferent season with some of their best running rugby. Inevitably mistakes accrued and a kind bounce gave Carleton his third try (England's first treble since Herbert Jacob scored three against France in 1924). But there was time yet for Rutherford, who had come together with Laidlaw, his chief ally, earlier in the season against Ireland, to make an outside break and score himself before the exultant England forwards chaired Beaumont, their leader, from the field.

Anything else paled by comparison though Ireland, given the rub of the green by the referee, would surely have beaten France in Paris rather than losing 19-18. Campbell's return of 46 points was a championship record but the comeback of the season belonged to Scotland. Struggling grimly against France at Murrayfield, Irvine inspired them to a burst of 18 points in the final 13 minutes and they won 22-14. It was one of those wonderful occasions which Irvine had the capacity to create, not once but again and again, taking charge by the sheer audacity of his running. He scored two tries, both from long distance and both through the quality of support running from the likes of Renwick, Rutherford and the newcomer in midfield, David Johnston. Irvine also kicked two penalties and a conversion, and would have scored all 18 points himself but for a brief injury which allowed Renwick to kick one conversion.

It was a game which hinted at what was to come in the new year, when Jim Telfer became Scotland's coach for the first time. Telfer never made a secret of his admiration for New Zealand rugby, of his belief in a swift, mobile game and the need for Scotland to tour frequently so they could learn at first hand the growing intensity of the game at international level that their own domestic competition did not give them. Then a school teacher, Telfer was a hard taskmaster, but personal popularity was far from his agenda. It is not overstating the case to say that his individual drive has been central to every Scottish achievement of the last twenty years.

Certainly there was a clarity of vision which England lacked and which Wales, still fresh from the golden 1970s, had lost. Since it was their centenary season, Wales hoped for better in 1981 but they were bracketed with England and Scotland on two wins while France, demonstrating once more their ability to go from the 'gor blimey' to the sublime, took an unexpected grand slam by reverting, under the coaching of Jacques Fouroux, to the massive methods which had served them well in 1977. Perhaps for the home unions the traditional post-Lions trauma set in, their leading players having worked so hard in South Africa during the summer of 1980 before losing the series 3-1 to the increasingly-isolated Springboks.

Yet no-one, not even France, celebrated too hard. Try-scoring was down (Wales scored only two in four matches) and the penalty goal was king. On the same day that Irvine's single penalty in Paris made the Scot the world's leading points scorer with 213, Hare kicked five for England yet could not stop Wales winning 21-19 in Cardiff. Indeed, the full back had the chance to win the game with the last kick of the match but he could not find the target. The game marked the conclusion of Fran Cotton's international career, though he was to distinguish himself as the 1997 Lions manager and for his role in the in-fighting which marred the first four years of the professional game in England.

Cotton had been affected by a heart condition, viral pericarditis, during the Lions tour but appeared to have recovered. Here he was forced off by a hamstring injury but illness subsequently forced him to retire from the game altogether. Thus passed one of England's best prop forwards, comfortable on either side of the scrum, adept with ball in hand and with an acute intelligence which brought him outstanding success as a businessman. With Neary and Uttley having retired, the England pack was suddenly not what it was nor, during the season, was the back division. John Horton gave way at fly half to the twinkle-toed Huw Davies while all Hare's heroics of the previous season could not save his replacement by Marcus Rose who, coincidentally, had preceded him at Leicester as a schoolboy.

England's best moments came in the 23-17 victory over Scotland, notable for two delightful tries from Woodward and Davies, and they went into the final weekend of the season capable of forcing a share of the championship against France. It was not to be. Fouroux had restored Jean-François Imbernon to his second row alongside the thirty-two-year-old newcomer, Daniel Revallier, described in French newspapers as a 'force of nature'. The powerful Basque prop, Pierre Dospital, confirmed a place in the front row and behind the pack two new half backs, Pierre Berbizier – destined to be so influential a figure in French rugby – and Guy Laporte made their mark. It did not matter that France had two wonderful attacking centres in Roland Bertranne and the 'petit prince', Didier Codorniou, nor that a certain Serge Blanco had been picked on the wing: Fouroux would win through his forwards and half backs.

'Right-wing Blanco set the French ball rolling by enterprisingly scoring an unconverted try,' *Rothmans Rugby Yearbook* reported of the game with Scotland, not knowing then just how much enterprise Blanco was to show over the next ten years. Bertranne added another and France won 16-9 without looking like a team of world-beaters. Nor did many give them a prospect of beating Ireland in Dublin when influenza forced Codorniou and Blanco out of the team and injury had removed Bernard Viviès from fly half; the Irish had a competitive pack, a distinctly-useful pair of halves in Campbell and John Robbie, and had been tipped for the championship.

Instead their 19-13 defeat was the prelude to a whitewash. Laporte, the cheerful fly half from Graulhet, marked his debut with two penalty goals and two dropped goals, the first from nearly fifty metres. Ireland worked their way briefly into a one-point lead with a try by the adventurous Hugo MacNeill from full back, but France created a fine try for Laurent Pardo and Serge Gabernet added a third penalty to round matters off. It was Gabernet, the Toulouse full back, who proved the downfall of the Welsh in Paris a month later. With only the final quarter of a hostile, often bitter, match to go, Wales led 15-9 thanks to a scintillating try by David Richards, the Swansea centre, and the kicking of Gwyn Evans. But the France scrum forced Wales into deep defence and Gabernet crossed for the only France try and kicked the final penalty which put France out of reach at 19-15.

Twickenham is not the ground where France would normally choose to play for a grand slam, so frequently have they lost there, but this time they made no mistake. They had forwards packed with what the New Zealanders call 'grunt', they had two scheming half backs – though the selection of Berbizier ahead of Jérôme Gallion had caused something of an outcry – and they had an ounce of luck. Their good fortune began when England chose to play against a strong wind and found themselves sixteen points down by the interval; it continued when Pierre Lacans, the flanker,

The France team that won the 1981 grand slam at Twickenham. Standing: P. Dintrans, R. Paparemborde, P. Dospital, P. Lacans, D. Revallier, J-L Joinel, J-F Imbernon. Seated: S. Blanco, P. Berbizier, R. Bertranne, G. Laporte, J-P Rives (captain), S. Gabernet, D. Codorniou, L. Pardo.

scored a try which should not have been allowed. The ball had gone deep into the West Stand and the law did not permit Berbizier to grab another one from a ball-boy to take a quick throw-in but he was allowed to do so, Rives chimed in and Lacans scored.

It proved to be the difference between the teams, though the French probably deserved to win. Their pack held the upper hand and England's backs could make little headway playing into the wind. Laporte landed two dropped goals at either end of the first half and Rives gave creative assistance when France scored their second try, through the long-haired wing, Pardo. When they had the wind behind them, England could score no more than four penalties through Rose and the French slam had been secured 16-12. It was a fitting way for Bertranne to bid the championship farewell; now thirty-one, the Bagnères centre had been playing since 1971. He collected two more caps against New Zealand in the autumn and then retired with the magnificent total of 69 appearances. Maybe he also knew that there was a youngster called Philippe Sella waiting in the wings.

Elsewhere there was little to enthuse over. The award of the first penalty try in the championship, by David Burnett during Scotland's game with Wales at Murrayfield, merits a footnote below the sadness that marked the departure after that 15-6 defeat of J.P.R. Williams and Steve Fenwick, captain in the first three internationals of that season. Williams, just short of his thirty-second birthday, had taken his total of appearances to 55 and left an indelible mark on the game. It may be no coincidence that in the four years that followed, Wales tried three full backs before settling on Paul Thorburn from Neath as the long-term successor to a player who had become an icon.

As if to mark how transient form can be, Ireland and France changed positions in 1982: France won only one game and Ireland assumed the championship and the triple crown (winning it, for the first time, in Dublin) before losing their grand-slam ambitions to the dispirited French in Paris. If one man can be said to make a difference to a team, even allowing for the goal-kicking achievements of Campbell, it was Ciaran Fitzgerald (13) who took over the captaincy from Fergus Slattery. It was a mantle that fell naturally on his shoulders. A comparative latecomer to the game, which he took up in his final year at St Joseph's School, Ballinasloe, Fitzgerald's leadership skills were honed with unfashionable Connacht as well as Ireland B and the Irish Army in which he was a serving officer.

He proved an utterly inspired choice when Slattery stood down. He had the ability to bring out the best from a talented group of players, some of them growing long in the tooth in their country's service. Slattery, Keane, Orr and Duggan possessed more than 150 caps between them while Fitzgerald, at twenty-nine, had 6 but he also held the key to the Irish psyche: to see the little hooker hanging on the neck of a big lock such as Keane, quite openly appealing to him for one last effort, was one of the more uplifting sights of the season and, whatever misfortunes Fitzgerald was to encounter as captain of the 1983 Lions in New Zealand – a role he should never have been invited to occupy – his value to Ireland was incalculable.

He did not inherit the most promising of situations. Ireland had lost seven successive internationals, the talented scrum half, John Robbie, had chosen to emigrate to South Africa, the Ward-Campbell controversy rumbled on and a clutch of new backs were trying to make their way into the side – among them Michael Kiernan, nephew to Tom who had now taken over as coach. Yet the side was not short of footballing ability: Paul Dean, for example, was a delightful player at fly half or centre, Moss Finn on the wing was a converted fly half, Trevor Ringland, the powerful Ulsterman, brought forthright skills to the wing and the tenacious Robbie McGrath was available at scrum half.

The trick was to stir the mixture to better effect and Fitzgerald, with his boyish fringe, did that. It is never a bad thing to begin the championship with home advantage and Ireland's campaign began well at Lansdowne Road with a 20-12 win over Wales, Campbell kicking the first eight points in what would become a season's haul of 46. The fly half also spelled out his running skills to anyone who doubted them, ghosting through the defence to create two tries for Finn and giving Ireland the confidence that better times lay ahead. That belief was confirmed at Twickenham where a 16-15 win failed to indicate Ireland's superiority.

England were still recovering from the enforced withdrawal of Beaumont, their captain. He had taken a blow to the head playing for Lancashire in the county final and had been advised to retire on medical grounds. The loss of so popular a leader shook the team and though Steve Smith took over the leadership with his customary ebullience, the players were still coming to terms with the abrupt change when Ireland piled into them; indeed the dominant image of that match is of 'Ginger' McLoughlin, the Shannon prop, driving over for a try festooned with white shirts but with his own colleagues providing the motivating force.

The try came from Campbell's quick wit – the fly half's drop at goal was charged down but he recovered the ball and instigated the move which McLoughlin finished. Slemen's late try helped England close the gap but time had run out on them, the match teeing up the meeting of Ireland and Scotland which was bound to settle the championship issue. Games between these Hibernian cousins have frequently been high-scoring and exciting affairs but seldom have great matters hung on them. This time was different, even though Scotland had played only once up to this point.

The triple crown was within Ireland's grasp, they were playing at home and had an unaccustomed self-confidence. When they had last won the crown, thirty-three years earlier, they had also been led by a hooker, Karl Mullen, and had also begun the season by losing to the touring Australians. It was a heady mixture but, for once, Ireland kept their cool: no-one, indeed, cooler than Campbell who kicked six penalty goals – equalling the world record for one match – and a dropped goal in his side's 21-12 victory. As the crowds streamed away, Tony O'Reilly, the former wing but now acknowledged throughout the commercial world for his business acumen on behalf of H.J. Heinz, said: 'I played in several satisfactory Irish defeats so I'm not going to moan about an unsatisfactory Irish victory.'

It was a day when a strong wind blew down the ground, a day for discipline and only once did Ireland allow their grip to relax, when Laidlaw skipped away in the first half and presented Rutherford, his partner, with the only try of the game. Ireland's scrum was so strong that they were able to walk the Scots back at times, leaving Campbell to direct operations in comfort. Every penalty was a hammer blow to Scottish aspirations and Irvine had few chances to respond. When they came he was inaccurate and before the end Renwick had taken over to score two penalties and keep his side nominally in the match.

Had they not had to wait a month for their final match, the momentum might have carried Ireland to the grand slam but in the intervening period the France selectors came to their senses. They restored the pack with which they had tinkered so much, recalled Berbizier at scrum half and stopped the Irish in their tracks with a 22-9 win. On the same day Scotland flowered in Cardiff, where they had not won for twenty years. The Scots might have known it would be a mixed bag of a season when they scrambled a 9-9 draw from their first outing, Irvine kicking a mammoth penalty from his own half in the dying moments against England.

But the ingredients of a championship side were being allowed to come together; there was no chopping and changing, save for injury, and though defeat in Ireland was a bitter pill, the French were beaten and Scotland's potential was then laid bare on the Arms Park stage. They won 34-18, scoring more points than any visiting side had ever achieved in Wales, and they played with an almost alarming sense of adventure, amply illustrated when Roger Baird collected a chip by Gareth Davies in his own 22, swept down the touchline and found Iain Paxton and Alan Tomes in support. The final surge came from Jim Calder, the Stewart's Melville flanker who was to be followed into the side by his twin brother, Finlay, and the try gave the Scots a confidence they did not lose.

On a day which saw Robert Norster, one of the finest lineout forwards Wales has ever produced, make his debut, every Welsh mistake was punished to the full. Renwick dropped a goal on the run then ripped Wales apart in a fifty-metre run; Jim Pollock, the Gosforth wing who became something of a lucky mascot for Scotland, scored a try on his debut and further tries went to Johnston and the all-purpose back-row forward, Derek White. It was as complete a demolition as any contractor could have sought and earned Scotland a share of second place in the table, alongside England whose season included a match in Paris almost as notorious for what happened afterwards as anything that occurred on the field itself.

England recalled Hare against France in a side of which four of the seven backs came from Leicester, winners of the national cup competition between 1979 and 1981. The Newark farmer

Clean-cut heroes of another era (clockwise): Ireland's George Beamish (1); the flying Scot, Ian Smith (2); the two brilliant Wales midfield men, Wilf Wooller (3) and Cliff Jones (4).

5. *J.P.R. Williams, Wales's full back, in full flow.*

6. *Gerald Davies, the supreme artist on Wales's wing – in the 1970s or any other period.*

7. Ian McGeechan, master tactician for Scotland as player or coach.

8. Mike Gibson, an ice-cool brain at work for Ireland.

9. Bill Beaumont and Fran Cotton at the hurly-burly that England-Scotland lineouts so frequently became.

10. Clive Woodward, wrong-footing David Johnston, with Andy Irvine to beat in another Calcutta Cup clash.

11. *Jim Renwick, the little Border maestro, on the run against Wales.*

12. *Graham Price, one-third of the renowned Pontypool front row.*

13. Ciaran Fitzgerald, inspirational as Ireland's captain.

14. Donal Lenihan, a mainspring in Ireland's second row and here supported by another long-serving forward, Phil Orr(1).

15. Jonathan Davies, the Wales fly half whose best years were given to Rugby League.

16. Finlay Calder, a granite-hard scourge of the English.

17. Philippe Sella, cutting another French angle against Wales.

18. England celebrate the winning of a grand slam in 1991. Standing: D. Morris, D. Richards, J. Webb, S. Halliday, W. Dooley, P. Winterbottom, J. Probyn, J. Leonard, B. Moore, M. Teague, M. Skinner. Kneeling: R. Hill, S. Hodgkinson, N. Heslop, R. Underwood, J. Guscott.

19. *The England pack with Mike Teague and Peter Winterbottom prominent.*

20. *Rory Underwood looks for the gap against Ireland.*

21. Patrice Lagisquet, all pace and balance, against Scotland.

22. Ieuan Evans, an ever-present comfort on Wales's wing when the dragon had lost its fire.

23. *Thomas Castaignède, the cheeky chappy of the French midfield.*

24. *Jeremy Guscott strides imperiously away for another try.*

25. *Christian Califano, a mighty bulwark in the French front row.*

26. *Scotland 1999, before the game with France. Twenty-four hours later they were the last Five Nations champions. Standing: S. Longstaff, P. Walton, C. Chalmers, A. Reed, J. Leslie, D. Hilton, M. Leslie, S. Murray, S. Grimes, A. Pountney, G. Metcalfe, S. Brotherstone, G. Graham, I. Fairley, Seated: P. Burnell, K. Logan, A. Tait, G. Armstrong (captain), G. Townsend, S. Reid, G. Bullock, C. Murray.*

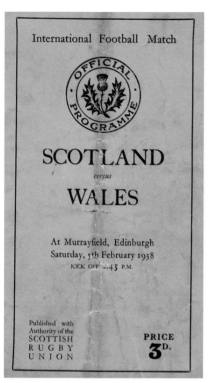

27. *Scotland v Wales, 1938.*

28. *England v Wales, 1949.*

29. *Ireland v Wales, 1949.*

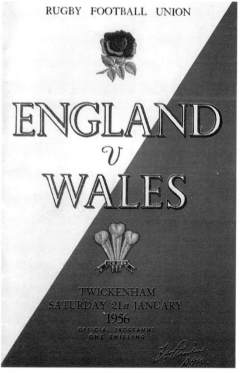

30. *England v Wales, 1956.*

31. *Ireland v Scotland, 1958.*

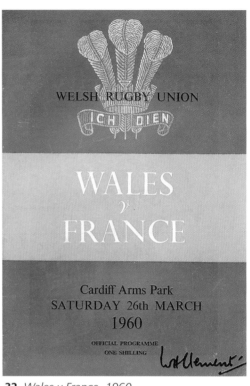

32. *Wales v France, 1960.*

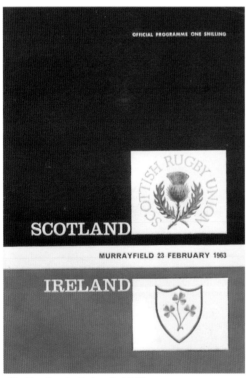

33. *Scotland v Ireland, 1963.*

34. *France v Scotland, 1965.*

35. *France v England, 1974.*

36. *Ireland v Scotland, 1980.*

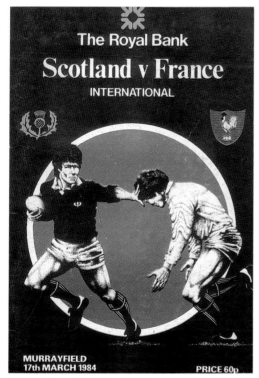

37. *Scotland v Wales, 1984.*

38. *Scotland v England, 1990.*

39. *Ireland v France, 1991.*

40. *England v France, 1991.*

41. *France v Scotland, 1999.*

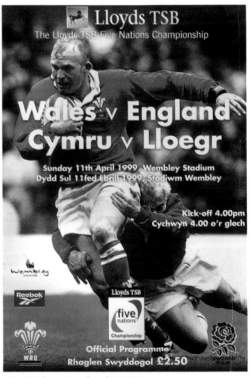

42. *Wales v England, 1999.*

Serge Blanco, the peerless France full back.

responded by kicking five penalties and two conversions in a 27-15 win, the England tries coming from Woodward and Carleton. The first was thanks to the quick wit of Slemen, the Liverpool wing whose footballing qualities were not always used to the full by his country (the same could be said of his attenuated coaching career): seeing the France backs turned for a drop-out, Slemen restarted quickly, kicked on upfield and found Woodward in support to complete the kick-and-chase try. Maybe it was in raising a cheery glass to his backs at the post-match banquet that Colin Smart, the Newport prop, fell prey to a practical joke by his colleagues: Smart quaffed deeply of the after-shave lotion thoughtfully provided as a gift by the French federation and ended the evening in hospital.

This was also the season in which the name of Peter Winterbottom **(19)** sprang to public attention, thanks to his play in a lightweight but wonderfully-creative Yorkshire side. The blond flanker was to spend the next ten years with his name in lights, but the bottom was dropping out of England's world. How ironic that, in a 1983 season when they came so close to breaking their Cardiff hoodoo by drawing 13-13, they should lose every other match and end at the foot of the table. Instead Ireland showed their championship win to be no fluke by repeating the feat, though this time they had to share the honours with France who had now moved Blanco to full back. It was the start of a phenomenal career and by the time it was over, in 1991, Blanco had played in 93 internationals and scored 38 tries, but, outweighing the statistics by far, he had written his name in capitals into the game's annals.

Born in Caracas, Blanco announced himself with a quite brilliant display in a 'B' international against Wales in 1979 when he was twenty. As a counter-attacking full back he had no peer: he could see space and had the speed to use it, even though he was often accused of being overweight and smoking too many cigarettes. His game possessed many of the effortless qualities of a player who is, mentally, three or four steps ahead of colleagues and opponents; his judgement of the pass made him a different kind of player from, say, J.P.R. Williams, who revelled in the physical contact of the game. Blanco had the ability to make a crowded field seem empty. He made his debut in 1980 on tour in South Africa, spent two seasons on the wing then came into the kingdom he was not to leave.

At the same time he was surrounded by talent: Philippe Sella (17), too, spent a season on the wing before he moved to centre at the start of a career which ended with 111 caps (the world record). On the other wing was Patrick Estève, a genuine sprinter, and the delightful Codorniou at centre. This was the season, too, in which Didier Cambérabéro, the son of Guy who had contributed so much to France's first grand slam in 1968, first made his mark at fly half – though his goal-kicking skills were not at their best when France opened a new championship season at Twickenham. If they had been, England would have been swept away by more than 19-15, Estève's try beginning a season in which he was to achieve the rare accomplishment of scoring in every championship game (joining England's Carston Catcheside, from 1924, and Scotland's Johnny Wallace, from 1925).

The backs were well served by a formidable pack, a strong front row having been joined by two classic spoiling locks in Jean Condom and Jean-Charles Orso. In an era when lifting was not allowed at the lineout and referees frequently turned a blind eye to illegality in the interests of keeping the game going, such grafting forwards were worth their weight in gold; throw in a back row which now had Laurent Rodriguez, the moustachioed No. 8 from Mont-de-Marsan, as a regular component and the reasons for French success become transparent.

It was a younger pack, too, than their Irish counterparts who were now being labelled *Dad's Army* after a popular television show. Yet the old guard still knew too much for most of their opponents, their experience dealing with Scotland 15-13 on the day that Princess Anne officially opened the new £3m stand at Murrayfield. They also dealt with France in Dublin, with a storming rally which overturned France's 16-15 lead – for which they had to thank Blanco – and left Ireland with a 22-16 win during which Finn scored two tries and Campbell, on his way to a championship record of 52 points, kicked the rest.

It was Wales, based squarely on the Pontypool pack, who brought the Irish down. After their slightly fortunate draw with England, Wales had won well in Murrayfield against a Scotland side lacking the injured Irvine and Rutherford. Pontypool had been steamrollering everything in their way and five of their forwards – Jeff Squire and Eddie Butler in the back row, John Perkins at lock and the two props, Graham Price and Staff Jones – played against Ireland and France. Behind them Terry Holmes, Cardiff's scrum half, thoroughly enjoyed himself: Holmes did not have the all-round skills or athleticism of the great Edwards but he was a powerful player possessed of a bruising hand-off and a good turn of speed, well able to play as a ninth forward or service a back division being encouraged by a new coach, John Bevan (the former fly half who died tragically young through illness), to express itself.

Against Ireland they did, by three tries to nil, which asked questions of the quality of the Ireland forwards. Holmes turned in his finest display of the season, as a runner and kicker of the ball, and under pressure the Irish committed a stream of errors. It left Wales with the prospect of the title but such hopes came to nothing during a running battle with France in Paris: antagonism between the teams already existed and Tom Doocey, the New Zealand referee and the first southern-hemisphere official to take charge of a Five Nations match (he had handled the Calcutta Cup match a fortnight earlier), could not coax a fluent game from either side.

Going into the final quarter Wales led 9-6 but Estève scored his fifth try of the championship – a French record, surpassing the four scored by Michel Crauste in 1962 and Christian Darrouy in 1965 – and Blanco's goal-kicking carried the French home 16-9. Thus they laid one hand on the title but only one since, on the same day, Ireland dispatched a badly-organised England side 25-15, only Hare's five penalties giving England respectability. Campbell scored his first try for Ireland in a match haul of 21 points, Slattery scored a second and England ended the season in a welter of recrimination between senior players and selectors.

That the championship had produced an aggregate of 325 points, the highest ever, did not make it one of quality. England managed only one try, Scotland two – both against England in their most-decisive win at Twickenham – and even Ireland only registered five. There were only 26 tries in all, less than half the record number of 55 registered in 1911. Instead the championship produced 56 penalties and nine dropped goals, accounting for 195 points and leading to a great debate about playing standards, a debate not allayed when the Lions returned from the summer tour to New Zealand beaten 4-0.

Among their other selection errors, the Lions had contrived to leave at home David Leslie, the Scotland flanker. Leslie had made his debut in 1975 but, after recovering from a broken leg, was now at the height of his considerable powers. Together with Jim Calder, John Beattie and Iain Paxton, he formed the prototype back row by which all subsequent Scotland back rows could be judged and, by and large, they lived up to an exceptional standard. It was an area of the game on which Jim Telfer, who coached the 1983 Lions, could safely be described as an expert, which makes Leslie's absence from the tour all the stranger. Besides the all-round skills of a back-row forward – he could play all three positions – Leslie was also a wonderful lineout performer, responding to the pinpoint accuracy of Colin Deans' throwing, which also set a model for future hookers.

In 1984, however, Scotland made up for much that had gone before. The clever money was on England for the title, because they had beaten a weakened New Zealand team at Twickenham before Christmas under the captaincy of Wheeler, now in his final international season. They did so with a crushing forward display but there was a cynicism about England, an air of too many players past their sell-by date and paying only half a mind to their new coach, the former flanker, Richard Greenwood. One should except from such criticism the two young Yorkshire backs who were chosen for the championship: Bryan Barley might have enjoyed an extended career at centre but for injury, whilst Rory Underwood **(20)** had the most extended career of any Englishman. When his international career ended in 1996, he had played for England 85 times and scored 49 tries (second only in the world rankings to Australia's David Campese).

Scotland left the captaincy with Jim Aitken, the Gala prop and a successful businessman who had taken over against England the season before. At thirty-five, the selectors left it late to recognise his leadership qualities, but they gave him a team with few weak links in the chain. Alongside him in the front row was the mobile, athletic Deans and Iain Milne, known to all and sundry as 'The Bear' and an immoveable force on the tight head. The locks – a selection from Alastair Campbell and the veterans, Bill Cuthbertson and Alan Tomes – both had nuisance value and, in Tomes, a player who could equal the best when roused (which was not always the case).

But the axis of the side was the middle five, the multi-faceted back row and the half backs, Laidlaw and Rutherford, who had been one of the Lions' better players in New Zealand. There was pace in the three-quarters and dependability at full back in the shape of Peter Dods, the Gala man who had replaced Irvine. The sadness of this successful campaign was that Irvine, so wonderful a servant of Scottish rugby in 50 internationals but now increasingly injury-prone, had to watch from the replacements bench and never had the opportunity to share actively in Scotland's second grand slam.

The 1984 championship did not make the most optimistic of starts. Leslie inspired Scotland to a 15-9 win in Cardiff, where Aitken himself scored one try with Paxton taking the other, and the visiting back row induced the jitters in a Wales back division seeking to run the ball but not always choosing the right place in which to do so. On the same day, however, France's 25-12 defeat of ageing Ireland was marred by the dismissal of Jean-Pierre Garuet, the Lourdes prop, for eye-gouging. Garuet, who was subsequently banned for three months, became the first Frenchman to be sent off in an international when Clive Norling, the Welsh referee, identified him as the culprit after John O'Driscoll reeled out of a maul, fists flailing.

Since France had started by scoring a delightful try through the recalled Jérôme Gallion within 100 seconds of the start, their afternoon could be said to have descended. Sella added another but otherwise Irish indiscretions gave Jean-Patrick Lescarboura, the lanky Basque fly half, numerous kicks at goal which earned him 17 points in a season which, by its conclusion, brought him a championship record of 54 points. France had a month in which to ponder their indiscretions while Scotland kept their ball rolling with success at Murrayfield in the 100th meeting with England, displaying their characteristic ability to adapt to circumstances which England, in this decade, so signally failed to do.

The Scots might not have achieved their 18-6 win had not Hare, normally so dependable, had such an indifferent day with the boot on an afternoon marred by wind and rain. He kicked two from eight attempts but the Scots, favouring the rucking game which allowed their half backs to control events, scored two tries. The first came when Leslie won lineout possession at the tail and Johnston, who enjoyed a flourishing football career in his youth, toed the ball through to score. Euan Kennedy, the 6ft 5in centre who played alongside Johnston for Watsonians, scored the second after Hare failed to reach Laidlaw's chip, leaving Calder and Rutherford to do the spadework.

With Dods kicking both conversions and two penalties, Scotland were well placed for their mid-season break, which left France to take centre stage against Wales. The Welsh, under the captaincy of the feisty Newport hooker, Mike Watkins, had picked themselves up against Ireland in a match featuring a fine individual try by Robert Ackerman, the London Welsh centre. On their own ground at Cardiff they gave France a tremendous run for their money but were undone by the kicking and tactical play of Lescarboura who fired over six assorted goals to go with Sella's try in a 21-16 win.

The two sides tilting for the championship both scored 32 points on the same day, France overcoming England 32-18 and Scotland dismissing Ireland 32-9 to ensure a triple crown at the very least – their first for forty-six years. It might have been worse for England, who had recovered a degree of equilibrium by beating Ireland 12-9 in a match where all the points came from kicks (which masks the fact that there was a lot of running rugby played on a day when seven players from Leicester appeared in England colours – a feat no English club had managed for ninety-eight years).

However, in Paris the sang-froid deserted them. It was reminiscent of the worst days of the 1970s as every France three-quarter scored a try and Gallion added a fifth. Three touch-downs were disallowed on an afternoon when France were without a first-choice wing, Patrice Lagisquet (21), the 'Bayonne Express'. In Lagisquet and Estève, France possessed probably the fastest pair of wings in the world at that time, but Lagisquet also possessed a delightful swerve and majestic acceleration as he demonstrated with utter clarity in his 45 international matches.

If England, for whom Underwood scored the first of his record tally of tries, thought that was bad, Irish heads must indeed have been low after Scotland had run in five glorious tries without response. Evidence of change was all around anyway: Campbell had been suffering from a virus and gave way to Ward, though no-one knew then that Campbell had played his last international. Slattery played when not fully fit against France, was dropped against England, restored against Scotland but had to pull out with illness – he, too, would not be seen again. Injury kept Fitzgerald out and the captaincy passed to Willie Duggan who, with true Irish generosity, gave the Scots first use of the wind.

Within fourteen minutes, Scotland had scored 15 points and Ireland had hardly touched the ball. Laidlaw, who so often tormented Ireland during his long career, dummied over for a try, Dods kicked a conversion and a penalty and then another conversion when Ireland's scrum collapsed and Fred Howard, the English referee, awarded Scotland a penalty try. Since Laidlaw promptly added another try it came as some relief to Ireland when he left with blurred vision. Kiernan scored what proved to be Ireland's only championship try of the season but Keith Robertson and Dods scored further tries for Scotland to complete a triumphant day for Aitken's team.

Hence two unbeaten teams vied for the honours on the final weekend of the championship, Scottish concern focusing on Laidlaw since Gordon Hunter, his replacement, fractured a cheekbone at Lansdowne Road when he collided with an enthusiastic spectator after the match was over. All was well for the Jed-Forest scrum half, which was more than could be said for the French who recalled François Haget, the Biarritz croupier, to play lock four years after his previous cap since Dominique Erbani was injured.

'We start off at a slight disadvantage because the players are not used to top-class rugby every week', Jim Telfer, Scotland's coach, said before 17 March dawned on Murrayfield. 'They have to rise to the occasion more than other countries and it is my job to get them to peak four times a season.' How they peaked against France, winning their first slam for fifty-nine years by 21-12 after a first half in which they looked likely to be overwhelmed. There were two schools of thought which suggested France might have won had not Gallion, their brilliant scrum half, come off second best in a collision with Leslie or if Winston Jones, the Welsh referee handling his first Five Nations game, had not caned them in the penalty count.

At one stage the Scots had received nine penalty awards and France none, a statistic calculated to bring the histrionics from any French team. Gallion scored their first-half try but it was scant reward for their domination and there was always Dods to kick the goals which kept Scotland in touch. It was the Gala full back's finest hour as he remorselessly kicked five penalties, even with one eye closing after a blow to the face. With Lescarboura kicking a conversion, a penalty and a dropped goal, it was knock for knock at 12-12 until Scotland's game-breaking try by Jim Calder – the result of a misdirected tap-down by France at a lineout on their own try-line. Dods' 17 points gave him a championship return of 50, which was 15 points better than Irvine's Scotland record. It was not a great match but it was, as is so frequently the case when Greek meets Greek, a great occasion.

Significantly, however, it was the two countries scoring most tries who decided the title: Scotland scored 10, France 9 in a championship which produced 27 tries in a record tally of 333 points. This, moreover, in a season when neither Irvine nor Renwick, those broken-field runners *par excellence*, played (Renwick returned for his 52nd and final cap against Romania two months later, a match which Scotland lost somewhat ingloriously). For Rives, in his 59th and last international, it was a bitter disappointment.

Moreover, France had to be content with second best a year later. In 1985 there were two unbeaten teams, though no grand slam. Scotland plummeted like a stone to a whitewash and Ireland bobbed up like a cork, denied the slam only by a hard-fought 15-15 draw with France in Dublin. To be fair, the championship came as something of an anti-climax after the marvellous and inventive rugby played before Christmas by the touring Australians captained by Andrew Slack. They took the grand slam that season, by beating all four home countries, but it was Ireland who seized the moment with an old captain and a new coach.

Fitzgerald was restored to the leadership and Mick Doyle, the former flanker, took over the coaching from Willie John McBride. 'Give it a lash' was the phrase which instantly identified Doyle's approach, though his thinking went far deeper than that. He also had new tools to hand, several fashioned in Ulster, who had dominated the inter-provincial championship during the 1980s. There was the abrasive back-five forward, Willie Anderson, and a pair of outstanding flankers in Nigel Carr and Philip Matthews. Such young blood took the championship by storm, while the introduction of a midfield cutting edge, where Brendan Mullin and Paul Dean played centre and fly half, created infinite possibilities.

Dean, while not so quick on his feet as the still-available Ward, possessed a softness of touch in his passing game which brought the best from a positive back division in which Keith Crossan had joined his fellow Ulsterman, Ringland, on the wing. Indeed, the two of them shared with Mullin the season's tally of five tries, though the most influential element was the kicking of Kiernan. At the start of the season, with no outstanding kicker in the starting XV, the choice lay between Kiernan and Moss Finn and the former confirmed his ability not only with 47 points but the dropped goal which beat England and earned the triple crown.

This was also the year in which the game's authorities finally acknowledged that there should be a World Cup; there had been intermittent threats of a professional circus and, indeed, the following year a rebel New Zealand party toured in South Africa. But the demands made upon the players' time had grown hugely as coaches called for ever more squad training and in Wales particularly, weighed down with a great tradition and a recent golden era, those demands became too much: in 1984 Graham Price, Jeff Squire and David Richards, three senior and influential figures, withdrew from international rugby and in 1985 three more followed them – Mike Watkins, Eddie Butler and Gareth Davies, all of whom had captained their country.

It was a reflection of the discontent felt by the players in all countries, and which grew after the inaugural World Cup of 1987, which brought the best in the world together for the first time, and when they learned how the game's regulations could or should be outmanoeuvred. England had tried to overcome the discontent of their old stagers by calling up a host of bright young backs, among them Rob Andrew, who was to prove so authoritative a figure in English rugby for the next ten years and in the professional club game for much longer. To counter-balance that, they unearthed a Lancashire policeman in Wade Dooley, who cast a long shadow. At twenty-six, Dooley was hardly in the first bloom of youth and Preston Grasshoppers, his club, were unaccustomed to having England selectors in their neck of the woods but at 6ft 8in, Dooley represented a formidable lineout presence who, in the course of 55 internationals, became a world-class lock.

However, hard though they tried, England lacked the judgement to make an impact. They surprised everyone, themselves included, by holding France to a 9-9 draw at Twickenham after the first weekend of the championship had been postponed through bad weather in Paris and Dublin. Andrew made his mark by scoring two penalties and a dropped goal but, in all probability, France would have won had not Richard Harding, the bouncy Bristol scrum half, knocked the ball from Estève's hands as he was in the act of grounding it behind the England posts. The bad weather, incidentally, persuaded the Rugby Football Union to press for the championship to be played later in the season but it was to be another decade before they were granted their wish.

England contrived a 10-7 win against Scotland, who had decided that at thirty-seven, Aitken was too old for international rugby (it was, of course, no more than ten months since his day of triumph) but that was the extent of their success. For Ireland, however, there was good news once they had started with an away win over the Scots; Ringland proved a deadly finisher with two tries in an 18-15 success, and when Kiernan kicked five penalties to force a 15-15 draw with France (who scored two tries), it seemed as though Doyle had put together a side of genuine character.

All Ireland's physical resources were required against the French, but a fortnight later they travelled to Cardiff and produced an outstanding game against a Wales side that could neither play fluent rugby nor kick their goals. Ireland did both: Ringland and Crossan scored tries and, in between, Kiernan kicked three penalties in a 21-9 win which left Ireland slavering to give England the warmest of welcomes at Lansdowne Road. When the day came, however, the Ireland backs were a bundle of nerves and if England had been more precise in their work, a day of celebration would have been abandoned; but Brendan Mullin was able to charge down Chris Martin's over-deliberate clearance and though England worked their way back to a 10-7 lead, they could not hold out. Kiernan levelled matters with a penalty and when Lenihan (14) led the Ireland forwards in one late rush, the ball was laid back for the centre to drop the goal that won the day.

The weather, though, had forced a further postponement which left Wales and England completing the championship as late as April 20. Wales had given a debut to the Neath full back, Paul Thorburn, against France and now found themselves forced to call up another Neath newcomer, Jonathan Davies (15), against England. The vacancy at fly half arose when Cardiff's Gareth Davies tired of being the pawn in selectorial games and stood down from the international game. As luck would have it, his twenty-two-year-old replacement dropped a goal and took advantage of an error by Martin, England's full back, to score the try which turned the game towards Wales.

Jonathan Davies became, in a sense, the fly half Wales never had. He played for the national side for three years at a time when their fortunes were at a low ebb, for all the third place they managed during the 1987 World Cup. But constant sniping drove him out just as surely as it had Gareth Davies, though in the case of Jonathan he took himself off to Rugby League and carved out an outstanding professional career. When Rugby Union went open in 1995, he was able to return but too late to have any lasting effect, even though he did add five more caps to his tally. This swansong served merely as a reminder of what Wales had missed, the elusive running, the deft ball skills, the bravery which was never seen to better effect than in 1988 when Wales were trounced in New Zealand but Davies offered convincing proof, in the worst possible circumstances, of his talent.

The approach of the first World Cup did serve to light something of a blue touchpaper underneath the home unions. There was a flurry of activity in England, who reintroduced a divisional championship in the hope of refining their talent, there were new coaches in England, Wales and Scotland and even before a blow had been struck in anger, three players were lost to the championship for – you might say – having struck blows in anger. Robert Norster and Richard Moriarty of Wales, and Steve Bainbridge of England (all, as it happened, lock forwards though Moriarty played much of his rugby in the back row) were suspended from international rugby after misconduct in club matches. Injury removed several leading Frenchmen, among them Philippe Dintrans, Didier Codorniou and Jean-Patrick Lescarboura.

But the newest stall was that set out by Scotland. Under the shrewd guidance of Derrick Grant, the former flanker – how often is it back-row forwards become top-class coaches? – they recast their side to play France by fielding six newcomers, two of them brothers, Gavin and Scott Hastings. It was no surprise: in the final trial, the Possibles had beaten the Probables 41-10. 'One suspects that Gavin Hastings at full back will never play as well again as he did in the trial,' one leading critic wrote before the start of a career which brought the powerful Watsonian 61 caps in the next nine years, along with the captaincy of his country and the Lions. His younger brother, Scott, in the centre made 65 appearances in the next 11 seasons.

They were a remarkable duo. Two of four rugby-playing brothers, both were blessed with huge self-confidence, Gavin with a dry wit and Scott with a generous sense of humour but their concentration where it mattered – on the pitch – was total. Gavin, two years the older, brought substantial presence being 6ft 2in and 15st, but he also possessed a sound footballing brain which allowed him to fit perfectly into the fast, mobile game that successive Scotland coaches wanted. There was a sense of adventure too, nourished perhaps by what amounted to his first experience of international football – his kick-off against France went straight into touch but the French took a quick lineout rather than the midfield scrum Scotland expected, and Hastings watched in horror as a phalanx of white jerseys bore down on him, the inevitable try going to Berbizier.

Like his Welsh precursor, J.P.R. Williams, Hastings revelled in defensive chores though no more than his brother, who was utterly reckless in the tackle. For a period in the late 1980s, Scott Hastings ranked among the best in his position in the world and it was no fault of his that, towards the end of his career, he was invited to play on the wing with unfortunate consequences. But they were not alone in giving a fresh, new look to the national side: they were joined by Matt Duncan (a chunky wing), Jeremy Campbell-Lamerton (scion of a distinguished rugby-playing family) and two future Scotland captains, David Sole and Finlay Calder (16).

The latter followed his twin, Jim, into the Scotland back row where he found a soul-mate in John Jeffrey, a Kelso farmer. The pair of flankers, initially with John Beattie but then with Derek White, formed a trio to strike panic into the heart of many an opponent, proving worthy successors to the retired David Leslie. There was an unforgiving hardness to their play, a mental edge more readily associated with New Zealand rugby upon which burgeoning Scottish success would be founded. That same quality was to be found in Sole, then loose-head prop for Bath having graduated from Exeter University; questions were sometimes asked of Sole's scrummaging but it seldom let Scotland down while his driving play in the loose made him a player for the modern generation.

The new combination was sufficient to give Scotland a share of the 1986 championship, along with France whom they beat 18-17 in the opening match. The French, led for the first time by the Agen hooker, Daniel Dubroca, were the most complete side in the championship but were let down by their own indiscretions, nowhere more than at Murrayfield where, despite scoring two tries, they were punished by six penalty goals from the boot of Gavin Hastings. France's second try came from Sella in what was to be a season of sustained excellence: he scored in every championship match – becoming only the fourth player to do so – and when the International Rugby Football Board celebrated their centenary at the season's end they were able to bring together on one pitch the two best centres in the world, Sella and Danie Gerber, the South African.

It is hard to convey the all-round ability Sella brought to a career which carried him through 111 internationals and two further years of professional club rugby with Saracens in London before he drew a line underneath it in 1998, at the age of thirty-six. He allied a physical dimension with absolute subtlety; he was hard and soft – hard in the tackle and powerful in his running, yet delicate in his distribution of the ball and the perceptive angles he ran. He learned his rugby playing with his friends on the streets of his native Clairac and the techniques of the game were so ingrained that he very seldom received an injury. Had he not been a centre of the highest class, he could also have served as a flanker, so strong was he on his feet. Sella scored 30 tries in his lengthy career for France, but it would be hard to count those he laid on for others.

Having opened so well, Scotland must have hoped for good fortune in Cardiff against a Wales side which had opted for the more refined skills at scrum half of Robert Jones, only twenty, from Swansea as opposed to the physical skills of Holmes (now departed to play Rugby League for

Dean Richards sets the ball up for Nigel Melville, England's scrum-half.

Bradford Northern), Mark Douglas and David Bishop. There must, therefore, have been a certain bleak satisfaction in France when they heard that the side that scored three tries to one had lost, primarily to the goal-kicking of Thorburn, whose five penalties included one monster which was subsequently measured at around sixty-five metres.

Indeed, two splendid matches were played on the same day since, while the Scots were going down 22-15 in a game where the lead changed hands seven times, France beat Ireland 29-9 and ended the game with a try of such sustained brilliance that even the greatest rugby cynic might have had his faith in the running game restored. From the moment the ball left Fitzgerald at a lineout, it passed through twenty pairs of hands during sixty-four seconds of magic before Sella (inevitably) crossed for the try. Considering the lineout was Ireland's most successful area of the game, in a season where the brave new world of the previous year seemed little short of a mirage, the fact that such a score began from an Ireland throw rubbed salt into a gaping wound.

England, meanwhile, had introduced a new centre pairing of Simon Halliday, the powerful Bath player who might have been capped three years earlier but for a bad ankle injury, and Jamie Salmon who had achieved the rare distinction five years earlier of playing for New Zealand. The captaincy had been returned to Nigel Melville, the Wasps scrum half who had displayed precocious talent as a teenager but whose career was so restricted by a debilitating series of injuries; Melville was probably the most naturally-gifted scrum half to have played for England since the war, but he was not alone in a certain fragility since Huw Davies, now playing full back, was plagued by a recurrent shoulder problem.

Whatever the personnel, it made no difference to Scotland who utterly crushed England at Murrayfield 33-6, equalling the 27-point margin of defeat England had suffered on tour against New Zealand the previous summer. Scotland held firm at the scrum, out-thought England at the lineout and left them bereft in the loose play; Gavin Hastings kicked five penalties and converted all three tries by Duncan, Scott Hastings and Rutherford – of which the last two stemmed from England possession. It was the most complete of victories and the only surprise was that, a month later, Scotland could only sneak home somewhat fortuitously by 10-9 against Ireland in Dublin, the match which earned Phil Orr his 50th cap in the Ireland front row and proved to be the final appearance of the inspirational Fitzgerald.

In recasting their disconsolate team to play Ireland at Twickenham, England opted for six changes in personnel, though only two newcomers: one was the tall Orrell centre, Fran Clough, who accumulated only four caps. The other stayed somewhat longer: Dean Richards, the Leicester No. 8, became a talisman to his countrymen, both those with whom he played and those who watched. Unorthodox in nearly everything he did, Richards had rare gifts for an Englishman – he could both read a game and control it. His great strength was crucial in the maul and in the tackle, his covering brought solace to many a lonely full back and he wrote his signature large in his first international, scoring two tries from pushover scrums while a third that he might have been given was construed as a penalty try as England won 25-20.

Yet England's future still looked tenuous. France scored four tries against them in Paris to force a share of the championship with a 29-10 win, demonstrating at the same time their conclusive power at the scrum. Melville once again could not complete the match after sustaining a neck injury which allowed Richard Hill to replace him for a third time. Hill, a contemporary of Sole's at Exeter University who also went to Bath, was far more durable than Melville and, by rigid application, made himself into an outstanding player. He disciplined himself to work at every aspect of his game, particularly his pass, and though he had an unfortunate 1987 as England captain, he ended his international career in 1991 as his country's most-capped scrum half.

It was, though, transparently obvious that the northern-hemisphere country best prepared for the World Cup was France. They possessed both the brawn and the brain; they toured extensively in 1986 to Argentina, Australia and New Zealand, and played three pre-Christmas internationals of which the third – against the All Blacks which they won 16-3 – has gone down in history as the 'Battle of Nantes'. It was, without exception, one of the most-overtly aggressive games produced by a Five Nations side and it was no surprise when France went through the 1987 championship like a dose of salts, carrying off their fourth grand slam in the process.

There was not one newcomer but a thoroughly experienced XV which changed only once in four matches, when Alain Lorieux gave way to François Haget. More to the point, Dubroca induced a greater sense of responsibility in his players in translating Fouroux's coaching. France conceded far fewer penalties while themselves handing the place-kicking duties to Philippe Bérot, the Agen full back whom they stored safely on the wing. There have been few taller back rows than that of Erbani (6ft 4in), Rodriguez (6ft 3in) and Eric Champ (6ft 5in), which extended the lineout options considerably, and there was great steadiness at fly half from Franck Mesnel, the gregarious player from Racing Club de France whose sense of style produced the fashionable Eden Park line in leisurewear.

Berbizier was Dubroca's eyes and ears behind the scrum, Sella and Denis Charvet the midfield lances with Blanco doing what he always did – offering the unexpected. It was to be a good season too for Eric Bonneval, the 'Bomb' from Toulouse who had played up and down the back division but now settled onto the wing where he scored 5 of France's 10 tries. The first of them came in an uncertain 16-9 win over Wales in Paris and was hotly contested by the three Wales players who felt they had pushed him into the cornerflag. There was some doubt over Mesnel's try too but both were allowed by Colin High, the English referee, and Bérot added eight points against nine by Thorburn, who broke his collarbone and did not reappear that season.

The match also marked the start of another extended career, that of Ieuan Evans (22) on the Wales wing. The geography student from Salford University had shown brilliant form for Llanelli but his debut had been delayed by a dislocated shoulder – indeed, had it not been for a variety of injuries, Evans would surely have collected more than his 72 caps in a career that did not end until 1998. France, meanwhile, moved on to Twickenham where an interception try by Sella was the difference between the teams as England went down 19-15. The French were more creative but had yet to translate their superiority into points against opponents constantly responding to being written off by their own media.

Bonneval's try, after a storming run by Champ, was the highlight of the game with Bérot adding a conversion and a penalty, Mesnel and Blanco kicking dropped goals. France, as it turned out, were saving themselves for the Scots in Paris: with Lorieux injured, Haget was recalled to the second row thirteen years after his first international appearance and for an hour France were superb. They played total rugby in every sense of the word, on the same day that Wales and England were serving up a sullen, bitter match in Cardiff. If the hero was Bonneval with two tries in the first half and one in the second, he was only the beneficiary of wonderful play by his colleagues, Rodriguez in particular.

Yet from a healthy lead of 22-7, France found a Scotland side unprepared to lie down and die. It was the Scottish response in the final quarter that made this such a classic match, a response engineered by Rutherford and Robertson who had replaced the injured Douglas Wyllie. At one stage it seemed that the visitors' momentum would carry them to a totally-unexpected win, but France battened down the hatches with two late penalty goals from Bérot. Bérot also scored France's other try, thanks to Blanco's intervention, helping France to an 18-7 lead, despite a well-marshalled defence in which Beattie was outstanding.

It was Beattie and Scott Hastings who scored Scotland's tries on the day when Deans, their captain, became the most-capped hooker in world rugby with his 46th appearance. Gavin Hastings kicked four penalties, but three from Bérot and a dropped goal by Mesnel kept the Scots at arm's length. Though they had to complete the slam in Dublin, there was seldom any doubt of French ability to do so, not even when the Irish careered into a ten-point lead through tries by Ringland and Michael Bradley. 'We have always felt that if France keep their heads they can beat anybody,' Doyle, Ireland's coach, said. For Fouroux, winning where he had won as player and captain in 1977, it was a matter of applying the *système correcte* – what the English would probably call the game plan.

Here it was best applied by Champ. The Toulon forward had a match to remember, whether at the set piece or in the loose, and scored both the France tries in the second half, against the wind. France could even shrug off the loss of Blanco with damaged ribs, bringing on the equally-elusive Jean-Baptiste Lafond. Three penalties and a conversion brought Bérot's total for the season to 37 and France a 19-15 win. Ireland acknowledged they had lost to a 'world-class side', the side indeed that would contest the first World Cup final (against New Zealand) after playing a semi-final against Australia generally regarded as one of the sport's greatest games.

While France were making their inexorable progress, England were the talk of the home unions, mostly for the wrong reasons. They played poorly in the rain in Dublin to crash 17-0, picked themselves up against France and then unravelled completely in Cardiff. Even before they played Wales there was dissent in the camp when Stuart Barnes, the Bath fly half handled badly by the selectors early in his career, withdrew from the replacements in the belief that he rather than Andrew should be in the starting XV. This was a debate, like that between Campbell and Ward in Ireland, which lasted throughout their respective careers and closed firmly in Andrew's favour – 71 caps as against 10 for Barnes. They were two very different players, Barnes the more elusive and adventurous fly half, Andrew far more considered and generally perceived to be a kicking pivot, though his initial impact showed quite clearly that he could run the ball.

'The spirit of rugby football died a little on Saturday,' Gerald Davies, the former Wales wing now writing for *The Times*, said after watching Wales beat England 19-12. Hill, England's captain, in a rabble-rousing team address in the changing room, may have overheated the situation but there had been a mean-spirited reception for England as they inspected the ground and when the punches began to be thrown, Wales players were as involved as anyone. That Ray Megson, the Scottish official, was refereeing his first major international did not help and the burden of penalties went against Wales but the surprise was that no player was dismissed.

If that was the case during the match, it was not so afterwards. The Rugby Football Union reviewed the ugly scenes and told the team management that the behaviour of some players had been 'totally unacceptable'. They spoke of a serious loss of discipline by both teams but only one was punished: a fortnight later, four players were suspended for one match – Hill, as captain, his Bath colleagues from the front row, Graham Dawe and Gareth Chilcott, and Dooley, the lock. It was an unprecedented step and salt was rubbed into English wounds when Wales found no cause to discipline any of their players.

Had there not been a World Cup imminent, the management themselves might have been at risk but, to their credit, England found a way out of their trough. They recalled Richard Harding at scrum half for the final match of the season, against Scotland at Twickenham, and gave him a new cap, Peter Williams from Orrell, as a partner having in effect agreed with Barnes that Andrew's form was not at its best. Dean Richards, who had missed the first three games with injury, returned to the back row and there was a new hooker from Nottingham, Brian Moore, of whom much more was to be heard. The captaincy went to the Yorkshire wing, Mike Harrison, who had led the North to great heights in the divisional championship and now found himself installed for the World Cup too.

Scotland arrived in search of a triple crown and departed, beaten 21-12. Victory did not remove England from the foot of the table, where they languished with Wales, but it was a far better closure than they could have hoped for. Bainbridge dominated the lineout, Bath's Nigel Redman performed with his customary zeal in the loose and Harding played a splendidly-selective game. Rose registered 17 points with a try, two conversions and three penalties to go with a penalty try awarded when Harrison was obstructed and though Robertson scored a late try, Scotland lacked the lustre that had attended defeat in Paris.

Ireland also ended the championship in victory, beating Wales 15-11 in Cardiff with a display of scrummaging that owed much to the advice of Syd Millar. It was, though, a bitter-sweet occasion: Nigel Carr, the Ards flanker who had become a regular over three seasons, was forced to withdraw from the Ireland party for the World Cup after injuries received in a terrorist bomb blast which killed Lord Justice Maurice Gibson and his wife. Carr had been travelling from Belfast to squad training in Dublin with his Ulster colleagues, Philip Rainey and David Irwin. His injuries were such that he was forced to retire, which placed in grim perspective any perceived ills within the game of rugby.

Thus the World Cup came and went with New Zealand the victors, leaving the northern hemisphere pondering the future. England had at last accepted the need for league rugby and created, in the Courage Clubs Championship, the biggest league in the world. The Rugby Football Union also chose a team manager rather than chairman of selectors, their gaze lighting upon Michael Weston. Three weeks later the former centre resigned, unable to have the coaching panel he favoured, and Geoff Cooke, a successful manager of the Northern Division, replaced him. It was the most significant move English rugby had made in years.

Cooke, a Cumbrian much of whose life had been spent in Yorkshire, knew what he wanted and had the advantage of being a new broom. He was joined in selection and coaching by Roger Uttley, the former England forward, and John Elliott, the former Nottingham and England trials hooker. For them the 1988 season was one in which to reconnoitre, to assess the talent available and make such changes as they wanted, among them the creation of a structure that would carry England upwards towards the 1991 World Cup rather than stumbling from hurdle to hurdle and their problem could hardly have been better illustrated than in 1988, the year of five captains.

Mike Harrison retained the leadership initially and when injury removed two first-choice centres, Halliday and John Buckton, England travelled to France with Les Cusworth restored at fly half after a four-year gap, John Orwin at lock after a three-year gap and Jonathan Webb – one of the few successes of the World Cup campaign – at full back. There were also three newcomers: Mickey Skinner, the brash Harlequin flanker, joined Jeff Probyn, the Wasps prop winning his first cap at the age of thirty-one, in the pack whilst the midfield included a young undergraduate from Durham University, Will Carling, whom Cooke knew well from divisional rugby.

Defeat by 10-9 was no disgrace, particularly since France's winning try by Rodriguez late in the game was a defensive blunder. Defeat by Wales at Twickenham, however, was not on the agenda, even in a season where Wales shared the championship with France and displayed an exuberant set of backs who hinted at the dash and glamour of a decade earlier. Heads promptly rolled: Melville resumed the captaincy, Andrew returned at fly half and Halliday to the centre, while the strongly-made Chris Oti, another Durham product, found a place on the wing. Not that wing play mattered at Murrayfield, where England ground out a 9-6 win over Scotland, but against Ireland it was the very essence. Another injury to Melville proved the spark: Orwin took over the captaincy and

England ripped the Irish to shreds in the second half, Oti scoring three tries, Underwood two and Gary Rees, the reliable Nottingham flanker, adding a sixth in a 35-3 win.

So at least there was mid-table respectability for the new regime, above Scotland – who had lost the services of Rutherford because of a knee injury which forced his retirement – and Ireland. But the honours lay between Wales and France: two tries by Adrian Hadley, the Cardiff wing, had helped the Welsh to their 11-3 win at Twickenham and France were fancied to win at Murrayfield until Gavin Hastings scored what was, in effect, an intercept kick-and-chase try, then hoofed over four penalties to produce a 23-12 win. The consequences were dramatic. Fouroux had already begun to dismantle the World Cup final side and half his pack was changed for the meeting with Ireland, while Didier Cambérabéro returned at fly half. The result was a comfortable victory but then came a month's wait while Wales built up a head of steam.

The Welsh recalled Thorburn for the meeting with Scotland, but the imprint left was that of Jonathan Davies. Twice Scotland led, by seven and then by ten points, but each time Davies reeled them back in supported by a side prepared to play rugby from anywhere. This was a team which had, in effect, three fly halves in that Bleddyn Bowen and Mark Ring were paired at centre. So there were decision-makers all over the park with the contrasting finishing skills of Evans and Hadley on the wings. Davies, turning bad ball into good with a grub-kick which he chased himself to the line hinted first at what was to come; then Ring and Hadley paved the way for Evans to dance past four defenders for the try of the season, the Llanelli wing making his way back to his own half with what became his trademark bouncy walk in which pride and modesty struggled to proclaim themselves.

Still Gavin Hastings embellished tries by Calder and Duncan with four penalties and it was time for the Wales forwards to earn their corn: Ian Watkins, the Ebbw Vale hooker, crossed for a third try after a long thrust by Thorburn, whose penalty reduced the Scotland lead to one point. Then Davies applied the matador's touch: beautifully served by Robert Jones, his first dropped goal wobbled over the bar but his second was a majestic strike and gave Wales their 25-20 victory in a magnificent game.

The same could not be said of their triple crown meeting with Ireland in Dublin. The 12-9 success was as mean in spirit as the previous game had been generous; the Irish set out to spoil but, their kicking being so poor, could not do so effectively. The Welsh seemed oppressed by the occasion, Davies overcome with the idea of dropping goals and the game had gone three minutes into injury-time before Thorburn kicked the angled penalty that brought victory. There was a try apiece by Terry Kingston, Ireland's hooker, and Paul Moriarty for Wales but little more that was memorable. Still, Wales had home advantage for their final game against a France side led for the final time by Dubroca.

The Agen hooker's imminent retirement may have been an additional motivating force for his colleagues in a team which fielded not only a huge pack but the muscular Marc Andrieu at centre while Lescarboura was recalled at fly half. It was as well he was there since he scored the try which gave France their desperately-close 10-9 win and a share in the championship. Played in pouring rain, France were happy with a tight game, leaving it to the lighter Wales backs to try and play rugby. But in difficult conditions they lacked precision – a couple of chances on the wings went begging – and France built up a 10-3 advantage before Evans found the space to kick past Lagisquet and make the touchdown. Thorburn's conversion reduced the lead to one point but Wales could not find the inspiration to make the final step.

The quality of the championship was summed up by David Kirk, the New Zealand scrum half who had lifted the Webb Ellis trophy at the World Cup the previous year: 'I can think of no rational reason for the unpredictability of the results,' Kirk said, 'except the old belief that much rugby is played by minds rather than bodies.' Wales did not then appreciate the chance they had missed as their rugby spent the next three years plunging downhill. Curiously it was Scotland, joint bottom with Ireland, who had as much cause for optimism as anyone, even if they were over-concerned with the fate this season of the Calcutta Cup. The old trophy had gone missing after the defeat by England and it was later discovered that two forwards, Jeffrey from Scotland and Richards from England, had taken it on something of a pub crawl. Each man received a comparatively modest playing suspension and the cup, which had sustained £1,000 worth of damage, was repaired; the joke that subsequently did the rounds was that when it left the post-match dinner it had been a cup but it was anonymously returned by being slid under the door of a match official as a shield. Like so many rugby stories, it was a slight exaggeration.

It became a year for comings and goings: the retirements included those of Laidlaw, so long Scotland's scrum half, Graham Price who hung up his club boots at Pontypool and the Ireland pair, Tony Ward and Ciaran Fitzgerald, who had not appeared in harness together as often as they might have done. Adrian Hadley, the Cardiff wing, departed to Rugby League with Salford and was followed, in January of the new year, by Jonathan Davies to Widnes. The departure of Davies was a bitter blow but the fly half had already felt the pain of rejection. He had returned from Wales' unsuccessful tour to New Zealand eager to impart opinions to the Welsh Rugby Union, and had been denied. Instead the union sacked the coach, Tony Gray, who had helped to win the triple crown and installed John Ryan. But Davies, the nucleus around whom any coach could build a team, became the seventh capped Welsh player in four years to go north.

England's adjustments included that of captain. Having been led by Harrison, Melville and Orwin during the 1988 championship, Orwin led a touring party to Australia and Fiji where he was briefly superseded by Harding. After a succession of stop-gaps, Cooke took a nation by surprise by turning to Carling to lead England up to the 1991 World Cup. It was a bold step to name the youngest member of the side, but Cooke seldom had cause to regret his decision. He recognised qualities of application in the centre which would change the role completely and make it, like football and cricket, one of the highest-profile jobs in English sport. That Carling was a most gifted player was undeniable: he was fast – as he had showed when Harlequins won the cup final that year – he was strong, with a low centre of gravity, and possessed of a delightful outside break. His family background was in the armed services – indeed he resigned an Army commission to further his sporting career – and Carling was also prepared to work at turning round the fly-by-night status that had become attached to the captaincy.

He was fortunate that his early years included such mature characters as Andrew, Winterbottom, Halliday and Richards, players who instinctively knew the best way forward. It is also a tribute to Carling that such individuals offered sustained support in the course of the world-record 58 games during which he led England. It is a truism that great leaders always have great players in their teams, and this was the season in which a great England team began to come together – aided, ironically enough, by a Frenchman, Pierre Villepreux, who was invited to lend his coaching skills during preparations in the Algarve for the Five Nations.

England had at last uncovered, too, the skills of Paul Ackford, at the age of thirty. Ackford had been spotted by the touring New Zealanders in 1979 as a lock forward full of potential but not until he joined Harlequins in 1986 did he make substantial progress; now he was to form, with Dooley, a classic second-row pairing which was central to England's subsequent success. As central, in its way, as the half-back pairing of Gary Armstrong and Craig Chalmers was to Scotland: there was a seamless translation from one Jed-Forest scrum half to another when Armstrong followed Laidlaw into the side and a similar approach too by a terrier-like player swift on the break, able to take responsibility and brave as a lion.

Chalmers, twenty, came from Melrose and was the player Scotland had sought since Rutherford's departure. His play at fly half was so mature that when he and Armstrong had played their way into the Lions party to go to Australia, there could be no possible argument against their selection; even so he was fortunate to have a knowledgeable New Zealand head alongside him in the shape of Sean Lineen, the Boroughmuir centre whose father, Terry, had played for the All Blacks. The captaincy went to Finlay Calder as Scotland prepared to play a Wales side now led from full back by Thorburn, whose recent fortunes also reflected a certain fickle approach by the selectors.

It was a championship in which the Scots jostled with France and England for superiority, their Celtic cousins left trailing sadly behind. Before it began, Jacques Fouroux, the least romantic of coaches and in the process of welding together another massive pack (three props in the front row), offered an analysis of the tournament: 'It's probably more than a rugby event, it's a social event which brings rugby to the forefront of sport in our country. For two months no other sport enjoys such a privilege. It's the best televised series ever devised – better than any American thriller series.

There is not one match in the history of the championship which resembles another. The development of the game in France is based on the attraction of the Five Nations.'

Fouroux's assertion was completely justified after France had beaten Ireland, now under the captaincy of Philip Matthews, 26-21 in Dublin: '*Match extraordinaire*,' he muttered. The Irish led 15-0 and 21-7 before Blanco inspired a wonderful response, scoring one try himself after a counter-attack sparked by Mesnel had flowed from one end to the other. The wings, Lagisquet (twice) and Lafond scored the other tries and Ireland's first-half ascendancy with the wind was overtaken six minutes from the end.

Wales would have enjoyed a similar comeback, when they found themselves trailing 19-0 at Murrayfield, but they had no Blanco. Armstrong, White and Chalmers scored Scotland's tries in a 23-7 victory which took them to Twickenham in assertive mood; not quite assertive enough, however, because a 12-12 draw ensured that neither Scotland nor England could claim the high ground. Jeffrey scored a charge-down try but Andrew had the winning of the game for England when he hooked a late penalty wide. It did mark, though, the start of a lengthy career in the front row for the London Scottish prop, Paul Burnell, and the resumption of a career which looked to have stalled for Mike Teague (19), the Gloucester back-row forward.

Matters improved materially for both teams: England came home from Dublin with a worthy 16-3 win and then knocked French hopes out of kilter with an 11-0 victory at Twickenham. France had disposed of Wales 31-12, but their muscular forwards ran up against a brick wall in the shape of Richards and his colleagues. It was England's first win over the French since 1982 and came on the day Andrew became his country's most-capped fly half, surpassing the mark of 22 set by W.J.A. Davies in the 1920s. A well-taken try by Carling, after a switch move had gone wrong, was confirmed by a late try from Andy Robinson, the Bath flanker, and left England with a real prospect of the championship if they could find a way of beating the Welsh bogey at Cardiff.

They could not. Even in a season when Welsh fortunes went from bad to worse, they found two players who could conjure up a home victory against the English, in this instance the two Roberts,

*Rob Andrew, England's most-capped –
though not always most-appreciated –
fly half.*

Jones and Norster. Playing in a downpour, Norster gave an extraordinary exhibition of lineout play in what was his last season; behind his forwards, Jones box-kicked in masterly fashion and England were pinned to the sidelines. Even so, they might still have won had not Underwood contrived to give Wales first an attacking scrum by knocking on, and then a try when he delayed his pass to Webb and the ball went down between them, leaving Arthur Emyr to kick on and Mike Hall to claim the points that gave Wales victory by 12-9.

The result saved Wales from a whitewash and let in France for the title, courtesy of a 19-3 victory over Scotland. Fouroux had restored Garuet, Dintrans and Louis Armary to his front row and their rugged play brought the Scots up short after the glories of the eight-try match with Ireland, which they won 37-21. Yet if it had all been, as Fouroux said at the start, so unpredictable, at least the Rugby Football Union were sufficiently encouraged to begin the transformation of Twickenham with a debenture issue to finance a new North Stand. There was, too, an important postscript to the season in the shape of England's 58-3 defeat of Romania which gave the young Bath centre, Jeremy Guscott (24), three tries on his first taste of international football while Ireland decided that Brian Smith, the former Australia utility back, was qualified to play for them which opened another period of controversy.

Wales, though, had a monopoly on controversy as the 1980s wended away. The covert involvement of committee members in organising players to attend the centenary of the South African Rugby Board led to the resignation of David East, the Welsh Rugby Union secretary, and Clive Rowlands, the president (though he was persuaded to return). Questions were asked on all sides about payments to players as amateurism struggled to keep its head above water, so it was as well that the players made the 1990 championship one to remember, particularly the players from England and Scotland who contrived a nail-biting shoot-out at Murrayfield which left Ian McGeechan coach to a grand-slam winning Scotland side only nine months after he had coached the Lions to a series win over Australia.

If the match against Romania had hinted at the genius of Guscott, it had also demonstrated the consistency as a goalkicker of Simon Hodgkinson, the Nottingham full back. Both players duly stepped forward for the opening championship weekend, against Ireland, while Richard Hill was restored at scrum half after a season in which Dewi Morris paraded his muscular skills. Crucially, in the light of subsequent events, England were without Richards for the entire campaign because of injury while Scotland were able to restore Gavin Hastings at full back after a groin injury had kept him out of the 1989 championship.

The first blow was struck by England, however, with a 23-0 win over an Ireland side which had introduced a former hammer thrower, Gary Halpin, the Wanderers prop, to international rugby. There were four tries, for Probyn, David Egerton, Guscott and Underwood, his nineteenth try for England (which therefore erased the record held by Cyril Lowe since 1923). Underwood had enjoyed himself with five tries against Fiji before Christmas and chalked up another four in the championship during a golden period in which he himself began to realise his importance to England's cause. The youngster who had wanted to fly fast jets and play international rugby seven years earlier had achieved both ambitions, as an RAF officer and as one of world rugby's outstanding finishers. Underwood combined speed and strength with an inherent athletic balance which made up for a certain absence of vision that sometimes plagued him. Now he had the maturity to use his ability to best effect. Moreover, England had come to believe they could play good, running rugby. They showed it at the Parc des Princes, forcing mistakes from France with the power of their forward play while Andrew pulled the strings from fly half. With Hodgkinson kicking quite beautifully across the swirling wind, France were crushed 26-7 with Underwood, Carling and Guscott scoring the tries. Returning to Twickenham, they repeated the dose against Wales with a 34-6 win which forced the resignation of the visiting coach, John Ryan. Underwood (two), Carling and Hill scored the tries and Hodgkinson carried his championship tally to 39 in three matches.

Elsewhere the engines were spluttering. There were two dismissals for foul play – both by Fred Howard, the English referee – of Kevin Moseley, the Pontypool lock, during Wales' defeat by France, and Alain Carminati, the Béziers flanker, during Scotland's 21-0 win over France. The Scots themselves had opened with an uncertain 13-10 win over Ireland in Dublin, under the leadership of David Sole; the prop forward, now playing with Edinburgh Academicals, took over from Calder who had been, at best, a reluctant captain even though his year of office included leadership of the Lions. His team included Tony Stanger, the Hawick wing making his debut, and Hastings at full back who proved so badly out of form with his kicking that the duty was passed to Chalmers for the rest of the season.

It was so close that had Kiernan kicked a late penalty, Ireland would have drawn. With Brian Smith playing fly half, they dominated the first half before the underrated White scored Scotland's first try after a diagonal run by Lineen. Chalmers added the conversion and kicked a penalty, leaving his side only a point in arrears, and White won the match by breaking powerfully from a scrum and catching the Ireland back row napping. If the London Scottish No. 8 had been the man of the match here, Sole and Jeffrey dominated events at Murrayfield as a petulant France team reduced to fourteen men went down to defeat. With the wind, all Scotland had to show for their first half was a penalty from Hastings but into the conditions they played far better, Calder and Iwan Tukalo scoring tries, Chalmers adding the conversions and kicking a further penalty.

Yet no-one would argue that the Scots were playing championship-winning rugby. They could only squeeze past Wales 13-9 in Cardiff, even though the Welsh – post-Twickenham – were in disarray with Ron Waldron, the Neath coach, trying to make something sensible from the tatters. They did score a delightful try through Emyr but Scotland's back row saw them through, helping create a try for Damian Cronin, the Bath lock, while Chalmers kicked three penalties. 'We have not played our best rugby for eighty minutes this season,' Sole said afterwards.

Yet on 17 March at Murrayfield they were in a position to win all the prizes: grand slam, triple crown, championship, Calcutta Cup, everything was up for grabs for the winner. England had the form, Scotland the home advantage and the support of a football-loving nation which had suddenly discovered rugby. There was a sense of nationalism in the air, some of it distinctly unlovely, of a proud country with limited playing resources pitting itself against the might of England. There were even the two coaches, McGeechan and Uttley, who had made the Lions into a team the previous year, face to face.

And there was the slow march. England took the field first, then Sole led his Scots at a walk onto the field, milking every moment of support from a tumultuous crowd. It was a moment of sheer theatre which even England must have felt for, playing into a strong wind, they went 6-0 down to two penalties kicked by Chalmers. Yet in the second quarter they had the winning of the match: Teague drove into the heart of the defence, Hill's pass gave Carling space and Guscott finished with a glorious dummy to Hastings. For the only time in the match the Scots found themselves pinned into defence but England chose not to kick at goal when awarded a series of penalties but to go for a pushover try. Another referee than New Zealand's David Bishop might have decided that Scotland collapsed the scrum and awarded a penalty try but, one way or another, England could not make their advantage tell and Scotland recovered from the period in which they adjusted to the loss of the injured White by bringing on Derek Turnbull.

Moreover, their tactical planning worked out in every sense. They concentrated on disrupting Hill so as to starve the dangerous England backs; their scrummage held up and their lineout play made Ackford and Dooley seem anonymous. England could seldom work out where the ball was going as Scotland's jumpers switched positions and Chalmers showed the folly of not going for goal when he kicked a third penalty before the interval. The decisive moment came immediately after half-time: Scotland restarted into touch but, given the scrum, Teague knocked on so it was Scotland who scrummaged on the centre spot. Jeffrey gave Armstrong the hint of a gap, the scrum half fed Hastings and the full back launched a high kick into England's right-hand corner where Stanger, leaping high above Underwood, collected the bounce and touched down the try.

There was virtually the whole of the second half to go but all England could retrieve was a single penalty through Hodgkinson and 13-7 was the final score. An heroic defence, in which Scott Hastings was outstanding, knocked England attackers down again and again: 'This match has captivated the heart of the Scottish nation,' Sole said. It also made a fundamental change to England's approach for the next five years.

9
SWING LOW SWEET CHARIOT
1991-1995

'If England ever get themselves organised, the rest of us could be in trouble,' Finlay Calder mused during his year of captaincy. In the final decade of the century they did, though the heart ached in contemplation of England's successful side of the 1990s against, say, the successful Wales side of the 1970s. In 1990/91, Wales were a shambles. They had suffered their first whitewash of the Five Nations in 1990 and a panel of distinguished retirees, Gareth Edwards and J.P.R. Williams amongst them, mused on television that the worst might be yet to come.

France, too, were in the throes of change with Daniel Dubroca and Jean Trillo taking over the coaching after the long reign of Jacques Fouroux finally ended. Ireland swept into a new championship with a new club league behind them, a new coach in Ciaran Fitzgerald and five newcomers of whom one, Rob Saunders, the London Irish scrum half, was invited to captain the side after the withdrawal through injury of Donal Lenihan. Scotland had to make do without that formidable competitor, Calder, whose retirement from international rugby lasted only until he was persuaded to return for the 1991 World Cup.

Wales, as they had done so successfully in times past, turned to youth: Neil Jenkins and Scott Gibbs, both nineteen and whose careers had started in Pontypridd's mini-rugby section, were named at fly half and centre respectively against England in Cardiff. Gibbs was one of six Neath players in the side named by Ron Waldron, the national coach who had turned Neath into the foremost club side in the country; the others included the Llewellyn brothers, Gareth and Glyn, in the second row. However, Waldron was to find that the all-court, mobile game that had brought Neath fame could not be translated to international rugby if the set-piece basics were insufficient.

The set pieces, of course, were where England are notoriously strong and this season they were, in the words of Geoff Cooke, determined to 'beard the dragon in its lair'. They wanted to absorb the Welsh atmosphere and so moved into Cardiff a day earlier than normal, listening all the while to taped renditions of the Welsh national anthem, leaving no stone unturned to achieve a psychological edge at a venue where they had been unsuccessful since 1963. Dean Richards was fit once more and Jason Leonard, who had made his debut at prop on tour in Argentina the previous summer, made his first championship appearance as did Nigel Heslop, the Orrell wing.

Not that wings had much of a day of it. The iron was in England's soul and their forwards, driven on by Richard Hill from scrum half, trampled all over their opponents, notably at the lineout. Such was the Welsh disarray that they conceded penalty after penalty, of which Simon Hodgkinson kicked seven in a 25-6 victory; the game's sole try was scored by Mike Teague, thrusting over from a scrum. Hodgkinson's was a championship record and the hoodoo was broken but England, in their hour of victory, refused to attend the normal post-match press conference amid claims that they were either drained by their efforts or annoyed that arrangements made by their commercial representatives had not been acknowledged.

There was an official reprimand for Cooke but no further action by the Rugby Football Union, some of whom may have recognised the inevitability of players exploring commercial possibilities as the International Rugby Football Board relaxed still further the bounds of amateurism. There were arguments between union and players over individual awards before minds turned once again to rugby and the Calcutta Cup match at Twickenham. Will Carling, their captain, reminded his players of the events of the previous season by strewing press cuttings around the team hotel of the day they lost the grand slam. Scotland duly lost 21-12, though theirs was the more inventive rugby and, in Gary Armstrong, they had a player bidding fair to be man of the match.

Again there was only one try – by Heslop – but five penalties and a conversion by Hodgkinson against four by Craig Chalmers. 'You stand or fall by your results,' Roger Uttley, the home coach, said. 'We're learning by experience.' Let others entertain, we're here to win, England were saying, and they did so again in Dublin to take the triple crown for the first time since 1980; there was nothing memorable about their rugby and if Ireland had been more precise in their work, they might not have lost 16-7. One man held England firm, the massive Richards who drew the game to him and wrapped it in his hand – little more than ten minutes remained when he rescued Guscott from trouble and set in motion the move which gave Underwood the chance to step off his wing, use Hodgkinson as a foil and cross for the try which finally broke Ireland. Teague scored another and, with Hodgkinson's limited return of nine points, England were on the verge of the slam they had missed a year earlier.

Would England have won that slam without Richards? Would they have won the World Cup final against Australia in November 1991 had Cooke not chosen to drop him for the knockout stages? Impossible to say, but both matches were close-fought and rested on tactical mistakes. Richards, the Hinckley policeman, had a way of making his point and he did so time and again when coaches thought his day was done. On 16 March there was another close-fought match at Twickenham, again the need to steady the ship at times, and Richards was at the heart of it as England won the grand slam by beating France 21-19 in a pulsating game.

The French, too, were unbeaten. They had introduced the Dax lock, Olivier Roumat, and added pace to their back row in the shape of Laurent Cabannes, the flanker from Racing Club whose career had, a few years earlier, apparently been written off in a bad car accident. They had Didier Cambérabéro at the height of his powers at fly half and Serge Blanco, who had suffered at the hands of the critics the previous season, determined to end his magnificent career (which was to close after the World Cup) in style. France had beaten Scotland, the champions, first time out and Cabannes enjoyed a runaway try in beating Ireland. When Wales were annihilated 36-3 in Paris, with Blanco scoring one of six tries, the stage was set for a mighty conflict.

It was graced, too, by a quite exceptional try. Hodgkinson had kicked one penalty but was wide with another in the eleventh minute (he missed five penalty attempts during the game) and his colleagues turned away for the drop-out. Except that Berbizier, in his own in-goal area, had caught the kick and passed to Blanco, he loped into the 22 and linked with Lafond who found Sella on the right wing under the East Stand. But the telling intervention was by Cambérabéro who put pace into the move, chipped over Underwood and caught the ball on the full. Streaming into the England half with the cover desperately trying to respond, Cambérabéro planted a cross-kick into a deserted midfield where Philippe Saint-André, who had made his championship debut only a few weeks earlier as a replacement for the injured Lagisquet, collected on the bounce and scored a stunning try.

It was a score worthy of winning a grand slam, except that England resolutely refused to be crushed by its brilliance. For a half-hour it was nip and tuck, Andrew dropping a goal and Hodgkinson kicking a second penalty while Cambérabéro's conversion and penalty kept the score to 9-9. But Underwood slipped Lafond, his marker, for an England try on the day he joined Tony Neary (on 43) as his country's most-capped player and Hodgkinson's boot brought an 18-9 advantage at the interval. Yet in the second half England tried to play for territory and left France to play the rugby: they did, Cambérabéro exploiting his own kick for one try and Mesnel, with no more than a minute left, adding another which carried France to within two points of an increasingly edgy England.

However, Hodgkinson's fourth penalty had given them just enough breathing space, besides giving him a championship record of 60 points. That France had scored three tries to one did not matter in the English scheme of things, nor to the crowd who carried their heroes off shoulder-high. That they carried, in some cases, the wrong ones did not matter: this was a victory for Winterbottom and Teague, for Hill and Underwood – players who had been involved in international rugby for seven, eight years and now understood the joy of winning.

This was a joy which the Welsh had all but lost. Another season without a win had passed, the only mitigation being the drawn match with Ireland who had plucked four backs from London Irish during the season, among them the blond wing, Simon Geoghegan, whose mercurial style illuminated the championship until a succession of foot injuries cut short his career. Geoghegan's course could seldom be charted by his colleagues, never mind his opponents, but he knew his way to the try line, scoring against Wales, England and Scotland. That Ireland had, like Wales, only one point to savour from the campaign did less than justice to their ambitious rugby and they were, justifiably, angered when Brian Smith left them to play Rugby League in Australia for Balmain. Ireland had embraced Smith, recognising both his footballing talent and desire to play international rugby, and had hoped to make him a linchpin of their World Cup side.

That tournament, though, marked the end of the line for many experienced and talented players: Blanco from France, Ackford from England, Calder and Jeffrey from Scotland, all retired while during or after the 1992 championship they were joined by White and Sole from Scotland, and Lenihan from Ireland. If only Lenihan, with 52 appearances in 11 competitive years, could have left on a higher note; there were few more loyal or hard-working servants of Irish rugby than the Cork Constitution lock – who has now become Ireland's team manager – but the promise of 1991 bore no fruit in 1992 as Ireland were whitewashed.

This time it was England first, the rest nowhere as Carling's team completed their back-to-back grand slams, a feat achieved only three times before – by England in 1913/14 and 1923/24 and Wales in 1908/09 (when the Five Nations proper had yet to come together). With Roger Uttley, the coach, having stood down, the role passed to Richard Best and they shrugged off the loss of Ackford, of Teague through injury, declined to restore Richards to the side and dropped Hill from scrum half. The newcomers to the team chosen to play Scotland in a reprise of the World Cup semi-final three months earlier included two Northampton forwards, Tim Rodber, an Army lieutenant at No. 8 and Martin Bayfield, a policeman standing 6ft 10in in his socks, at second row.

There was also a reversion to England's traditional all-white strip, though not before a legal spat over details of the contract regarding the World Cup shirt, which had included coloured stripes here and there. It was a passing phase, since all countries had cottoned on to the cash to be made from international jerseys and not many months had passed before distinguishing marks, and finally commercial logos, had become the norm. More to the point, England's reconditioned pack found themselves being shunted around Murrayfield in a most undignified way by, it might almost be said, some of their own: Scotland had dipped into England's pot and come up with Neil Edwards (Harlequins) and Ian Smith (Gloucester) – both of whom had played in junior representative England teams – for their own side. It was a measure of English frustration that Dooley chose to elbow in loose play Doddie Weir, the coltish lock from Melrose who was playing in his first championship match.

It was not until the second half that England gained an air of control, at 16-7, at which stage Rodber was forced off by a neck injury and Richards took his place. All of a sudden the game shot away from Scotland at a rate of knots. Dewi Morris added a second try to one in the first half by Underwood and Webb kicked 14 points to go with a rare dropped goal from Guscott. But if victory by 25-7 did less than justice to the Scots, the Irish had nowhere to look after crashing 38-9 at Twickenham to an England side inspired by Morris and given a cushion by Webb in his most successful and articulate season. The 6ft 2in Bath full back had been in and out of the side since 1987, balancing the requirements of sport with the demands of a burgeoning medical career and a young family but, at his best, there have been few better England full backs and none who scored the points that Webb did.

Here he finished with 22 – including two tries – which equalled the record championship haul of Doug Lambert against France in 1911. Webb's first try was timed at twenty-three seconds into the match, his second came in the final minute, while in between Morris, Underwood, Guscott

ENGLAND		FRANCE
ENGLAND	Referee: L. J. Peard (Wales) Touch Judges: C. Norling (Wales) D. Bevan (Wales)	**FRANCE**
White Jerseys, White Shorts		Blue Jerseys, White Shorts
15. **S. D. HODGKINSON** Nottingham	FULL BACK	15. **S. BLANCO (captain)** Biarritz
	THREE QUARTERS	
14. **N. J. HESLOP** Orrell	RIGHT WING	14. **J.-B. LAFOND** Racing Club
13. **W. D. C. CARLING (captain)** Harlequins	CENTRE	13. **P. SELLA** Agen
12. **J. C. GUSCOTT** Bath	CENTRE	12. **F. MESNEL** Racing Club
11. **R. UNDERWOOD** RAF & Leicester	LEFT WING	11. **P. SAINT-ANDRÉ** Montferrand
	HALF BACKS	
10. **C. R. ANDREW** Wasps	STAND-OFF	10. **D. CAMBERABERO** Béziers
9. **R. J. HILL** Bath	SCRUM-HALF	9. **P. BERBIZIER** Agen
	FORWARDS	
1. **J. LEONARD** Harlequins	PROP	1. **G. LASCUBÉ** Agen
2. **B. C. MOORE** Harlequins	HOOKER	2. **P. MAROCCO** Montferrand
3. **J. A. PROBYN** Wasps	PROP	3. **P. ONDARTS** Biarritz
4. **P. J. ACKFORD** Harlequins	LOCK	4. **M. TACHDJIAN** Racing Club
5. **W. A. DOOLEY** Preston Grasshoppers	LOCK	5. **O. ROUMAT** Dax
6. **M. C. TEAGUE** Gloucester	FLANKER	6. **X. BLOND** Racing Club
7. **P. J. WINTERBOTTOM** Harlequins	FLANKER	7. **L. CABANNES** Racing Club
8. **D. RICHARDS** Leicester	No. 8	8. **A. BENAZZI** Agen

Replacements: 16. J. M. Webb (Bath)
17. S. J. Halliday (Harlequins) 18. C. D. Morris (Orrell)
19. P. A. G. Rendall (Wasps) 20. C. J. Olver (Northampton)
21. M. G. Skinner (Harlequins)

Replacements: 16. T. Lacroix (Dax)
17. E. Bonneval (Toulouse) 18. H. Sanz (Narbonne)
19. C. Deslandes (Racing Club) 20. M. Cécillon (Bourgoin)
21. P. Gimbert (Bègles)

KICK-OFF 2.45 p.m.

The Rugby Football Union gratefully acknowledge the support of Save and Prosper

The teams for the vital match in the 1991 championship. England won 21-19 and went on to take the grand slam, with France finishing second.

and Halliday all crossed Ireland's line. It was as complete a performance as England's harshest critics could have wished, though it did not impress their own management in every respect, since Rodber was dropped and Richards recalled for the meeting with France in Paris. Control at the back of the lineout and in the loose were the reasons for change, though the challenge was for England to play the same running game at the Parc des Princes.

During the World Cup, England's quarter-final against France (for which Richards was dropped) contained some notable flash points and left an element of bitterness behind. Daniel Dubroca, the coach, had been dismissed after a verbal assault on David Bishop, the New Zealand referee who had handled the quarter-final, his role passing to Pierre Berbizier, who played down any motives of revenge as England prepared for the third leg of the championship. But the combustibility of his front row, which included the Bègles pair of Vincent Moscato and Philippe Gimbert, had already been in evidence during the 12-9 win over Wales and Brian Moore, England's hooker, was not slow to scratch French sores in print.

Moore, who ended his career as England's most-capped hooker with 64, was one of the most interesting characters in the team that dominated the northern-hemisphere game in the early 1990s. Indeed, it could be argued that the character of the whole team sometimes appeared to be a reflection of one player: opinionated, abrasive, ever willing to cross swords with authority, Moore was nonetheless a worthy successor to Evans, Pullin and Wheeler. His technical work was sound, his loose play sometimes inspiring and he appealed so much to the crowd that his nickname of Pit Bull seemed at times to be affectionate. As a lawyer he had been at the forefront of the squad's negotiations over commercial rights, which gave him a public profile in which he revelled.

France had half a dozen players new to the championship and a new captain in Philippe Sella; crucially they had no father figure in the pack and that is where England dismantled them in the course of a 31-13 victory – the first time since 1914 they had passed 30 points against the French. Unfortunately, much of the good rugby played by both sides was lost in the welter of recrimination that followed the second-half dismissal by Stephen Hilditch, the Ireland referee, of two French forwards, Grégoire Lascubé (prop) and Moscato (hooker), the first for stamping on Bayfield, the second for head-butting at a scrum. Both were justified and Jean-François Tordo was fortunate to remain, though by that stage the destiny of the match was decided.

The first half had been well-contested, a try by Sébastien Viars overtaking Webb's early penalty, but England scored two tries immediately before the interval despite the loss (a rare injury for the fly half) of Andrew after a collision with Sella which left the France captain groggy and eventually forced him off the field. The first was a penalty try, after the France scrum collapsed, the second a delightful dummy by Webb who sailed serenely through as the defence converged on Underwood. England's third try left the French in complete disarray: Alain Penaud collided with Jean-Luc Sadourny and Underwood collected the loose ball to score, leaving Sadourny (himself a replacement for Sella) to stagger off the pitch along with Christophe Mougeot, the lock who had strained a muscle.

That Penaud scored a charge-down try meant little as French morale disintegrated, their two front-row forwards departed and Morris stole a fourth try from under French noses. Webb concluded with 19 points and, for all the remonstrations made as Hilditch left the field under police escort, Lascubé and Moscato were suspended until the start of the following season. Many French critics, too, felt that the loss of control reflected no more than what was happening in club rugby in France, though it was to Berbizier's credit that there were no disciplinary problems on their next outing, a 10-6 defeat in Scotland, and his players finished with a record 44-12 win over Ireland.

England, though, were left to complete the final hurdle of the grand slam at Twickenham, against Wales. It was a Wales side coached by Alan Davies, once of Nottingham and once assistant coach to England, and it knew its way around in defence; there was, therefore, no win in the grand manner but, by the same token, England were never in danger of losing. Victory by 24-0 featured tries by Carling (after only ninety seconds), Skinner and, in his fiftieth international, Dooley with Webb limited to only 12 points from his kicking. The crowd roared for Underwood to score a try, the wing having announced his intention of retiring (a decision he had reversed by the end of the year), but it was never a game which flowed his way as he tussled with Ieuan Evans.

During the season England had scored 118 points, breaking their own record of 90 (set in 1990) and the championship record of 102 set by Wales in 1976. Webb registered 67 points, another record since it surpassed Hodgkinson's 60 a year earlier and also made him England's leading points scorer ahead of Dusty Hare. Whatever the frailties of the opposition, England had never shown to better effect the ability to score when opportunity beckoned or when their territorial advantage suggested they should. It was a magic touch which deserted them all too soon.

For the rest, there was not too much to be said. Wales, after a disastrous summer tour in 1991 to Australia which had ended in disgraceful exhibitions off the field as well as on it, had brought in new management in Davies and Bob Norster, and a new captain in Ieuan Evans, and their most notable achievement was to restore discipline and indicate that there might be some way out of the bottomless pit in which the national game found itself. Such qualities were enough to produce a win over Ireland and did bring the saving grace of a win over Scotland by 15-12, their first championship win in Cardiff for three years.

Scotland, crucially without the injured Armstrong at scrum half all season, could not sustain the momentum that had carried them to fourth place in the World Cup, though they did find in Rob Wainwright, the Army doctor from Edinburgh Academicals, a talented successor to the retired Derek White. Ireland, even in a season when they introduced to the championship the busy mobility of Nick Popplewell, the Greystones prop, lost their way completely. Ralph Keyes, the Cork Constitution fly half recalled to great effect for World Cup duty, was out of touch and

Saunders, whose star had shone so brightly the season before, was dropped. Adding to their difficulties, Philip Matthews, the captain, withdrew with injury and the experienced Brendan Mullin retired before the season's denouement, when France cast off their woes in a 44-12 drubbing – Sébastien Viars, the Brive wing, establishing a championship record of 24 points with two tries, five conversions and two penalties.

The championship as a whole produced 326 points and 34 tries, largely through England's efforts and France's seven-try finale against Ireland. It was also the season in which the Five Nations committee agreed to accept a trophy for the tournament, proposed by Lord Burghersh on behalf of the Sporting Trophies Exhibition Ltd, a decision which meant that, after so many years, a formula had to be devised to determine the sole winner – no more five-way ties for the Five Nations. In true rugby tradition, however, the details only emerged halfway through the 1993 championship as though the authorities had taken some persuading of the idea.

Nor were the International Rugby Football Board inactive: their meeting in Wellington confirmed the arrival of the five-point try and a new ruck-maul law which swiftly became known as 'use it or lose it', awarding as it did possession to the defending side if the attackers could not sustain their momentum in the maul or produce quick ball to sustain continuity of play. Since it invariably takes time for coaches, referees and players to pick their way through new legal minefields, the impact on the 1993 championship was largely negative, though there was no lack of excitement, if only because England subsided from the heights of the previous two years.

Instead France emerged from a chaotic 1992, during which they sacked Pierre Berbizier as coach only to reinstate him, and put together a thoroughly hard-nosed side. All of a sudden they became convinced about players who previously had seemed peripheral figures, floating in and out of touring squads: Thierry Lacroix, the Dax midfield player, found a home at centre, Laurent Seigne came from Mérignac to prop and Abdelatif Benazzi was given the chance to display his multi-faceted talents. Benazzi, born in Morocco, joined Agen and survived the experience of being sent off in his first international, against Australia in 1990. Capable of playing anywhere in the back five, he matured to become a mainstay of the pack and captain of his adopted country, a forward of genuine world standing until affected by injury. His initial impression was at lock since the back row contained not only Cabannes but Philippe Benetton, another extremely effective Agen forward, and Marc Cécillon, the rock of Bourgoin who was approaching the height of his lengthy career.

Since Cambérabéro also returned to the side, France took on the appearance of a team living in the present rather than the future. England, with two Underwoods available to them since Rory was back in action and Tony, his younger brother, had been capped against Canada in the autumn, chose only the older and omitted Richards from their back row where Ben Clarke, the rapidly-improving Bath No. 8, was preferred. But twenty-four hours before opening the defence of their title at Twickenham, they lost Dooley with a thigh injury and called up the young Leicester lock, Martin Johnson, to start an international career which set fresh standards as rugby changed into a professional sport.

In retrospect, England should have kept Johnson in the team rather than restoring Dooley for the rest of the season. Though they won 16-15, the plaudits were all for the discipline of the French, who lost Sella and Lacroix to injury during a windy afternoon but maintained their structure and, had not Lafond's dropped goal hit the crossbar, would probably have won. Saint-André added two more tries to his tally against one distinctly fortunate score to Ian Hunter, the strapping Northampton wing, otherwise a featureless England had to fall back on Webb's kicking. It was as though they believed all the publicity about England and France climbing clear of their Celtic cousins; if so, England were in for a nasty surprise.

Lacroix, meanwhile, recovered in time to score the only try of the 11-3 win over Scotland and Saint-André was there yet again when France beat Ireland 21-6. The wing scored one try, Sella another, and the French made sure of becoming the first name on the new championship trophy when they beat Wales 26-10 in Paris, Benetton claiming two of their three tries. It had been an honest, hard-working season for France, the perfect antidote to the preceding year

England hooker Brian Moore sets up the ball against Wales, with support from Tim Rodber, Dean Richards and Nigel Redman.

while the home unions were left to savage each other. Scotland, knowing that McGeechan was to step down as coach at the season's end, began well when a side including four newcomers beat Ireland 15-3. Derek Stark, the Boroughmuir wing and one of the new quartet, scored one of the tries and Andy Reed, the lock from Cornwall via Bath, did well in the forward exchanges as did another exile, Iain Morrison, the London Scottish flanker.

Ireland were under new management, Gerry Murphy having replaced Fitzgerald as coach after a difficult (to put it mildly) summer tour in New Zealand, and the long-serving scrum half, Michael Bradley, took over as captain. Bradley, the Cork Constitution scrum half, was one of those players whose all-round enthusiasm and organisation made up for technical limitations at the highest level. It always felt as though Ireland enjoyed having him there, a known quantity in a time of change with a footballing brain which did not always receive the respect it deserved. Among the changes was the raw-boned Paddy Johns from Dungannon, the quiet lock who in due course was to captain his country, and he was joined that season by Peter Clohessy, the prop who had caused the touring Australians so much anguish when he played against them in Munster's colours before Christmas.

Ireland's time, though, was to come. Wales were first to put a spoke in the English wheel when their inexperienced XV brought joy to a beleaguered nation by winning 10-9. England had every opportunity to win the match but could not do so, their lineout was out-manoeuvred and they did not enjoy the rub of the green with the refereeing decisions of Joel Dumé from France. Yet Wales, working to a limited game plan, deserved their win: they tackled manfully, no-one more than Gibbs, and sustained pressure even when two penalties by Andrew and a dropped goal by Guscott had put them 9-3 in arrears. Even so, danger did not obviously threaten when Emyr Lewis, the flanker, popped up in midfield and placed a delicate grub-kick towards England's left wing; Underwood turned slowly and seemed to think the ball would roll into touch. Too late did he realise that Evans, the Wales captain, was scooting past him, hacked the ball on and beat a horrified Webb to the touchdown.

Jenkins, who had kicked an early penalty, hammered over the conversion and the English goose was cooked. The sadness for Wales was that they failed to build upon their success: Scotland took them apart 20-0 and Ireland, as was becoming their habit, won 19-14 in Cardiff when the Wales team included for the first time Nigel Walker, the international hurdler who had turned to rugby. By the end of the season the experienced Robert Jones, the scrum half, was so lacking in confidence that he was replaced with Rupert Moon, the Englishman who had opted for Wales just as Dewi Morris had done the reverse journey from Crickhowell to England. Behind the scenes, confrontations between leading committeemen were once more ensuring that the game lacked vision and drive and, by the autumn, the Welsh Rugby Union had dismissed Denis Evans, their secretary.

England's response to defeat was swift. Andrew's head rolled, after 52 internationals, and his place against Scotland went to his great rival, Stuart Barnes, who had long since made his peace with the team management. Hunter, the wing, was also dropped for Tony Underwood but it was Andrew's demotion that puzzled – true, he was less than match fit after an enforced suspension consequent upon his return from a spell with Toulouse to rejoin Wasps (for whom he had to re-qualify to comply with competition rules) but his play had not been so undistinguished in Cardiff. Yet now Barnes could start a championship match for the first time, nine years after making his international debut against Australia.

He did so in style, though Scotland were leading 6-3 when they lost Craig Chalmers with a broken forearm. The injury to their fly half allowed Gregor Townsend to win his first cap at centre but the reorganisation left the Scots vulnerable and Barnes attacked them brilliantly. His break from his own 22 was supported by Guscott and a try for Rory Underwood was the result. The younger Underwood also scored, as did Guscott himself, in a burst which effectively won the match 26-12 and denied Scotland the triple crown, but it was noticeable that England's set pieces were not so effective as they should have been and their penalty count regrettably high.

A week later, moreover, Bradley inspired Ireland to victory in Wales, aided by a newcomer at fly half, Eric Elwood from unfashionable Connacht. The warning signs were there as England made their way to Dublin, needing to win by a hatful of points if they were to win the championship trophy, though the bookmakers made them 6-1 on favourites (not that the bookies have ever been an accurate guide in rugby). Ireland won 17-3 on the day that Bradley became Ireland's most-capped scrum half, overtaking Mark Sugden's tally of 28 which had survived since 1931. Elwood, the fifth fly half to wear the green in a calendar year, kicked two penalty goals and two dropped goals and Mick Galwey scored a storming try near the end.

Elwood's control of the match was absolute, whereas England could seldom release their backs into space. It was a sad conclusion to the careers of Dooley (55 caps) and Winterbottom (58), though both went with the Lions to New Zealand that summer, nor did Probyn play again after 37 appearances. All Probyn's caps had come after he had passed his thirtieth birthday, a commentary itself on his fitness and the problems he continually posed in the front row with his awkward angles of packing on the tight-head side; he was thirty-six on his final appearance and still justified a place with the Lions. He did not get it, though sixteen of his colleagues did. It was, too, the final season for Webb at full back, who left the game as England's highest points scorer with 296.

A few weeks later the International Board paved the way for former Rugby League players to play Rugby Union and, as if to demonstrate how commercial the game had become, Scotland announced a sponsor for the national team in the shape of The Famous Grouse, the Scotch whisky company. But it was unfancied, down-in-the-mouth Wales – seldom more so than after losing to Canada in Cardiff during the autumn – who came through on the rails to take the 1994 title with the twenty-year-old Scott Quinnell in their back row. Quinnell was the oldest son of Derek, the back-row forward whose utility value had served Wales and the Lions so well twenty years earlier, and his arrival on the scene, brash, powerful and fast, offset the loss to Rugby League of Richard Webster, the Swansea flanker and, at the season's end, Scott Gibbs.

Wales based their XV around the Llanelli club, eight of whose players started the game with Scotland. Under the direction of Gareth Jenkins, now the assistant Wales coach, Llanelli had played some marvellous rugby but it was two of their forwards, Quinnell and the experienced Phil Davies, who gave them control on a wet day. There was, too, Neil Jenkins who justified his coach's faith in him at fly half with some deft decision-making as Wales, with Mike Rayer scoring two tries as a replacement wing, won 29-6.

In little more than five weeks, Wales stood on the verge of a grand slam, although admittedly the game with Ireland in Dublin might, perhaps should, have been lost had Elwood kicked with his customary composure. But, having kicked five penalties, he failed with a sixth from fifteen metres which would have snatched the lead with only a few minutes left. Jenkins, with a try and four penalties, scored all Wales' points in a 17-15 win and left the country in good heart for the arrival of the French; the country was in even better heart when the French left, since not only had Wales won 24-15 but England, on the same day, had gone down once again to the Irish.

It was one of those Five Nations days, not necessarily rich in quality but chock full of surprise. One of those days too when one player steals all the thunder: that player was Quinnell whose try in the first quarter laid down a benchmark for his colleagues. Lunging away from a lineout he fended off two tackles and sprinted forty metres to the corner for the try that laid down an obvious gauntlet. But the Wales forwards played so well that France could not respond and they turned round 17-3 down, thanks to the kicking of Jenkins. Yet this was a Freance team of no little talent: only Olivier Merle, the giant Grenoble lock, and Emile Ntamack, the Toulouse wing who was making his debut, had not played in the championship before and gradually they nibbled away that lead to only two points, tries by Roumat and Sella testing Wales' fragile self-confidence.

However, they held firm, Quinnell surging into the France half, from the ruck Wales ran to the short side and Quinnell, yet again, laid on the pass that sent Walker sprinting clear for the decisive try. It teed up a final championship weekend for the Welsh at Twickenham, but they had to wait a month for the day to dawn; in the meantime the opposition was experiencing mixed fortunes. Elwood kicked five out of seven penalties for Ireland but was still trumped by Lacroix who scored 20 points as France dispatched Ireland 35-15. Scotland, drubbed by New Zealand in the autumn, made eight changes before playing Wales and a further nine before playing England, among them the successful persuasion of Gary Armstrong back into international rugby after a hiatus in which the balance between work, play and family had become too much for the Jedburgh lorry driver.

England were deprived of Guscott all season with a groin injury and Richards by an elbow injury rather than selectorial vagaries, but went for old and new in the back row to play at Murrayfield: old in the shape of John Hall, the Bath forward who had not played international rugby for four years, largely because of injuries, and new in the smaller shape of Neil Back. England, embarrassed with back-row riches, were in the throes of a sizeist debate which declared big to be beautiful now that Winterbottom had gone into retirement. Back, the Leicester flanker, had been a known quantity for five years but, at 5ft 10in, was judged too small for the modern game. That he possessed all the required skills and a few not always connected with flankers did not seem to matter but with Richards and Rodber injured, his chance came.

There were four others starting a championship match for the first time on the day Carling passed the world record of the Australian, Nick Farr-Jones, in captaining his country for the 37th time. Scotland had two debutants, Alan Sharp and Peter Walton, in an inexperienced pack and moved Townsend to fly half. Few, even among their own countrymen, gave them a hope, yet with a minute of injury-time played, they led 14-12. At that stage Jonathan Callard, the Bath full back who had succeeded Webb, stepped up to kick a penalty, his fifth of the match, from forty metres which reduced even as strong a character as Gavin Hastings, Scotland's captain, to tears. The new-look Scotland had done everything their captain and new coach, Douglas Morgan, could have asked save in one respect – Hastings, on the day, could kick only two goals from seven.

In many respects it was a poor game except that the lead changed hands so frequently that no-one could predict the outcome. Wainwright scored the only try and Townsend dropped the angled goal which seemed to have won the match until Scottish hands were detected in a ruck which gave Callard his chance for fame. After the match, video analysis suggested that it was a white shirt with a blue flash (a cunning England ploy) that had been illegally at work, but the result could not be changed. At all events, England deemed the back row to have been at fault and restored Rodber for Hall to play against Ireland. When Clarke was forced to withdraw with injury, the uncapped Steve Ojomoh stepped into what became another Irish whirlwind.

Ireland had Conor O'Shea, the Lansdowne full back in his first championship season, and a new centre in Maurice Field, but they also had an age-old lack of respect for a team they perceived to be in transition. Twelve of their number had played in the victory over England a year earlier and, though the margin was closer at 13-12, they deserved the spoils. Ireland played with passion and invention to post their first win at Twickenham since 1982 and inflict England's first home defeat in the championship for six years. If the architects were the half backs, Elwood and Bradley, the inspiration was Geoghegan who scored a quite beautiful try coming off his right wing and scoring on the left while O'Shea and Field made the dummy runs up the centre.

If England needed a jolt to the system, they received it when Geoff Cooke announced his intention to stand down as manager at the end of the season. After seven years he had, he said, grown tired of life in the goldfish bowl, his every action subject to public scrutiny and, quite frequently, criticism from committeemen who did not always appreciate the strength he brought to the squad. Cooke's contribution to the rise of English rugby can never be underestimated. He brought a consistency and a loyalty to which the players were unaccustomed and they responded like wildfire, never more so than in going to Paris five days later and beating France 18-14 thanks to five penalties and a dropped goal from Andrew, first-choice goalkicker for the first time since 1989.

The fly half had been restored before Christmas and once again proved how thoughtful a player he was and remains. When World XVs are debated, Andrew will fall short of the required standard but England has seldom enjoyed a more composed or productive player. The subject of criticism for much of his career, Andrew learned to shrug off the slings and arrows in the pursuit of being the best player he could make himself; formidably well-organised, he would have been a successful surveyor but for his decision to become a professional director of rugby with Newcastle. He was, in all respects, a player for the modern era in the course of winning 71 caps over 11 years, all but one at fly half. He has not been replaced.

Even so, England had completed a calendar year without scoring an international try so no-one expected them to run amok as Wales, with Ieuan Evans restored to fitness, came searching for the grand slam and triple crown. Nor did they, but they had Richards in the back row to oppose the up-and-coming Quinnell and did manage tries through Rory Underwood and Rodber. Even though the margin of victory was no more than 15-8, Wales seldom looked as though they believed they could win. Yet they did prevent an England win by a clear 16 points, which left them losers of the battle but victors in the war as Evans, looking slightly abashed, collected the trophy from the Queen. On the same day Scotland collected the wooden spoon after a reshaped France team under the leadership of Saint-André won at Murrayfield for the first time in sixteen years.

Could the championship pot have been upended more conclusively than it was in 1995? The game was heading for the World Cup and for professionalism, but the last throw of the 'amateur' championship, which had been in thrall to commercial interests for over a decade, was a full house. Wales, the champions, lost their young hero, Scott Quinnell, to Rugby League, lost their way on the field and lost their management team only a few days before the World Cup was due to begin in South Africa. Scotland, despite the loss through injury for the entire season of Gary Armstrong, came storming up from the foot of the table and were runners-up in Gavin Hastings' last season. England, under the new management of Jack Rowell, the man who had done so much to turn Bath into perennial champions, won another grand slam yet ended the season with a whiff of controversy after Will Carling referred, in a televised programme, to the '57 old farts' who constituted the Rugby Football Union committee. France, who had won 2-0 their series in New Zealand during which Philippe Sella won his 100th international cap – he and Australia's David Campese remain the only players to have reached a century – suffered disciplinary problems and had to settle for mid-table respectability. Ireland, unhappy at half back, had only the comfort of their regular success in Cardiff.

It was, as it turned out, the final throw of England's old guard: Guscott returned but the most interesting newcomer was Mike Catt, born in South Africa but brought to prominence by Bath.

Will Carling was captain of the England side when they won three grand slams in five years between 1991 and 1995.

Catt had played against Wales the previous season as a late replacement but he leapfrogged ahead of Callard, his club colleague, and Bristol's Paul Hull on the strength of his play at full back as a replacement against Canada before Christmas. That most of his rugby had been at fly half or centre seemed not to matter then and, in fact, future England managements had difficulty in pigeon-holing him, aware only that he had gifts of pace and vision which they had to use somewhere.

He played against an Ireland side including a rejuvenated Brendan Mullin at centre and at fly half Paul Burke, all of whose representative rugby had previously been with England's junior sides. Keith Wood, the Garryowen hooker who had made such an explosive impact on tour in Australia the summer before, also made his first championship appearance. Wood was a born ball-carrier (which not every front-row forward claims to be) who followed his late father, Gordon, into an Ireland pack. He was also blessed with pace and a penchant for the chip kick, which reached its apogee playing for the Lions in South Africa two years later. Furthermore, at twenty-two, he was given the responsibility for leading the pack on the day at Lansdowne Road, where the wind blew and England's back row took complete control.

If there were any English fears as a result of defeat in 1993 and 1994, they were laid to rest by the muscular mixture of Dean Richards, Ben Clarke and Tim Rodber. Clarke scored one of England's three tries but also became the first player to be 'carded' in a championship match – referees were now empowered to show yellow warning cards for disciplinary offences and red cards for dismissals and Clarke's colour was yellow after a stamping incident. There should have been a try for Rory Underwood on his 70th appearance (a home unions record), but Guscott chose not to pass; instead Tony, his brother, scored as did Carling who was back to his best form.

Victory by 20-8 meant much; victory over France at Twickenham by 31-10 meant even more and sustained an unbroken six-year run of success against England's inveterate rivals that was to end four months later in the World Cup third-place play-off. If the France try by Viars, from seventy metres, was a thing of wonder it was no more so than England's control of long passages of play which brought two tries for the younger Underwood and a third for Guscott.

Gavin Hastings in full stride for Scotland, for whom he scored 667 points.

Understandably there was a mood of confidence in the side that moved, still unchanged and would remain so throughout the championship, to Cardiff to play Wales, with Malcolm Phillips – the former centre, now chairman of a RFU working party into commercial earnings – forecasting £15,000 a man in the following season. He little knew that, by then, the game would have changed forever.

Again England scored three tries in a 23-9 win, even though their half-back combination was disrupted by, among others, Robert Jones playing his 50th game for Wales at scrum half. Though by now past the height of his powers, Jones was as great a servant of Welsh rugby as Ieuan Evans, his captain who had fought back from an horrific ankle injury sustained in a club match early in the season to reclaim his international place. Both deserved to play in a more successful era but the lithe, nimble Jones, son-in-law to Clive Rowlands – himself an international scrum half – reminded everyone of the inherent skills required by the position at a time when the emphasis seemed to be on size. He had a sympathetic pass, an eye for the gap and developed his tactical kicking until he was among the finest exponents of the art. Jones finished level with Gareth Edwards as Wales' most-capped scrum half, but won a 54th cap as a replacement in the three-quarters against Ireland in 1994.

Victor Ubogu, the Bath prop, was first to cross the Wales line and was followed in the second half by Rory Underwood, making up for never having scored in a Cardiff international by doing so twice. Completing Welsh misery, John Davies, the Neath prop, was sent off for kicking – they had earlier lost Anthony Clement, the full back, and winger Nigel Walker through injury and the management must have felt that little more could go wrong. Events were to show that, when you are down, friends are in short supply. But while Wales suffered, England moved on to another showdown with Scotland, themselves unbeaten and going for the grand slam five years after they had unexpectedly lifted all the prizes at Murrayfield.

This time, though, England had home advantage and were a side of immense experience. Even so, there was a consistency about Scotland that boded well: they had averaged 25 points a match with a team in which Bryan Redpath, the little Melrose scrum half, had become a key component in the absence of Armstrong. England's larder had been raided for the Bath forwards, David Hilton and Eric Peters, and Damian Cronin recalled after two years, this time from Bourges since his diverse business interests had taken the one-time Bath lock to France. Moreover, Hastings was determined to exit on the highest possible note: the full back, now thirty-three and troubled by a back injury, intended to retire after the World Cup but, on the way, he became Scotland's most-capped player and the first championship player to pass 600 points in an international career.

They took time to gel against Ireland before a try by Cronin put them on their way to a 26-13 win, Hastings contributing 16 points. But joy was unconfined when Scotland won in Paris, their first victory in the French capital since 1969, and Hastings was central to the 23-21 result. For a team that had been roundly panned in defeat by South Africa before Christmas it was a startling reversal of form, even though it cost them the services of Ian Jardine and Cronin, both injured. The signs were there by the interval, when Scotland led 13-5, helped by a delightful try from Gregor Townsend after Saint-André had scored a soft try two minutes into the match. Even though Lacroix was wayward with his place-kicking, the French could still score tries and did so through Sadourny and then, with six minutes remaining, Saint-André again after Townsend had failed to find touch. It seemed to signal the end for the Scots, trailing 21-16, but Hastings, consoling Townsend, told his young centre to give his elusive talent full rein. Townsend responded and found a midfield gap; support came from Hastings himself, the full back accepting a deft flip behind the back to storm through to the posts for a try he also converted for a match tally of 18 points.

It was a remarkable success and was confirmed when Wales were beaten 26-13 at Murrayfield. Only Jones offered much response to a confident Scotland side in which the two new boys, Peters and Hilton, scored tries and Hastings added another 16 points in a season which ended with an aggregate record of 56 for the championship, surpassing his individual best of 52 which had been set in his first international season nine years earlier. But this time there was to be no slam, no triple crown, no Calcutta Cup; all those honours went to England who, when push came to shove, played pragmatic rugby and won 24-12.

The executioner was Andrew: seven penalty goals and a dropped goal made him England's record points scorer, carrying him past Webb's total of 296 and matching the championship record for points in one match held by Sébastien Viars. On a day when both sides seemed intent on cancelling out each other's strengths, England shrugged their shoulders and won in workmanlike style; Scottish attempts at long-range counter-attacking foundered on stern English tackling, yet it was still a substantial achievement to have come so far with such a new team. Two penalties for Hastings and two dropped goals by Chalmers was their return on a day when Carling became the only player ever to have led a side to three grand slams.

French hopes had been doused in the first half of the championship, first when they dropped Olivier Merle, the towering Montferrand lock, for a head-butt during the Wales match which led to Ricky Evans, the Llanelli prop, breaking his leg as he fell off balance. When England demolished them and Scotland mugged them, there was little to play for but the recall of two experienced campaigners, Mesnel and Cécillon, contributed towards a 25-7 defeat of Ireland and shrewder critics realised that, in Christian Califano (**25**), the Toulouse prop, France had uncovered a gem of a front-row forward.

Ireland dropped Wood halfway through the season and changed their half backs for every game: Burke and Niall Hogan started the championship, Michael Bradley came and went, and the season finished with Elwood and Hogan in the pivotal area. It was, therefore, not surprising that their only solace was the 16-12 win in Cardiff which pushed the wooden spoon the way of Wales. Nine days later Robert Norster and Alan Davies, manager and coach respectively, read the tea leaves and resigned before they were dismissed by the Welsh Rugby Union, who subsequently appointed Alex Evans, Cardiff's Australian director of rugby, as coach to the World Cup squad. It was a little ironic that a week later plans were announced for the £100m refurbishment of Cardiff Arms Park in readiness for the 1999 World Cup which Wales were to host – there seemed other areas of the national game in greater need of repair.

10
THE GRAND FINALE
1996-1999

The 1995/96 season began in confusion and ended in utter turmoil, amid speculation that the Five Nations Championship would be no more. England had been expelled by the other home unions for striking their own television agreement with a satellite television company, the format for a new four nations tournament was drawn up and the world stood on its head. Not only that, Will Carling announced his retirement from the England captaincy, a post he had enjoyed with singular success for 59 internationals.

It is too simplistic to say that the decision by the International Rugby Football Board, taken in France in August 1995, that the game should go open was responsible for this Pandora's Box. Rugby Union had been making continuous concessions for a decade, stretching the amateur regulations to the limit, the pace always being forced by the southern-hemisphere powers. When South Africa, New Zealand and Australia announced in June, on the eve of the World Cup final, an agreement worth £370m with News Corporation, the media company owned by Rupert Murdoch, the Australian businessman with global interests, it was the final shove.

There was no way that professionalism could now be held back and, in any case, even before the last kick of the World Cup the predators were circling, sports-minded businessmen keen to establish a professional circuit of their own with a series of global franchises involving the world's best players. In what remains a masterly analysis of the situation, lacking all sentimentality, Vernon Pugh, the chairman of the Welsh Rugby Union and by now a guiding figure on the International Board, wrote a critique which, in effect, told his colleagues on the board that if the game did not go open, large parts of it would be taken away from them by commercial interests.

One hundred years, almost to the day, after the split in England which created Rugby League, Pugh's colleagues agreed. But whereas the southern-hemisphere countries were ready for the inevitable, the home unions were caught totally unprepared. Pugh's own union, Wales, was in disarray, its administration having been constantly changing throughout the 1990s. England were in the process of handing over from one chief executive with firm ideas on the benefits of amateurism, Dudley Wood, to another, Tony Hallett, whose views were more liberal. Scotland had just paid millions in the refurbishment of their Murrayfield stadium, while England had debts hanging over them for the same reason. Ireland were in the middle of a playing slump.

Now the unions were being asked to contract all their leading players and ensure that beneath this there was a structure that would finance a professional game while catering still for the traditional needs of thousands of players who sought merely recreation. The answer of the southern hemisphere, chiefly to ward off the prospects of commercial interests luring away their best players, had been to throw money at long-term contracts, which they would live to regret. But at least they had the money, courtesy of the deal with NewsCorp, and had drawn up plans for a Super 12 provincial tournament designed to be a money-spinner. The home nations did not have the money, and the only new competition in the pipeline was an embryo European club championship. Governing bodies took one view, leading clubs another and less than a month had passed since the momentous Paris decision when a new breed of administrator entered the game – the wealthy businessman who saw in rugby the chance to make money, expand local interests, even to help the game in its hour of need (though altruism is not always a characteristic of individuals who make a lot of money).

The effect was to break the traditional hegemony of the game. Sir John Hall, chairman of Newcastle United Football Club, threw his influence behind the Newcastle Gosforth club and offered Rob Andrew a substantial five-year contract to move from Wasps to become the director of rugby at Newcastle. The move spelled the end of Andrew's long international career (with one curious blip) but it was merely the start of the comings and goings; Saracens, once the poor relations of the better-known London clubs, brought Michael Lynagh, the world's leading points scorer, from Australia, and Philippe Sella from France to North London, where they were subsequently joined by François Pienaar, the South African who had lifted the 1995 World Cup.

The search for overseas talent, which was to continue for the next four years with baleful effects upon ambitious home-grown youngsters, was matched by returning Rugby League players. The two codes, which had been at each other's throats for 100 years, now found themselves in amicable discussions and players previously barred from the union game were free to return. The most substantial of these was Jonathan Davies, after seven years away, who was brought to Cardiff to see out his playing career. Bath and Wigan, so long cock-of-the-walk in Rugby League circles, arranged a challenge series against each other and Wigan guested at the Middlesex sevens.

Most interesting of all, however, were the reactions of the respective governing bodies. England declared a year-long moratorium before bringing professionalism into effect, which destroyed the Rugby Football Union's prospect of contracting large numbers of players. Instead the clubs – or at least, those who attracted private money or sufficient sponsorship – took up the implications of the International Board decision and contracted players themselves. The RFU also became involved in a committee power struggle which was to continue for three years and throttled effective administration of the domestic game. France, by contrast, declared that they would leave their system largely alone – an admission that they had been semi-professional before and there was no great obligation to change. The Scots and the Irish, seeing many of their better players attracted to the salaries on offer in England, looked within for the most effective structure which would allow them to compete on a broader stage, and eventually found the answer in modifications to their provincial system. Wales, subject to the same kind of raids and with little corporate money on offer at home, remained in a state of confusion.

In such circumstances the arrival of the 1996 Five Nations came as a relief, a building block amid a sea of shifting allegiances, though it was instructive to compare the benefits of professionalism then on display: England players received a retainer of £24,000 with a match fee of £2,000, the French very similar save that they also incorporated a win bonus. Ireland (£7,500) and Scotland (£5,000) had much smaller retainers with match fees of £3,000, though the Scots had a substantial win bonus of £5,500. Wales players were able to earn around £25,000 from involvement in six games though, true to form, details of their retainers were a dark secret as the championship began.

With Andrew and Morris departed, England chose new half backs against France in the shape of the Northampton pair, Paul Grayson and Matthew Dawson. They also recast the back row and brought in Steve Ojomoh and Lawrence Dallaglio, the Wasps flanker, to operate with the established figure of Ben Clarke. Dallaglio had made his debut before Christmas but he had seemed destined for great things from the moment, three years earlier, when he had been plucked more or less from Wasps' second XV to play in the England side that won the inaugural World Cup sevens in Murrayfield. Fast and strong with good hands, he was played initially at open-side flanker while Rodber and Richards were cast aside.

Ireland, with a New Zealander as their coach in Murray Kidd, also found a New Zealander, Kurt McQuilken, to play centre, though both coach and player had given good service to Irish club rugby. Wales, as always, turned to youth: Leigh Davies, only nineteen but a strapping 15st, was one of five newcomers in the pre-championship match against Italy who had already justified their pleas for inclusion in the championship by beating Scotland. Yet, just as critics were poised to write off a Scotland team without the retired Gavin Hastings – Rowen Shepherd, from Melrose, was first to take his place – they came rattling through the championship to lose the title to England only on points difference. They did so thanks largely to their middle five, the back row of Rob Wainwright, the new captain, Eric Peters and Ian Smith with Bryan Redpath and Gregor Townsend at half back. Of that quintet Townsend was by far the most charismatic but Redpath was the more effective mainspring as the Scots charged through their first three matches with three wins.

On the way Michael Dods, whose brother Peter had been so strong a bulwark at full back for Scotland during the 1980s, scored all 19 points against the French at Murrayfield – two tries and three penalties – and kicked the goals that mattered to beat Wales in Cardiff. Suddenly they stood on the verge of a grand slam, which is what most had predicted for France after they had beaten England for the first time in the championship since 1988. The French, under the exciting management of Jo Maso, Jean-Claude Skrela and Pierre Villepreux – all great players during the 1960s and 1970s – had restored a touch of unpredictability by selecting two young centres, Richard Dourthe from Dax and Thomas Castaignède (23) from Toulouse. With the sleek Rolls Royce of a full back, Sadourny, and the wise head of Lacroix at fly half, France now possessed a back division of infinite promise.

Not that back play was the order of the day in Paris. Grayson kicked two penalty goals and two dropped goals for England, Lacroix three penalties and a dropped goal for France, but the game was won, at 15-12, by the cheeky chappy, Castaignède. Barely three minutes remained when the little gamin, whose twenty-first birthday was the following day, struck the mishit dropped goal that won the match and sent him galloping with glee back to his own half, tongue stuck out of a corner of his mouth. The downside was that Dourthe had been caught by television cameras stamping on Clarke and was subsequently suspended for two matches.

Maybe that was what upset France's season; having lost to Scotland they then scored 45 points against Ireland whose prop, Peter Clohessy, was disciplined after the match for stamping on Roumat and suspended for twenty-six weeks. Yet again it was a record score conceded by Ireland, with Castaignède now at fly half to pull the strings as his side scored seven tries in a 45-10 win. It was all of a piece with this crazy season that Ireland then went on to beat Wales 30-17, before the Welsh concluded the season by beating France 16-15 in Cardiff. There was no rhyme or reason to it, save that the championship throws up contradictory results like this with telling frequency.

Wales had hopes of their new half-back combination, Robert Howley at scrum half and Arwel Thomas, the slim youngster from Trebanos who had made his initial impression with Neath before crossing the Severn Bridge to play for Bristol. At 5ft 8in and 10st 10lb, Thomas looked unlikely to survive the rough and tumble but his footballing skills more than compensated. However, in a semi-concussed state against the Irish, after a heavy tackle in the first half, his skills deserted him and Ireland celebrated with four tries. Clohessy's suspension allowed them to introduce Paul Wallace to their front row – his brother, Richard, had already made several appearances on Ireland's wing – and the pack included another who was to make a vital contribution to the Lions' success in South Africa the following year, Jeremy Davidson, the Dungannon lock.

Still Wales stuck to the broad-brush approach encouraged by Kevin Bowring, their new coach. The vital component in Bowring's plan was a speedy open-side flanker and in Gwyn Jones, the quiet young medical student from Llanelli, he found the perfect tool. Articulate and intelligent, Jones was a worthy successor to some great Llanelli back-row forwards, the perfect support to fast-breaking halves of whom Howley had demonstrated, by the season's end, that Wales had uncovered another gem. Admittedly it had taken them some time, but while an ill-advised move from Bridgend to Cardiff then back again had affected Howley's club form a couple of years earlier, tries against England and France demonstrated his speed of thought and action.

There was little to distinguish England after their defeat by the French; it was as though they were still traumatised by the New Zealand side that had steamrollered over them during the World Cup semi-final the previous summer, their rugby was strained and devoid of creativity. The 21-15 win over Wales told observers more about the Welsh than the winners, though they also had the chance to see Rory Underwood score his 50th and last international try – 49 for England and 1 for the Lions. Though he never formally retired, this was Underwood's last international season in a remarkable career which had started in 1984. It brought him 85 England appearances and six for the Lions (a tally yet to be surpassed by another home unions player) while the number of tries he scored is second only to David Campese's 64 in world terms.

Tries, though, were in short supply when England arrived at Murrayfield and squashed Scottish hopes of the slam, the triple crown or anything else. Richards, now thirty-two and poised to become the most-capped No. 8 in the world, had been recalled one final time to the back row and seldom has a restoration proved more effective. Exercising an elemental control on the game, Scotland were denied their priority, loose ball, and the chance to run. At one point Townsend cut England's defence to shreds but lost contact with his support, otherwise it was a game for the kickers, Grayson scoring six penalty goals and Dods three in England's 18-9 win which left them, ironically, the chance to win at least the triple crown and championship. They even got away with a citing on Jason Leonard, the prop who was accused of punching Wainwright. The evidence was judged inconclusive, though the Scottish Rugby Union made evident its dismay at the ruling, but any lingering controversy was overtaken by Carling's decision to stand down as England captain. That he made his decision public in his column in a Sunday newspaper was an indication itself of how much the game had changed since he took charge in 1988, and the business career which Carling himself had built on his England profile. But during the preceding year he had become increasingly the focus of the media because of his friendship with Diana, Princess of Wales, and the breakdown of his own marriage; it was time for the limelight to fall elsewhere after one last bask in the public affection at Twickenham.

He duly received it in the course of a 28-15 win over Ireland, though not quite in the grand manner. With thirty-three minutes played Carling caught his studs in the turf and fell awkwardly, tearing ankle ligaments which forced him off the field; he hobbled up the steps of the West Stand to receive the championship trophy which had become England's property thanks to Wales' win over France on the same day. Again, with so many points, there was only one try and that by Jon Sleightholme, the England wing; otherwise Grayson filled his boots again with six penalties, a dropped goal and a conversion for a championship return of 64 points, only three behind Webb's record.

The greater affection, at the end, appeared to be for Richards who, after 48 games, would not be seen again and there was a tendency to damn England with faint praise. Kidd, Ireland's coach, summed up the problems: 'They have been much maligned for the way they have played the game,' he said. 'They are a very strong side and, in my opinion, have been criticised unfairly. There is a certain amount of arrogance in people thinking that England should win comfortably. There are no easy-beats in the championship.'

But even if the 1996 championship was over, the in-fighting which threatened its existence was only just beginning to warm up. The Rugby Football Union, at odds with its own clubs on the appropriate playing structure, had also fallen out with the other three home unions over the issue of television rights. The RFU contended that its bigger constituency – 2,045 clubs and 3,056 schools as opposed to 212 and 196 (Scotland), 419 and 810 (Wales) and 209 and 203 (Ireland) – entitled England to a larger share of the fees paid by television for showing the Five Nations Championship. They had flagged this belief during the negotiations over television rights in 1994, but now found in BSkyB, the satellite television company which is part of the Murdoch empire, a willing wooer.

England, of course, possessed the substantial population and commercial interest that the other home·unions did not and decided to break off joint negotiations with the other unions (which, historically, had kept Rugby Union on terrestrial television) in the hope of achieving a far greater financial return. Their three erstwhile partners argued that the championship was a joint venture and was not England's alone to sell and that the absence of any individual country irredeemably weakened the whole. The RFU's position was driven, also, by the need to find cash to satisfy their unruly clubs and to help pay off the £34m debt incurred on the West Stand at Twickenham, which completed the refurbishment of the national ground.

In April and May one crisis meeting followed another, delegates from the various countries slipping in and out of hotels in Heathrow and Dublin. Rumours abounded – that even if the RFU was cast into darkness, the clubs could form an 'England XV' that would be acceptable to the other unions, that an official England team would be entered into a high-powered global tournament. In June the extent of the differences between the countries became clear when the RFU, having apparently reached accord with its clubs in what became known as the Leicester Agreement, announced a five-year deal with BSkyB worth £87.5m which would come into effect in September 1997; the by-now entirely predictable response of the other home unions was an accusation of betrayal and a plan for a new four nations tournament, played home and away, to replace the Five Nations.

As a comparison, England hitherto had received £4.25m from the existing three-year agreement, boosted by a side agreement with BSkyB; the other unions received £2.38m. Even at this early stage there were those within the RFU warning that putting England rugby solely into satellite television could harm the game's long-term interests. They argued that the game would be exposed to far fewer customers and that the business world would resent the lack of terrestrial exposure in advertising terms. BSkyB offered £40.5m to the Welsh Rugby Union over the same five-year period, and £28m each to Scotland and Ireland, the whole package of £184m being directly comparable with the £370m over ten years which NewsCorp had given the three southern-hemisphere powers in 1995. The offer was, so far as Vernon Pugh was concerned, 'patronising and unfair'.

As the summer moved on, the RFU reached new heights in the scale of its internal strife during which Cliff Brittle, the chairman of the executive committee, claimed he had been marginalised by union officers and supporters of his beaten opponent for the chairmanship, John Jeavons-Fellows. The blow fell after a stormy annual meeting, during which there was a strong defence of the BSkyB deal and no indication to the membership that England would be expelled as a consequence; yet twenty-four hours later the Five Nations was, to all intents, dead as the other unions activated an accord reached in Paris three days earlier which committed them to a four nations tournament over a ten-year period. England's bluff, if that is what it was, had been called with a vengeance.

'None of the four unions will play England in the period between January 1 and the end of that, or any subsequent, season,' a statement read. Links were not only to be severed at senior level but at all representative levels below that, while individual playing contracts suddenly seemed thinner than before as far as England internationals were concerned and doubt was cast over the British Isles tour to South Africa the following year (for which, ironically, an Englishman, Fran Cotton, had already been appointed as manager). Brittle sought a review of the actions of England's representatives on the Five Nations television committee and Twickenham debenture holders threatened legal action against the RFU.

Over the next seven weeks the wrangling went on as both sides, knowing the ultimate value of England to the championship, sought a compromise that avoided expulsion. It was not until the first week of September that a meeting in Bristol provided a glimmer of light. Between them, representatives of the four home unions thrashed out an agreement designed to last for ten years and which was committed to paper, rather than the gentlemen's agreement which had hitherto been the basis for their dealings. Since England had a binding contract with BSkyB, there were limits to what the RFU could do but the nub of the matter was the acknowledgement that the Five Nations should remain a joint venture with no one party predominating, and that an independent valuation of the championship as a whole should be made.

England's home games were to be broadcast live by satellite with a highlights programme going out subsequently on terrestrial television; the other games remained the property of terrestrial television, an agreement with which France concurred since the French federation already had its own deal in place – an example frequently cited by England as justifying their own course of action. It was a bitter-sweet pill for the English to hear Jim Telfer, the Scottish Rugby Union's director of rugby, admit that 'to be honest, Wales, Scotland and Ireland need England more than they need us. They are the country everybody wants to beat.'

The championship had been saved but at a price, which was not so much a matter of pounds and pence but the severance of old loyalties and friendships. The distrust and discord created during the summer of 1996 informed many subsequent meetings of the home unions; individual dislikes came to play far too great a role, as they did when the RFU turned to negotiating with its own clubs – or rather, their owners. Three years later, the exercise was to be repeated.

For now, though, the championship was back on track and, as if to make some kind of point, England smashed the other home unions aside in the course of a record-breaking season: 511 points were scored in the ten games, obliterating the previous best of 363 in 1991. There were 53 tries – a post-war record but still second best to the 1911 tally of 55 – and England posted a record 141 points, but it was not enough to beat France who were about to embark on back-to-back grand slams. The new European club competition had been of substantial benefit to the French, who won the inaugural event in 1996 through Toulouse and then repeated their success in 1997 through Brive. The new tournament accustomed their leading players to winning away from home, which had always been a major weakness in their domestic club rugby, besides which there were some talented newcomers, among them David Venditti and Christophe Lamaison, both from the Brive back division.

The French drive to the top of the table began in Dublin where they shrugged off the late withdrawal of Dourthe, not only their first-choice centre but their goal-kicker. The Irish, now under the coaching of Brian Ashton (once England's assistant coach and subsequently part of the Bath panel), introduced the talented Eric Miller to their back row and looked for encouragement after defeat at home by Italy, now knocking ever louder upon the Five Nations door. What they received, however, was a 32-15 defeat, more points than France had ever scored at Lansdowne Road which included a three-try return for Venditti on the wing; Elwood, with five penalties, accounted for all the Ireland points but France won with some ease, considering that Penaud at fly half was limping for much of the match.

However, they lost Franck Tournaire, the formidable Toulouse prop, after a stamping incident, the French federation suspending him for one match amid claims that it was more than time for the home unions to act against their own players whom the French believed to be guilty of disciplinary offences. France brooded for a month and then, as only they can, came up with a combination to play Wales which showed six changes from that successful against Ireland: with five first-choice players ruled out by injury, Benazzi swopped places with Pelous and moved into the second row, the chunky Lamaison moved up to fly half with a new partner in Philippe Carbonneau and when Merle crossed the Wales line after only three minutes, they seemed set fair.

Yet how unfortunate Wales were to lose 27-22 in Paris where they had not won since 1975. Who knows if a more experienced full back would have coped with the bounce of David Aucagne's failed dropped goal but Neil Jenkins, playing out of position, and Gareth Thomas could not cover the danger and Lamaison arrived to send Laurent Leflamand, the Bourgoin wing, over for his second try. With Venditti having also crossed, France had a cushion to withstand valiant Welsh attempts late in the game to add to their three tries.

Given their erratic form in this game, few backed France to win at Twickenham. Had not England caught fire by scoring 41 points against Scotland, then 46 against Ireland? The quiet authority of Phil de Glanville, the Bath centre who had succeeded Carling as captain, seemed to be working though few could understand why he had not been partnered with Guscott in the centre. Instead Jack Rowell, the manager, conceded Carling's wish to have one more season of international rugby as 'one of the boys' and shuffled his pack to include bright newcomers like Richard Hill, the Saracens flanker, and Simon Shaw, the athletic lock from Bristol.

France restored Penaud at fly half and called up Olivier Magne, the talented and swift flanker from Dax, to their back row. Benazzi, the captain, gave his team a 30 per cent chance of success and when France stood 20-6 down after an hour to a confident, purposeful England team, few would have given France even that much of a chance. Into the wind England carved out a 14-6 advantage, Dallaglio striding magnificently away for a try and Grayson kicking his goals to the manner born; yet midway through the second half the tide turned as France, playing with

The France team that beat Scotland in Paris to win the 1997 grand slam. Standing: J-L. Jordana, D. Casadei, F. Tournaire, M. Dal Maso, R. Castel, O. Magne, H. Miorin, F. Pelous, O. Merle. Seated: M. de Rougemont, U. Mola, G. Accoceberry, D. Aucagne, L. Leflamand, S. Glas, A. Benazzi (captain), C. Lamaison, D. Venditti, J-L. Sadourny, P. Bondouy.

an unexpected maturity all the more impressive when injury removed Benazzi, seized the match by the scruff of the neck.

Lamaison was the architect: the twenty-five-year-old sports instructor ran through the gamut of scores, from try to dropped goal, for a return of 18 points in a remarkable 23-20 victory. His first act, after England had lost their own lineout, was to chip into the wind for Leflamand, who snatched the try under Tony Underwood's nose. Then, after a series of blind-side raids, Lamaison scored himself and converted to level the scores; finally offside by England gave him the match-winning penalty from fifteen metres, a win which told France that, for all the trials and tribulations they had suffered, this could be their season and an appropriate way to leave their home at Parc des Princes for the new stadium then rising in the north Parisian suburb of Saint Denis.

So it was. Scotland, struggling throughout the season, were the sacrificial lambs where, two years earlier, they had been the surprise package. The 47-20 victory gave France their fifth grand slam, but the first to be decided on their own soil; that they had changed their half backs yet again, along with half their pack, mattered little so intoxicated were they with a season that had turned to champagne. It was their highest score in the championship and Lamaison, with 24 points, equalled the record held by Andrew and Viars. This time all his scores came from kicks – three conversions and six penalties – which tell the tale of remorseless pressure on the Scots; there was a dropped goal from Sadourny and four tries, from Benazzi, Leflamand, Tournaire and, with a final long-drawn out flourish, Magne.

'Today they played modern rugby,' Villepreux said afterwards. 'They ran with the ball and when they were stopped, they kept it and ran with it again.' How simply the game can be described. Never before had France scored as many as 14 tries and 129 points in the championship, with so many good players – Roumat, Castaignède, Saint-André – missing. If only for making light of adversity, France deserved their success, and cared little that England scored 15 tries and 141 points.

Even so, England contrived to steal a little thunder on the championship's final day. They went down to Cardiff and won 34-13 in a match in which three old favourites said farewell – Jonathan Davies, Carling and, very strangely, Andrew. It had been a curious season, replete with points yet ultimately unsatisfying because of the way that victory against France had been squandered. There was still a triple crown to go for but that was an insufficient reward for the English, whose sights had been raised in recent years; there was also a strong sentimental nip in the air, since this was the last match at Cardiff Arms Park, that great repository of history and dreams. The stadium was to be demolished and a new edifice to rise on the same site, fit to host the 1999 World Cup and funded – to the tune of some £120m – in part with public money from the National Lottery.

Davies, now thirty-four, had made cameo appearances against Scotland and France, but was an original selection against England for a match when Wales were without Ieuan Evans, Scott Gibbs and Colin Charvis, the promising Swansea flanker. In a sense there was an inevitability about it after injury also removed Arwel Thomas while Kevin Bowring, the coach, persisted with Neil Jenkins at full back. There was nothing inevitable about Andrew's recall to an England squad, also at the age of thirty-four and having retired from the international game in 1995, but when Paul Grayson withdrew injured, instead of turning to the clever Wasps fly half, Alex King, as a replacement, Jack Rowell invited Andrew to sit on the bench. It was a retrograde step for which even Andrew himself could find little justification.

Carling spent the week hinting at retirement without saying so, after a season in which his form had been as good as ever. By the end of the match, he had been joined by his old henchmen, Andrew and Jeremy Guscott, the latter as a straightforward injury replacement of Jon Sleightholme on the wing, the former a gesture of questionable sentiment when Mike Catt gave way at fly half for the final few minutes. Along the way England won 34-13, the best of their rugby coming when Guscott was opening up the field in the second half. In their slipstream the Celtic nations were left in a bedraggled heap, each having achieved one victory. A week after the championship was over, a weakened France team lost 40-32 to Italy in Grenoble, a result which went a long way towards clinching Italy's place at the Six Nations table in 2000.

A month later Carling did, indeed, announce his retirement after 72 appearances. At the age of thirty-one he had plenty still to offer but the motivation had declined; at his best, a wonderfully-aggressive and assertive player, Carling had made his point – that he could no longer be captain but still command a place in the national side. Whatever problems he encountered, or created, in his private life and which soured his reputation later, his commitment to England's cause was never in doubt; cynics might say that such commitment boosted his business enterprises but, at bottom, Carling cared deeply about the teams on which he left so strong a personal mark.

Change was in the air, as sure as the vituperation that accompanied the Rugby Football Union's troubled summer and led to the resignation of Tony Hallett, their secretary. Jack Rowell resigned as England's coach after it became apparent his employers were looking elsewhere – one of their ports of call was upon Graham Henry in Auckland, though it was to Wales that the New Zealander finally turned. The Five Nations committee arranged a schedule in which, for the first time, two matches in the 1998 championship were to be played on a Sunday to suit television interests: 'We believe,' Roger Pickering, the former England scrum half and now chief executive to the committee, said, 'it will be an exciting new concept that will enhance the competition.' Not everyone agreed.

The committee was also looking at sponsorship. For the first time, the Five Nations dipped their hands into the lucrative corporate pool and, in November 1997, pulled out an agreement with the banking company, Lloyds TSB. The deal, worth around £12m, gave the bank title rights to the 1999 and 2000 championships with a further option, as well as sponsorship of the home games played by England, Ireland and Wales in 1998. The latter agreement allowed for the conclusion of longstanding deals by the French federation with Société Generale, and by the Scottish Rugby Union with the Royal Bank of Scotland, since there was an obvious conflict of interests between the various financial institutions. Old friends from the world of business, such as the Royal Bank, found that loyalty (in their case over fifteen years) was not enough.

Such dry detail, however, was overshadowed by the human tragedy suffered by Wales when their young captain, Gwyn Jones, suffered a spinal injury so severe that his career was terminated at the age of twenty-five. Playing for Cardiff against Swansea, Jones damaged his spinal cord in a ruck and spent many months in hospital learning to walk again; that he has managed to resume an active life is a tribute not only to medical science but to his own spirit and the encouragement of his family and close friends. Leadership of the national side passed to Robert Howley, Cardiff's scrum half, for a championship in which Wales suffered two humiliations for so proud a rugby-playing country yet still finished in mid-table.

Elsewhere England, Scotland and Ireland all shuffled their coaches. England voted in Clive Woodward, the will o'the wisp centre of the early 1980s whose subsequent *curriculum vitae* included exposure as a player in Sydney club rugby to two Australian gurus, Alan Jones and Bob Dwyer, and whose coaching approach was developed with Henley, London Irish and, briefly, Bath. Scotland, unhappy with Richie Dixon, turned once more to their old faithful, Jim Telfer, who might have believed he had put away the tracksuit for good after operating in harness with Ian McGeechan during the 1997 Lions tour in South Africa but who was, and remains, never happier than when he is out on a pitch with players. Then, with the first round of the 1998 championship already played, Brian Ashton resigned as coach to Ireland. There had been rumours that, despite a six-year contract, the Englishman and some of his Irish colleagues did not see eye to eye and that Ashton was frustrated at the slow progression of the game in Ireland. Equally, there was a clear sense of shock after Ireland had lost 37-22 to Italy in December, a triumph that Italy built on when they beat Scotland 25-21 in Treviso. They also ran Wales to 23-20 in Llanelli, the game that marked Ieuan Evans' 72nd and final appearance in a Wales jersey, which he had never worn with less than distinction whatever the vicissitudes of the national team.

Italy, therefore, possessed all the evidence they needed to convince the Five Nations that the time had come to be six. They made their pitch in Paris in January 1998 and came away exultant at their acceptance at the high table of northern-hemisphere rugby; they had finally succeeded where Romania, fifteen years earlier, had failed. They offered a secure infrastructure, a proven club championship and quality venues in Rome, Milan or Bologna accessible to supporters travelling by air from Britain and France. It was time for the game's traditional powers to open the door.

While all this was going on, France were once more lying in wait. They had not concluded 1997 in the grandest of styles, losing their final international of the year 52-10 to South Africa at the Parc des Princes, but they had a flamboyant new £270m home, the Stade de France (built to host football's World Cup), and were poised to embark on their richest season ever – a second successive grand slam and (with 144) more points than they had previously scored in a championship. In a season that produced 55 tries, equalling the record season of 1911, France scored 18 of them, one more than England whose points aggregate was 146. More significantly, the France defence conceded a meagre 49 points in four matches while the three Celtic nations all conceded 100 or more.

It started so well in February. There may have been some nails bitten down to the quick when icy weather threatened the opening game between France and England but, with assistance of an English firm, the ground staff produced a playable – albeit slightly yellow – surface for 80,000 to enjoy the performance of a much-changed France team. Gone were players with an English club connection – Thierry Lacroix, Philippe Saint-André, Laurent Cabannes, goal-kicker, try-scorer and flank forward extraordinaire – and the captaincy passed to Raphaël Ibañez, the Dax hooker of Spanish extraction who could do for France what Ciaran Fitzgerald did for Ireland sixteen years earlier.

At half back the French linked the little imp Castaignède (now dyed blond), with Philippe Carbonneau, the brains – and sometimes the brawn – behind Brive's rise to European distinction. New and old were linked in a potent mixture against an England team hardened by a succession of games during the autumn against the three southern-hemisphere powers. True, they had not been uniformly successful – two draws from four matches – but Woodward had struck out boldly for a new look. 'To my mind, I have every scenario covered,' he said before the match, holding out a hostage to fortune with a XV who were still shaking down together.

France duly won more convincingly than the 24-17 scoreline suggests: their defence was exceptional and their set-piece play a revelation in an area which traditionally has been so strong a source of English pride. Philippe Bernat-Salles and Christophe Dominici, the Stade Français wing making his debut, scored the France tries and they were unfortunate not to register at least three more. Neil Back's try and Paul Grayson's goalkicking brought England within touching distance just after the interval, but the goal-kicking of Lamaison and the drop-kicking of Castaignède and Sadourny carried France well clear. Adding insult to injury, the French drew English attention to the possibility that Jason Leonard had stamped on Thomas Lièvremont and caused him a rib injury.

The complaint was dismissed and Lièvremont, the Perpignan No. 8 whose play was reminiscent of Dean Richards, leaped from his bed of pain to play against Scotland a fortnight later. In doing so he became part of France's highest Five Nations win, by 51-16, over a Scotland team that simply had no answer to the pace and precision of players spearheaded by Magne. The flanker, with speed and vision to burn, was ubiquitous, in creating chances for colleagues and snuffing out Scotland attacks at birth. There were seven tries to set against one by Tony Stanger on his fiftieth appearance. Bernat-Salles led the way with two and the forwards scored three of the others which is an indication of the fluid game played by the French.

The downside was that, less than halfway through the tournament, it was clear that France were heading for a grand slam; their confidence was high, that of their remaining opponents from Ireland and Wales, low. Perhaps it was too high and they believed what everyone told them; perhaps they were deceived by the cunning Irish ploy of seeking inspiration in the third division of their club championship. The rise of Andy Ward to international status was remarkable. The New Zealand-born flanker had played for Ballynahinch for four years, rising to Ulster's provincial team and, on one occasion, being called up to train with the national side. Now, at twenty-seven, he was capped by Ireland's new coach, Warren Gatland (also a New Zealander) and played the debut of his life in an 18-16 defeat in Paris.

This was not in the script at all. Ireland had lost their previous outing, against Scotland, by one point; now they lost by two in a game where they led until seven minutes from time. Cruelly, the winning try came from an Ireland lineout throw near their own line, just after a tactical substitution had removed Paddy Johns, the Saracens lock, from the field. The French mauled forward and Ibañez ended up over the line under a heap of bodies. It was a wake-up call of seismic proportions and France had a month to ponder their shortcomings. They did so to glorious effect. With history beckoning – only England, in the history of the championship, had put together back-to-back grand slams before – Ibañez and his men wrote their names large in the book of records by dismissing Wales 51-0 at Wembley on a gloriously sunny April day.

Castaignède tore the Welsh to shreds, making so good a player as Neil Jenkins seem leaden-footed by comparison. If his name did not appear on the try sheet, his influence appeared all over Wembley where a large French contingent among the 72,000 roared their side on. Stuart Davies and Neil Boobyer put as many fingers in the dyke as they could but still the French tide washed them away, Sadourny scoring two tries in the opening quarter merely as an indication of the fate that awaited Wales. Lièvremont, enjoying life in the back row with his brother Marc, added a third and Stéphane Glas, Fabien Galthié and Xavier Garbajosa (twice), completed the erasure of the Wales defence; had not France lost direction in the third quarter the rout would have been even worse.

It was a superb display of fifteen-man rugby from a team that seemed likely to become even better; a fitting reward for the coaching combination of Skrela's practical head and the vision of Villepreux. It justified the selection of Ibañez as captain; there were strong competitors at hooker, such as Marc Dal Maso, but Ibañez, the contemplative fisherman who had led France to victory in the Student World Cup of 1992, had proved his worth. Significantly the spine of the team, from Ibañez through the younger Lièvremont at No. 8 to Sadourny at full back, was in commanding form which made the shock all the greater when France collapsed like a pricked balloon in 1999.

It also forced their British rivals to look inward and confess that the vibrant traditions of the Five Nations had to be sustained rather better. England had swept the Celts before them with a side well short of maturity, in a season when their squad included for the first time the eighteen-year-old Jonathan Wilkinson, fresh from school and yet to play a full match for Newcastle in the Allied Dunbar Premiership. They had humiliated Wales 60-26 at Twickenham, scoring eight tries; beaten Scotland 34-20 at Murrayfield on a dull Sunday afternoon and clinched the triple crown by dispatching Ireland 35-17, playing good rugby only in fits and starts but giving Wilkinson, a fly half by trade, his debut on the wing late in the game. Dallaglio was Woodward's choice for the captaincy, which seemed a long-term appointment until, in May 1999, the flanker was the subject of a tabloid exposé and resigned the honour (he was subsequently cleared to play but the leadership by then rested in the powerful hands of Martin Johnson).

Wales conceded 145 points, despite winning two of their games. It presaged the summer visit to South Africa where one more try would have given the Springboks a century of points. It also ended Kevin Bowring's reign as coach and set in motion the events that would bring Graham Henry from New Zealand to become the great redeemer of Welsh rugby. That Wales retained some character was shown by their 19-13 win over Scotland, at Wembley just a few miles away from the 'hurt' of Twickenham a fortnight earlier; players such as Scott Gibbs, Allan Bateman and Robert Howley could always do some damage given something of a platform by their forwards but they, like England during the summer, visited the southern hemisphere with a team hugely weakened by absentees and paid the penalty in full.

Scotland were probably a better side than their record suggested, and proved as much the following season; with two such shrewd heads as Jim Telfer and Ian McGeechan helping to stir the pot, only against France were they less than competitive and, against England, Stanger equalled the record of 24 tries which had stood to Ian Smith's sole credit since 1933. For Ireland there was only frustration. While at junior level they ruled the roost, winning the world youth (under-19) tournament in France, and proving competitive in schools and under-21 representative games, the translation of such talent to senior rugby was, and is, their major problem.

Nor did the off-field rows subside: the RFU and their leading clubs arrived at the Mayfair Agreement, designed to last seven years but due to suffer some dubious bending within seven months. The RFU and the International Board seemed permanently at odds though the Welsh Rugby Union, struggling to find a way forward, secured their man when Henry agreed terms for a five-year contract worth over £1m. The Scottish union, too, was trying to convince member clubs that the best way forward was to establish two 'super' clubs, and the Edinburgh Reivers and Glasgow Caledonians duly appeared, though without a decent fixture list. Only in Ireland did there appear to be a degree of harmony, possibly because the Irish Rugby Football Union was the only one with the financial clout to be able to contract leading players either to the national or the provincial cause.

As the last season of the Five Nations Championship approached, however, frustrations with England finally boiled over. In January 1999, the Five Nations committee met in Dublin with England pressing for a reworking of the 1996 concord to allow for the inclusion of Italy the following year; at issue, yet again, was the distribution of broadcasting fees and sponsorship monies. On 18 January, less than three weeks before the championship was due to begin, the game of bluff and counterbluff ended when England were formally expelled for failing to meet a deadline for agreement over the distribution of income. 'I bet my ear to a bag of sweets this will be sorted out within three days,' Mike Burton, the England prop of the

1970s turned entrepreneur, said and he was right; within twenty-four hours England had been readmitted.

A flight to Edinburgh by Brian Baister, in only his sixth month as chairman of the RFU management board, effected a reconciliation with Allan Hosie, the Scottish chairman of the Five Nations committee. Wisely, Baister took with him Bill Beaumont, the much-respected former England captain and now chairman of the union's playing subcommittee. Over a pint in a Glasgow public house, differences were set aside amid the unavoidable sounds of an English climbdown and the championship could take its course.

What a climax it proved. France, the champions, retained their pack from the previous season but chopped their back division to accommodate both injured absentees and the desire to see Emile Ntamack, the lithe wing, at full back. Ireland, bolstered by Ulster's success in winning the European Cup, fielded what appeared to be one of the most competitive packs in the championship. Scotland summoned a brigade of 'kilted Kiwis', New Zealanders with Scottish qualifications of whom John and Martin Leslie – sons of a former New Zealand captain, Andy – were the most able. Wales had the magic of Henry and a promising display against South Africa in the autumn behind them, as well as the practical ability of another New Zealander, Shane Howarth, at full back, and the mobile Chris Wyatt from Llanelli as their secret weapon in the second row. England, fittingly some thought, were standing in the corner when the rest kicked off under the sponsored banner of Lloyds TSB.

Within nine seconds of the opening whistle of the game between Scotland and Wales at Murrayfield, John Leslie had scored a try. Maybe then we should have known it would be Scotland's season; from the very first the decision-making of Leslie, the Otago centre consistently overlooked by New Zealand, was invaluable while the organised flank-forward play of his younger brother complemented it. With Eric Peters outstanding at No. 8 and Gregor Townsend restored at fly half after a sickening injury to Duncan Hodge (carried off with a broken leg) there was a rhythm and purpose to Scotland that boded well. Scotland won 33-20 and suddenly Henry's status as the redeemer was looking shaky. It was not a title the New Zealander wanted but an advertising stunt that took wing and when Ireland beat the Welsh 29-23 at Wembley, the stunt appeared to have gone horribly wrong.

That win made up in part for Ireland's cruel blow in losing 10-9 to France in Dublin on the opening day. Sixteen long years had passed since an Irish win over France, yet here the scales seemed to have turned: with the players daubed in blue and red dye from the sponsor's logos on the pitch which, in heavy rain, soon covered both teams, Ireland led 9-0 then 9-7 as the minutes ticked away. It was not until the eightieth minute that Castaignède kicked the penalty that nosed France ahead after Paul Wallace was controversially given offside; in injury-time David Humphreys, the Dungannon fly half who had kicked so well for Ulster in the European final, was given the chance to kick a fourth penalty. It drifted wide and the champions had won.

It was a wonderful sporting weekend, fit to banish the political blues. Enter England, the bad boys but with the memory of a 13-7 win over South Africa two months earlier still strong. With Will Greenwood and Phil de Glanville unavailable at centre, Woodward gave young Wilkinson – still only nineteen – his first championship start in the position he had been playing at Newcastle, alongside Rob Andrew. 'The Five Nations is fundamental,' Woodward said as his team prepared: 'As a player and a coach, you treat it with the utmost respect. It's a tournament that must be treasured.' With a World Cup only eight months away, every country sought consistency and, more importantly, the balm of victory.

Scotland, with Peters, Martin Leslie and the stalwart Peter Walton, thought they possessed a good back row. England with Dallaglio, Richard Hill and Neil Back – Lions all – thought they had a better one, but neither gained a significant advantage as England clung on to the Calcutta Cup with a 24-21 victory. Fourteen points to the good in the first quarter, one of two tries going to Tim Rodber who had been converted from the back row into a lock, suggested a comfortable win for England; but Scotland matched them try for try through Alan Tait, who scored two, while Townsend scored a third after his former colleague from Northampton, Nick Beal, had crossed for England.

It was the second of four in the season for Townsend, one in each fixture, which allowed him to join the exclusive club of Catcheside, Wallace, Estève and Sella. Controversy followed the game, Scottish indignation abounding after Johnson conceded only a yellow warning card after treading on John Leslie's throat at a ruck; there was, though, no further action and the spotlight promptly veered to Wales when Henry uncovered yet another Kiwi, but this time one with an allegiance to the dragon rather than the thistle. Against Ireland, for once, Jenkins had been outscored by the kicking of Humphreys and Henry wanted a player at open-side with greater vision – he chose Brett Sinkinson, late of Waikato Chiefs but only on the periphery of representative teams in New Zealand. He also gave a delayed debut to Peter Rogers, English-born, educated in Wales, played provincial rugby in South Africa and now playing with London Irish. Rogers added bulk and hard-earned know-how at loose-head prop.

The criticism of the policy of introducing overseas players, however old the tradition, was threefold: first there was too much of it, second it negated the efforts of home-bred players, third it gained no respect from southern-hemisphere opponents who knew that these were players who had not made it on their home turf. Against that was the differing skills and disciplines such players introduced and the ability of the championship itself to enlarge the man. Even Henry admitted that he had underestimated the intensity of the Five Nations, which for a man steeped in success with New Zealand 'A' and Auckland was tantamount to an apology. But also players such as Sinkinson and Rogers could expand within the framework of the championship, appreciating the opportunity they had been given all the more for the fact that it was unexpected.

Thus a reshaped Wales went out to battle against an unchanged France team in Paris, where they had not won since 1976, with the credo ringing in their ears that 'boldness wins matches'. Woodward agreed: he had changed three core players in the England side to play Ireland, restoring Kyran Bracken and Paul Grayson at half back and recalling Matt Perry, the young Bath full back on whom the coach pinned such hopes. He was aptly rewarded, Perry scoring a try from Wilkinson's perceptive pass in the course of a 27-15 win in Dublin; an England victory was not unexpected, a Wales one came out of the blue.

A game of pace, vision and seven tries – three of them by Ntamack – ended in a breath-taking 34-33 win by Wales and destroyed both French hopes of a third successive grand slam and a smooth progress towards the World Cup. If it was the breaking of one, it was the making of the other, the first of eight successive victories carrying Wales forward as host nation to the World Cup on a sea of expectation. First the Welsh led, before half-time France had recovered the ground lost, but a try by the younger of the Quinnell brothers, Craig, thrust the visitors into a ten-point lead at half-time. With the final quarter still to come France were level; Jenkins kicked his fourth penalty but Castaignède scored the try that gave the French a 33-31 lead with nine minutes remaining. He could not convert it and, with six minutes remaining, Jenkins came up with his fifth penalty and nineteenth point of the afternoon. Still there was drama when Castaignède, in injury-time, had the chance to steal the game with another penalty but the attempt drifted wide and Jim Fleming, the experienced Scottish referee whose contribution to the momentum of the match should not be overlooked, blew time.

Wales were left for a month to dwell over their change of fortune. France had to take their wounded pride to Twickenham and, to no-one's surprise, they lost in a game that produced one try in injury-time and 26 points from kicks. The greater share was England's, thanks to seven penalties from Wilkinson, and England happily celebrated their first win over the French for four years. More to the point, Scotland resuscitated their challenge with a 30-13 win over Ireland at Murrayfield, scoring four tries against a solitary penalty try. Kenny Logan, the Wasp with a kick rather than a sting, kicked his goals and another of the immigrant Kiwis, Glenn Metcalfe, settled to his role at full back.

The weekend left the championship in a state of suspense, with England favourites to carry off the grand slam even though injuries deprived them of David Rees and Jeremy Guscott in their back division. They were replaced by debutants, Steve Hanley, only nineteen but 6ft 4in and a regular try-scorer in his first senior season at Sale, on the wing and a former Rugby League player, Barrie-Jon Mather, at centre. Mather had been an England Schools lock before turning to Rugby League and stood at 6ft 6in, so there was no lack of physical presence in the side that faced Wales in their final match at Wembley before their return to the Millennium Stadium in Cardiff.

First, though, it was Scotland's turn. They, too, had suffered the misfortune of losing Peters with a knee severely damaged playing for Bath; Tom Smith, the mobile prop, had a broken leg and a reshuffled back row brought Budge Pountney, the Northampton flanker, back into the frame. It was Jim Telfer's final championship match before surrendering the coaching position (for the second time) to Ian McGeechan but above all was the knowledge that an injury-ravaged France team, indifferently selected all season, was there for the taking.

Quite remarkably the match was won by half-time. Castaignède created the first try, by Ntamack, after only two minutes but was injured in the process and had to be replaced. Then Scotland proceeded to ram home five tries with a finesse which launched comparisons with their grand slam sides of 1984 and 1990. By the interval they led 33-22 and the only score of the second half was Logan's penalty goal. There were two tries each for Tait and Martin Leslie – the latter a reward for shrewd support – and of course one for Townsend, all the sweeter now that the fly half was now playing his rugby in Brive. The forwards galloped around like backs, the backs rucked like forwards and Metcalfe, splitting the defence time after time, displayed his finest form.

Over the season Scotland scored 120 points – a year earlier they had conceded the same number – but still they had no trophy for the season. Twenty-four hours later they had. Wembley felt like a Welsh suburb as the build-up to the final Five Nations match was under way, rather less so as England scored three tries in the first half through Dan Luger, the Harlequins wing who was one of the successes of the season, Hanley and Hill. With seconds to go before the interval they enjoyed a comfortable ten-point lead, playing exciting rugby and disturbed only by the boot of Jenkins who kept Wales in the game.

The fly half's sixth penalty made the difference only seven points, a profligate return by England which led to their downfall. Barely had the second half begun than Jenkins had made a try for Howarth, who proved himself an inspiration in every game five years after winning four caps for New Zealand. Wilkinson kicked two penalties to push England back ahead but, for all the opportunities they created, they could not finish; Dallaglio, the captain, chose to kick for touch rather than at goal, Rodber was harshly penalised for a late charge but ninety seconds of injury-time had been played when Wyatt, rising at the lineout yet again, tapped down the ball and Gibbs, raging like a bull, hit a flat pass from Scott Quinnell. The centre's power and footwork carried him past four defenders and over the line to bring Wales within one point. He knew, all Wembley knew, that the unerring Jenkins would not miss the conversion, nor did he and England's slam wafted gently away into the warm air as countless Scots leaped from their television sets and toasted their renascent team. That, you might say, is the Five Nations Championship for you. The Six Nations has a hard act to follow.

BIBLIOGRAPHY

The International Rugby Championship 1883-1983 by Terry Godwin (Collins Willow)

The Complete Who's Who of International Rugby by Terry Godwin (Blandford Press)

The Phoenix Book of International Rugby Records by John Griffiths (Phoenix House/J.M. Dent)

The Five Nations Championship 1947-1993 by John Griffiths (Methuen)

The Book of English International Rugby 1871-1982 by John Griffiths (Collins Willow)

Centenary History of the Rugby Football Union by U.A. Titley and Ross McWhirter (Rugby Football Union)

The History of Scottish Rugby by Sandy Thorburn (Johnston and Bacon)

The Story of Irish Rugby by Edmund van Esbeck (Stanley Paul)

Fields of Praise by David Smith and Gareth Williams (University of Wales Press)

Welsh Rugby: The Crowning Years 1968-1980 by Clem Thomas and Geoffrey Nicholson (Collins)

The Rise of French Rugby by Georges Duthen and Alex Potter (A.H. and A.W. Reed)

Rugger by W.W. Wakefield and H.P. Marshall (Longmans, Green and Co. Ltd)

Rugby Football by W.J.A. Davies (Webster's Publications Ltd)

Rugby Football Up-to-date by E.H.D. Sewell (Hodder and Stoughton)

Passion in Exile by Peter Bills (Mainstream Publishing)

Dai for England by David Duckham (Pelham Books)

Fran Cotton: An Autobiography by Fran Cotton (Queen Anne Press)

Pride in England by Roger Uttley (Stanley Paul)

Great Contemporary Players by J.B.G. Thomas (Stanley Paul)

Giants of Irish Rugby by John Scally (Mainstream Publishing)

Playfair Rugby Football Annuals from 1948-49 to 1972-73

Rothmans Rugby Union Yearbooks from 1972-73 to 1999-2000

The Times

FIVE NATIONS
CHAMPIONSHIP RECORDS

Most points scored in a season:
England 146 (1998), Scotland 120 (1999), Ireland 71 (1983), Wales 109 (1999), France 144 (1998)

Most points conceded in a season:
England 100 (1986), Scotland 132 (1997), Ireland 141 (1997), Wales 145 (1998), France 100 (1999)

Most tries in a season:
England 20 (1914), Scotland 17 (1925), Ireland 12 (1928 and 1953), Wales 21 (1910), France 18 (1998)

Best points aggregate in a season:
511 (1997); 501 (1998)

Best try-scoring aggregate in a season:
55 (1911 and 1998); 53 (1924 and 1997); 50 (1914)

Most individual tries in a season:
England 8 – Cyril Lowe (1914), Scotland 8 – Ian Smith (1925), Ireland 5 – Jack Arigho (1928), Wales 6 – Maurice Richards (1969), France 5 – Patrick Estève (1983), Eric Bonneval (1987) and Emile Ntamack (1999)

Most individual points in a season:
England 67 – Jonathan Webb (1992), Scotland 56 – Gavin Hastings (1995), Ireland 56 – David Humphreys (1999), Wales 64 – Neil Jenkins (1999), France 54 – Jean-Patrick Lescarboura (1984)

Highest match score:
60, by England v Wales (60-26) 1998

Highest winning margin:
51, by France v Wales (51-0) 1998

Most points in one match:
24 Sébastien Viars (France v Ireland, 1992), Rob Andrew (England v Scotland, 1995), Christophe Lamaison (France v Scotland, 1997)

Tries in all four games of one season:
Carston Catcheside (England) 1924, Johnny Wallace (Scotland) 1925, Patrick Estève (France) 1983, Philippe Sella (France) 1986, Gregor Townsend (Scotland) 1999

Appendix 2

SEASONAL RESULTS AND CHAMPIONSHIP TABLES SINCE THE INCLUSION OF FRANCE IN 1910

1909/10		W	D	L	For	Ag
Wales 49 France 14 (Swansea)	England	3	1	0	36	14
England 11 Wales 6 (Twickenham)	Wales	3	0	1	88	28
Scotland 27 France 0 (Inverleith)	Scotland	2	0	2	46	28
Wales 14 Scotland 0 (Cardiff)	Ireland	1	1	2	11	36
England 0 Ireland 0 (Twickenham)	France	0	0	4	20	95
Ireland 0 Scotland 14 (Belfast)						
France 3 England 11 (Paris)						
Ireland 3 Wales 19 (Dublin)						
Scotland 5 England 14 (Inverleith)						
France 3 Ireland 8 (Paris)						

1910/11		W	D	L	For	Ag
France 16 Scotland 15 (Paris)	Wales	4	0	0	78	21
Wales 15 England 11 (Swansea)	Ireland	3	0	1	44	31
England 37 France 0 (Twickenham)	England	2	0	2	61	26
Scotland 10 Wales 32 (Inverleith)	France	1	0	3	21	92
Ireland 3 England 0 (Dublin)	Scotland	0	0	4	43	77
Scotland 10 Ireland 16 (Inverleith)						
France 0 Wales 15 (Paris)						
Wales 16 Ireland 0 (Cardiff)						
England 13 Scotland 8 (Twickenham)						
Ireland 25 France 5 (Cork)						

1911/12		W	D	L	For	Ag
France 6 Ireland 11 (Paris)	England	3	0	1	44	16
Scotland 31 France 3 (Inverleith)	Ireland	3	0	1	33	34
England 8 Wales 0 (Twickenham)	Scotland	2	0	2	53	37
Wales 21 Scotland 6 (Swansea)	Wales	2	0	2	40	34
England 15 Ireland 0 (Twickenham)	France	0	0	4	25	74
Ireland 10 Scotland 8 (Dublin)						
Ireland 12 Wales 5 (Belfast)						
Scotland 8 England 3 (Inverleith)						
Wales 14 France 8 (Newport)						
France 8 England 18 (Paris)						

1912/13		W	D	L	For	Ag
France 3 Scotland 21 (Paris)	England	4	0	0	50	4
Wales 0 England 12 (Cardiff)	Wales	3	0	1	35	33
England 20 France 0 (Twickenham)	Scotland	2	0	2	50	28
Scotland 0 Wales 8 (Inverleith)	Ireland	1	0	3	55	60
Ireland 4 England 15 (Dublin)	France	0	0	4	11	76
Scotland 29 Ireland 14 (Inverleith)						

France 8 Wales 11 (Paris)
Wales 16 Ireland 13 (Swansea)
England 3 Scotland 0 (Twickenham)
Ireland 24 France 0 (Cork)

1913/14

France 6 Ireland 8 (Paris)
England 10 Wales 9 (Twickenham)
Wales 24 Scotland 5 (Cardiff)
England 17 Ireland 12 (Twickenham)
Ireland 6 Scotland 0 (Dublin)
Wales 31 France 0 (Swansea)
Ireland 3 Wales 11 (Belfast)
Scotland 15 England 16 (Inverleith)
France 13 England 39 (Paris)

	W	D	L	For	Ag
England	4	0	0	82	49
Wales	3	0	1	75	18
Ireland	2	0	2	29	34
Scotland	0	0	3	20	46
France	0	0	3	19	78

Championship suspended during the First World War

1919/20

France 0 Scotland 5 (Paris)
Wales 19 England 5 (Swansea)
England 8 France 3 (Twickenham)
Scotland 9 Wales 5 (Inverleith)
Ireland 11 England 14 (Dublin)
France 5 Wales 6 (Paris)
Scotland 19 Ireland 0 (Inverleith)
Wales 28 Ireland 4 (Cardiff)
England 13 Scotland 4 (Twickenham)
Ireland 7 France 14 (Dublin)

	W	D	L	For	Ag
Wales	3	0	1	58	23
England	3	0	1	40	37
Scotland	3	0	1	37	18
France	1	0	3	23	26
Ireland	0	0	4	22	76

NB: Scotland and France did not meet

1920/21

England 18 Wales 3 (Twickenham)
Scotland 0 France 3 (Inverleith)
Wales 8 Scotland 14 (Swansea)
England 15 Ireland 0 (Twickenham)
Wales 12 France 4 (Cardiff)
Ireland 9 Scotland 8 (Dublin)
Ireland 0 Wales 6 (Belfast)
Scotland 0 England 18 (Inverleith)
France 6 England 10 (Paris)
France 20 Ireland 10 (Paris)

	W	D	L	For	Ag
England	4	0	0	61	9
France	2	0	2	33	32
Wales	2	0	2	29	36
Scotland	1	0	3	22	38
Ireland	1	0	3	19	49

1921/22

France 3 Scotland 3 (Paris)
Wales 28 England 6 (Cardiff)
Scotland 9 Wales 9 (Inverleith)
Ireland 3 England 12 (Dublin)
Scotland 6 Ireland 3 (Inverleith)
England 11 France 11 (Twickenham)
Wales 11 Ireland 5 (Swansea)
England 11 Scotland 5 (Twickenham)
France 3 Wales 11 (Paris)
Ireland 8 France 3 (Dublin)

	W	D	L	For	Ag
Wales	3	1	0	59	23
England	2	1	1	40	47
Scotland	1	2	1	23	26
France	0	2	2	20	33
Ireland	1	0	3	19	32

1922/23

	W	D	L	For	Ag
England	4	0	0	50	17
Scotland	3	0	1	46	22
Wales	1	0	3	31	31
France	1	0	3	28	52
Ireland	1	0	3	21	54

Scotland 16 France 3 (Inverleith)
England 7 Wales 3 (Twickenham)
Wales 8 Scotland 11 (Cardiff)
England 23 Ireland 5 (Leicester)
Ireland 3 Scotland 13 (Dublin)
Wales 16 France 8 (Swansea)
Ireland 5 Wales 4 (Dublin)
Scotland 6 England 8 (Inverleith)
France 3 England 12 (Paris)
France 14 Ireland 8 (Paris)

1923/24

	W	D	L	For	Ag
England	4	0	0	69	19
Scotland	2	0	2	58	49
Ireland	2	0	2	30	37
Wales	1	0	3	39	71
France	1	0	3	25	45

France 12 Scotland 10 (Paris)
Wales 9 England 17 (Swansea)
Ireland 6 France 0 (Dublin)
Scotland 35 Wales 10 (Inverleith)
Ireland 3 England 14 (Belfast)
England 19 France 7 (Twickenham)
Scotland 13 Ireland 8 (Inverleith)
Wales 10 Ireland 13 (Cardiff)
England 19 Scotland 0 (Twickenham)
France 6 Wales 10 (Paris)

1924/25

	W	D	L	For	Ag
Scotland	4	0	0	77	37
Ireland	2	1	1	42	26
England	2	1	1	42	37
Wales	1	0	3	34	60
France	0	0	4	23	58

France 3 Ireland 9 (Paris)
England 12 Wales 6 (Twickenham)
Scotland 25 France 4 (Inverleith)
Wales 14 Scotland 24 (Swansea)
England 6 Ireland 6 (Twickenham)
Ireland 8 Scotland 14 (Dublin)
Wales 11 France 5 (Cardiff)
Ireland 19 Wales 3 (Belfast)
Scotland 14 England 11 (Murrayfield)
France 11 England 13 (Paris)

1925/26

	W	D	L	For	Ag
Scotland	3	0	1	45	23
Ireland	3	0	1	41	26
Wales	2	1	1	26	24
England	1	1	2	38	39
France	0	0	4	11	49

France 6 Scotland 20 (Paris)
Wales 3 England 3 (Cardiff)
Ireland 11 France 0 (Belfast)
Scotland 8 Wales 5 (Murrayfield)
Ireland 19 England 15 (Dublin)
Scotland 0 Ireland 3 (Murrayfield)
England 11 France 0 (Twickenham)
Wales 11 Ireland 8 (Swansea)
England 9 Scotland 17 (Twickenham)
France 5 Wales 7 (Paris)

1926/27

	W	D	L	For	Ag
Scotland	3	0	1	49	25
Ireland	3	0	1	39	20
England	2	0	2	32	39
Wales	1	0	3	43	42
France	1	0	3	19	56

France 3 Ireland 8 (Paris)
England 11 Wales 9 (Twickenham)
Scotland 23 France 6 (Murrayfield)
Wales 0 Scotland 5 (Cardiff)
England 8 Ireland 6 (Twickenham)
Ireland 6 Scotland 0 (Dublin)
Wales 25 France 7 (Cardiff)
Ireland 19 Wales 9 (Dublin)
Scotland 21 England 13 (Murrayfield)
France 3 England 0 (Paris)

1927/28

	W	D	L	For	Ag
England	4	0	0	41	22
Ireland	3	0	1	44	30
Wales	1	0	3	34	31
France	1	0	3	30	48
Scotland	1	0	3	20	38

France 6 Scotland 15 (Paris)
Wales 8 England 10 (Belfast)
Ireland 12 France 8
Scotland 0 Wales 13 (Murrayfield)
Ireland 6 England 7 (Dublin)
England 18 France 8 (Twickenham)
Scotland 5 Ireland 13 (Murrayfield)
Wales 10 Ireland 13 (Cardiff)
England 6 Scotland 0 (Twickenham)
France 8 Wales 3 (Paris)

1928/29

	W	D	L	For	Ag
Scotland	3	0	1	41	30
Wales	2	1	1	30	23
Ireland	2	1	1	24	26
England	2	0	2	35	27
France	0	0	4	12	36

France 0 Ireland 6 (Paris)
England 8 Wales 3 (Twickenham)
Scotland 6 France 3 (Murrayfield)
Wales 14 Scotland 7 (Swansea)
England 5 Ireland 6 (Twickenham)
Ireland 7 Scotland 16 (Dublin)
Wales 8 France 3 (Cardiff)
Ireland 5 Wales 5 (Belfast)
Scotland 12 England 6 (Murrayfield)
France 6 England 16 (Paris)

1929/30

	W	D	L	For	Ag
England	2	1	1	25	12
Wales	2	0	2	35	30
Ireland	2	0	2	25	31
France	2	0	2	17	25
Scotland	1	1	2	26	30

France 7 Scotland 3 (Paris)
Wales 3 England 11 (Cardiff)
Ireland 0 France 5 (Belfast)
Scotland 12 Wales 9 (Murrayfield)
Ireland 4 England 3 (Dublin)
England 11 France 5 (Twickenham)
Scotland 11 Ireland 14 (Murrayfield)
Wales 12 Ireland 7 (Swansea)
England 0 Scotland 0 (Twickenham)
France 0 Wales 11 (Paris)

1930/31

		W	D	L	For	Ag
France 3 Ireland 0 (Paris)	Wales	3	1	0	74	25
England 11 Wales 11 (Twickenham)	Scotland	2	0	2	47	44
Scotland 6 France 4 (Murrayfield)	France	2	0	2	24	44
Wales 13 Scotland 8 (Cardiff)	Ireland	2	0	2	17	28
England 5 Ireland 6 (Twickenham)	England	0	1	3	38	59
Ireland 8 Scotland 5 (Dublin)						
Wales 35 France 3 (Swansea)						
Ireland 3 Wales 15 (Belfast)						
Scotland 28 England 19 (Murrayfield)						
France 14 England 13 (Paris)						

France suspended from the championship

1931/32

		W	D	L	For	Ag
Wales 12 England 5 (Swansea)	Ireland	2	0	1	40	29
Scotland 0 Wales 6 (Murrayfield)	England	2	0	1	32	23
Ireland 8 England 11 (Dublin)	Wales	2	0	1	28	17
Scotland 8 Ireland 20 (Murrayfield)	Scotland	0	0	3	11	42
Wales 10 Ireland 12 (Cardiff)						
England 16 Scotland 3 (Twickenham)						

1932/33

		W	D	L	For	Ag
England 3 Wales 7 (Twickenham)	Scotland	3	0	0	22	9
Wales 3 Scotland 11 (Swansea)	Ireland	1	0	2	22	30
England 17 Ireland 6 (Twickenham)	England	1	0	2	20	16
Ireland 10 Wales 5 (Dublin)	Wales	1	0	2	15	24
Scotland 3 England 0 (Murrayfield)						
Ireland 6 Scotland 8 (Dublin)						

1933/34

		W	D	L	For	Ag
Wales 0 England 9 (Cardiff)	England	3	0	0	28	6
Scotland 6 Wales 13 (Murrayfield)	Wales	2	0	1	26	15
Ireland 3 England 13 (Dublin)	Scotland	1	0	2	25	28
Scotland 16 Ireland 9 (Murrayfield)	Ireland	0	0	3	12	42
Wales 13 Ireland 0 (Swansea)						
England 6 Scotland 3 (Twickenham)						

1934/35

		W	D	L	For	Ag
England 3 Wales 3 (Twickenham)	Ireland	2	0	1	24	22
Wales 10 Scotland 6 (Cardiff)	England	1	1	1	24	16
England 14 Ireland 3 (Twickenham)	Wales	1	1	1	16	18
Ireland 12 Scotland 5 (Dublin)	Scotland	1	0	2	21	29
Ireland 9 Wales 3 (Belfast)						
Scotland 10 England 7 (Murrayfield)						

1935/36		**W**	**D**	**L**	**For**	**Ag**

Wales 0 England 0 (Swansea)
Scotland 3 Wales 13 (Murrayfield)
Ireland 6 England 3 (Dublin)
Scotland 4 Ireland 10 (Murrayfield)
Wales 3 Ireland 0 (Cardiff)
England 9 Scotland 8 (Twickenham)

	W	**D**	**L**	**For**	**Ag**
Wales	2	1	0	16	3
Ireland	2	0	1	16	10
England	1	1	1	12	14
Scotland	0	0	3	15	32

1936/37		**W**	**D**	**L**	**For**	**Ag**

England 4 Wales 3 (Twickenham)
Wales 6 Scotland 13 (Swansea)
England 9 Ireland 8 (Twickenham)
Ireland 11 Scotland 4 (Dublin)
Scotland 3 England 6 (Murrayfield)
Ireland 5 Wales 3 (Belfast)

	W	**D**	**L**	**For**	**Ag**
England	3	0	0	19	14
Ireland	2	0	1	24	16
Scotland	1	0	2	20	23
Wales	0	0	3	12	22

1937/38		**W**	**D**	**L**	**For**	**Ag**

Wales 14 England 8 (Cardiff)
Scotland 8 Wales 6 (Murrayfield)
Ireland 14 England 36 (Dublin)
Scotland 23 Ireland 14 (Murrayfield)
Wales 11 Ireland 5 (Swansea)
England 16 Scotland 21 (Twickenham)

	W	**D**	**L**	**For**	**Ag**
Scotland	3	0	0	52	36
Wales	2	0	1	31	21
England	1	0	2	60	49
Ireland	0	0	3	33	70

1938/39		**W**	**D**	**L**	**For**	**Ag**

England 3 Wales 0 (Twickenham)
Wales 11 Scotland 3 (Cardiff)
England 0 Ireland 5 (Twickenham)
Ireland 12 Scotland 3 (Dublin)
Ireland 0 Wales 7 (Belfast)
Scotland 6 England 9 (Murrayfield)

	W	**D**	**L**	**For**	**Ag**
Wales	2	0	1	18	6
Ireland	2	0	1	17	10
England	2	0	1	12	11
Scotland	0	0	3	12	32

Championship suspended during the Second World War

1946/47		**W**	**D**	**L**	**For**	**Ag**

France 8 Scotland 3 (Paris)
Wales 6 England 9 (Cardiff)
Ireland 8 France 12 (Dublin)
Scotland 8 Wales 22 (Murrayfield)
Ireland 22 England 0 (Dublin)
Scotland 0 Ireland 3 (Murrayfield)
England 24 Scotland 5 (Twickenham)
France 0 Wales 3 (Paris)
Wales 6 Ireland 0 (Swansea)
England 6 France 3 (Twickenham)

	W	**D**	**L**	**For**	**Ag**
England	3	0	1	39	36
Wales	3	0	1	37	17
Ireland	2	0	2	33	18
France	2	0	2	23	20
Scotland	0	0	4	16	57

1947/48

	W	D	L	For	Ag
Ireland	4	0	0	36	19
France	2	0	2	40	25
Scotland	2	0	2	15	31
Wales	1	1	2	23	20
England	0	1	3	16	35

France 6 Ireland 13 (Paris)
England 3 Wales 3 (Twickenham)
Scotland 9 France 8 (Murrayfield)
Wales 14 Scotland 0 (Cardiff)
England 10 Ireland 11 (Twickenham)
Wales 3 France 11 (Swansea)
Ireland 6 Scotland 0 (Dublin)
Ireland 6 Wales 3 (Belfast)
Scotland 6 England 3 (Murrayfield)
France 15 England 0 (Paris)

1948/49

	W	D	L	For	Ag
Ireland	3	0	1	41	24
England	2	0	2	35	29
France	2	0	2	24	28
Scotland	2	0	2	20	37
Wales	1	0	3	17	19

France 0 Scotland 8 (Paris)
Wales 9 England 3 (Cardiff)
Ireland 9 France 16 (Dublin)
Scotland 6 Wales 5 (Murrayfield)
Ireland 14 England 5 (Dublin)
England 8 France 3 (Twickenham)
Scotland 3 Ireland 13 (Murrayfield)
Wales 0 Ireland 5 (Swansea)
England 19 Scotland 3 (Twickenham)
France 5 Wales 3 (Paris)

1949/50

	W	D	L	For	Ag
Wales	4	0	0	50	8
Scotland	2	0	2	21	49
Ireland	1	1	2	27	12
France	1	1	2	14	35
England	1	0	3	22	30

Scotland 8 France 5 (Murrayfield)
England 5 Wales 11 (Twickenham)
France 3 Ireland 3 (Paris)
Wales 12 Scotland 0 (Swansea)
England 3 Ireland 0 (Twickenham)
France 6 England 3 (Paris)
Ireland 21 Scotland 0 (Dublin)
Ireland 3 Wales 6 (Belfast)
Scotland 13 England 11 (Murrayfield)
Wales 21 France 0 (Cardiff)

1950/51

	W	D	L	For	Ag
Ireland	3	1	0	21	16
France	3	0	1	41	27
Wales	1	1	2	29	35
Scotland	1	0	3	39	25
England	1	0	3	13	40

France 14 Scotland 12 (Paris)
Wales 23 England 5 (Swansea)
Ireland 9 France 8 (Dublin)
Scotland 19 Wales 0 (Murrayfield)
Ireland 3 England 0 (Dublin)
England 3 France 11 (Twickenham)
Scotland 5 Ireland 6 (Murrayfield)
Wales 3 Ireland 3 (Cardiff)
England 5 Scotland 3 (Twickenham)
France 8 Wales 3 (Paris)

1951/52

	W	D	L	For	Ag

Scotland 11 France 13 (Murrayfield)
England 6 Wales 8 (Twickenham)
France 8 Ireland 11 (Paris)
Wales 11 Scotland 0 (Cardiff)
Ireland 12 Scotland 8 (Dublin)
Ireland 3 Wales 14 (Dublin)
Scotland 3 England 19 (Murrayfield)
Wales 9 France 5 (Swansea)
England 3 Ireland 0 (Twickenham)
France 3 England 6 (Paris)

	W	D	L	For	Ag
Walesa	4	0	0	42	14
England	3	0	1	34	14
Ireland	2	0	2	26	33
France	1	0	3	29	37
Scotland	0	0	4	22	55

1952/53

France 11 Scotland 5 (Paris)
Wales 3 England 8 (Cardiff)
Ireland 16 France 3 (Belfast)
Scotland 0 Wales 12 (Murrayfield)
Ireland 9 England 9 (Dublin)
England 11 France 0 (Twickenham)
Scotland 8 Ireland 26 (Murrayfield)
Wales 5 Ireland 3 (Swansea)
England 26 Scotland 8 (Twickenham)
France 3 Wales 6 (Paris)

	W	D	L	For	Ag
England	3	1	0	54	20
Wales	3	0	1	26	14
Ireland	2	1	1	54	25
France	1	0	3	17	38
Scotland	0	0	4	21	75

1953/54

Scotland 0 France 3 (Murrayfield)
England 9 Wales 6 (Twickenham)
France 8 Ireland 0 (Paris)
England 14 Ireland 3 (Twickenham)
Ireland 6 Scotland 0 (Belfast)
Ireland 9 Wales 12 (Dublin)
Scotland 3 England 13 (Murrayfield)
Wales 19 France 13 (Cardiff)
France 11 England 3 (Paris)
Wales 15 Scotland 3 (Swansea)

	W	D	L	For	Ag
Wales	3	0	1	52	34
England	3	0	1	39	23
France	3	0	1	35	22
Ireland	1	0	3	18	34
Scotland	0	0	4	6	37

1954/55

France 15 Scotland 0 (Paris)
Ireland 3 France 5 (Dublin)
Wales 3 England 0 (Cardiff)
Scotland 14 Wales 8 (Murrayfield)
Ireland 6 England 6 (Dublin)
England 9 France 16 (Twickenham)
Scotland 12 Ireland 3 (Murrayfield)
Wales 21 Ireland 3 (Cardiff)
England 9 Scotland 6 (Twickenham)
France 11 Wales 16 (Paris)

	W	D	L	For	Ag
Wales	3	0	1	48	28
France	3	0	1	47	28
Scotland	2	0	2	32	35
England	1	1	2	24	31
Ireland	0	1	3	15	44

1955/56

	W	D	L	For	Ag
Wales	3	0	1	25	20
England	2	0	2	43	28
Ireland	2	0	2	33	47
France	2	0	2	31	34
Scotland	1	0	3	31	34

Scotland 12 France 0 (Murrayfield)
England 3 Wales 8 (Twickenham)
France 14 Ireland 8 (Paris)
Wales 9 Scotland 3 (Cardiff)
England 20 Ireland 0 (Twickenham)
Ireland 14 Scotland 10 (Dublin)
Ireland 11 Wales 3 (Dublin)
Scotland 6 England 11 (Murrayfield)
Wales 5 France 3 (Cardiff)
France 14 England 9 (Paris)

1956/57

	W	D	L	For	Ag
England	4	0	0	34	8
Wales	2	0	2	31	30
Ireland	2	0	2	21	21
Scotland	2	0	2	21	27
France	0	0	4	24	45

France 0 Scotland 6 (Paris)
Wales 0 England 3 (Cardiff)
Ireland 11 France 6 (Dublin)
Scotland 9 Wales 6 (Murrayfield)
Ireland 0 England 6 (Dublin)
England 9 France 5 (Twickenham)
Scotland 3 Ireland 5 (Murrayfield)
Wales 6 Ireland 5 (Cardiff)
England 16 Scotland 3 (Twickenham)
France 13 Wales 19 (Paris)

1957/58

	W	D	L	For	Ag
England	2	2	0	26	6
Wales	2	1	1	26	28
France	2	0	2	36	37
Scotland	1	1	2	23	32
Ireland	1	0	3	24	32

Scotland 11 France 9 (Murrayfield)
England 3 Wales 3 (Twickenham)
Wales 8 Scotland 3 (Cardiff)
England 6 Ireland 0 (Twickenham)
France 0 England 14 (Paris)
Ireland 12 Scotland 6 (Dublin)
Ireland 6 Wales 9 (Dublin)
Scotland 3 England 3 (Murrayfield)
Wales 6 France 16 (Cardiff)
France 11 Ireland 6 (Paris)

1958/59

	W	D	L	For	Ag
France	2	1	1	28	15
Ireland	2	0	2	23	19
Wales	2	0	2	21	23
England	1	2	1	9	11
Scotland	1	1	2	12	25

France 9 Scotland 0 (Paris)
Wales 5 England 0 (Cardiff)
Scotland 6 Wales 5 (Murrayfield)
Ireland 0 England 3 (Dublin)
England 3 France 3 (Twickenham)
Scotland 3 Ireland 8 (Murrayfield)
Wales 8 Ireland 6 (Cardiff)
England 3 Scotland 3 (Twickenham)
France 11 Wales 3 (Paris)
Ireland 9 France 5 (Dublin)

1959/60

	W	D	L	For	Ag
France	3	1	0	55	28
England	3	1	0	46	26
Wales	2	0	2	32	39
Scotland	1	0	3	29	47
Ireland	0	0	4	25	47

Scotland 11 France 13 (Murrayfield)
England 14 Wales 6 (Twickenham)
Wales 8 Scotland 0 (Cardiff)
England 8 Ireland 5 (Twickenham)
France 3 England 3 (Paris)
Ireland 5 Scotland 6 (Dublin)
Ireland 9 Wales 10 (Dublin)
Scotland 12 England 21 (Murrayfield)
Wales 8 France 16 (Cardiff)
France 23 Ireland 6 (Paris)

1960/61

	W	D	L	For	Ag
France	3	1	0	39	14
Wales	2	0	2	21	14
Scotland	2	0	2	19	25
England	1	1	2	22	22
Ireland	1	0	3	22	48

France 11 Scotland 0 (Paris)
Wales 6 England 3 (Cardiff)
Ireland 11 England 8 (Dublin)
Scotland 3 Wales 0 (Murrayfield)
England 5 France 5 (Twickenham)
Scotland 16 Ireland 8 (Murrayfield)
Wales 9 Ireland 0 (Cardiff)
England 6 Scotland 0 (Twickenham)
France 8 Wales 6 (Paris)
Ireland 3 France 15 (Dublin)

1961/62

	W	D	L	For	Ag
France	3	0	1	35	6
Scotland	2	1	1	34	23
England	1	2	1	19	16
Wales	1	2	1	9	11
Ireland	0	1	3	9	50

Scotland 3 France 11 (Murrayfield)
England 0 Wales 0 (Twickenham)
Wales 3 Scotland 8 (Cardiff)
England 16 Ireland 0 (Twickenham)
France 13 England 0 (Paris)
Ireland 6 Scotland 20 (Dublin)
Scotland 3 England 3 (Murrayfield)
Wales 3 France 0 (Cardiff)
France 11 Ireland 0 (Paris)
Ireland 3 Wales 3 (Dublin) – postponed to 17.11.62 because of smallpox epidemic

1962/63

	W	D	L	For	Ag
England	3	1	0	29	19
France	2	0	2	40	25
Scotland	2	0	2	22	22
Ireland	1	1	2	19	33
Wales	1	0	3	21	32

France 6 Scotland 11 (Paris)
Wales 6 England 13 (Cardiff)
Ireland 5 France 24 (Dublin)
Scotland 0 Wales 6 (Murrayfield)
Ireland 0 England 0 (Dublin)
England 6 France 5 (Twickenham)
Scotland 3 Ireland 0 (Murrayfield)
Wales 6 Ireland 14 (Cardiff)
England 10 Scotland 8 (Twickenham)
France 5 Wales 3 (Paris)

1963/64

	W	D	L	For	Ag
Wales	2	2	0	43	26
Scotland	3	0	1	34	20
France	1	1	2	41	33
England	1	1	2	23	42
Ireland	1	0	3	33	53

Scotland 10 France 0 (Murrayfield)
England 6 Wales 6 (Twickenham)
Wales 11 Scotland 3 (Cardiff)
England 5 Ireland 18 (Twickenham)
France 3 England 6 (Paris)
Ireland 3 Scotland 6 (Dublin)
Ireland 6 Wales 15 (Dublin)
Scotland 15 England 6 (Murrayfield)
Wales 11 France 11 (Cardiff)
France 27 Ireland 6 (Paris)

1964/65

	W	D	L	For	Ag
Wales	3	0	1	55	45
France	2	1	1	47	33
Ireland	2	1	1	32	23
England	1	1	2	15	28
Scotland	0	1	3	29	49

France 16 Scotland 8 (Paris)
Wales 14 England 3 (Cardiff)
Ireland 3 France 3 (Dublin)
Scotland 12 Wales 14 (Murrayfield)
Ireland 5 England 0 (Dublin)
England 9 France 6 (Twickenham)
Scotland 6 Ireland 16 (Murrayfield)
Wales 14 Ireland 8 (Cardiff)
England 3 Scotland 3 (Twickenham)
France 22 Wales 13 (Paris)

1965/66

	W	D	L	For	Ag
Wales	3	0	1	34	26
France	2	1	1	35	18
Scotland	2	1	1	23	17
Ireland	1	1	2	24	34
England	0	1	3	15	36

England 6 Wales 11 (Twickenham)
Scotland 3 France 3 (Murrayfield)
France 11 Ireland 6 (Paris)
Wales 8 Scotland 3 (Cardiff)
England 6 Ireland 6 (Twickenham)
France 13 England 0 (Paris)
Ireland 3 Scotland 11 (Dublin)
Ireland 9 Wales 6 (Dublin)
Scotland 6 England 3 (Murrayfield)
Wales 9 France 8 (Cardiff)

1966/67

	W	D	L	For	Ag
France	3	0	1	55	41
England	2	0	2	68	67
Scotland	2	0	2	37	45
Ireland	2	0	2	17	22
Wales	1	0	3	53	55

France 8 Scotland 9 (Paris)
Scotland 11 Wales 5 (Murrayfield)
Ireland 3 England 8 (Dublin)
England 12 France 16 (Twickenham)
Scotland 3 Ireland 5 (Murrayfield)
Wales 0 Ireland 3 (Cardiff)
England 27 Scotland 14 (Twickenham)
France 20 Wales 14 (Paris)
Ireland 6 France 11 (Dublin)
Wales 34 England 21 (Cardiff)

1967/68		**W**	**D**	**L**	**For**	**Ag**
Scotland 6 France 8 (Murrayfield)	France	4	0	0	52	30
England 11 Wales 11 (Twickenham)	Ireland	2	1	1	38	37
France 16 Ireland 6 (Paris)	England	1	2	1	37	40
Wales 5 Scotland 0 (Cardiff)	Wales	1	1	2	31	34
England 9 Ireland 9 (Twickenham)	Scotland	0	0	4	18	35
France 14 England 9 (Paris)						
Ireland 14 Scotland 6 (Dublin)						
Ireland 9 Wales 6 (Dublin)						
Scotland 6 England 8 (Murrayfield)						
Wales 9 France 14 (Cardiff)						

1968/69		**W**	**D**	**L**	**For**	**Ag**
France 3 Scotland 6 (Paris)	Wales	3	1	0	79	31
Ireland 17 France 9 (Dublin)	Ireland	3	0	1	61	48
Scotland 3 Wales 17 (Murrayfield)	England	2	0	2	54	58
Ireland 17 England 15 (Dublin)	Scotland	1	0	3	12	44
England 22 France 8 (Twickenham)	France	0	1	3	28	53
Scotland 0 Ireland 16 (Murrayfield)						
Wales 24 Ireland 11 (Cardiff)						
England 8 Scotland 3 (Twickenham)						
France 8 Wales 8 (Paris)						
Wales 30 England 9 (Cardiff)						

1969/70		**W**	**D**	**L**	**For**	**Ag**
Scotland 9 France 11 (Murrayfield)	France	3	0	1	60	33
France 8 Ireland 0 (Paris)	Wales	3	0	1	46	42
Wales 18 Scotland 9 (Cardiff)	Ireland	2	0	2	33	28
England 9 Ireland 3 (Twickenham)	Scotland	1	0	3	43	50
England 13 Wales 17 (Twickenham)	England	1	0	3	40	69
Ireland 16 Scotland 11 (Dublin)						
Ireland 14 Wales 0 (Dublin)						
Scotland 14 England 5 (Murrayfield)						
Wales 11 France 6 (Cardiff)						
France 35 England 13 (Paris)						

1970/71		**W**	**D**	**L**	**For**	**Ag**
France 13 Scotland 8 (Paris)	Wales	4	0	0	73	38
Wales 22 England 9 (Cardiff)	France	1	2	1	41	40
Ireland 9 France 9 (Dublin)	England	1	1	2	44	58
Scotland 18 Wales 19 (Murrayfield)	Ireland	1	1	2	41	46
Ireland 6 England 9 (Dublin)	Scotland	1	0	3	47	64
England 14 France 14 (Twickenham)						
Scotland 5 Ireland 17 (Murrayfield)						
Wales 23 Ireland 9 (Cardiff)						
England 15 Scotland 16 (Twickenham)						
France 5 Wales 9 (Paris)						

1971/72		W	D	L	For	Ag
England 3 Wales 12 (Twickenham)	Wales	3	0	0	67	21
Scotland 20 France 9 (Murrayfield)	Scotland	2	0	1	55	53
France 9 Ireland 14 (Paris)	Ireland	2	0	0	30	21
Wales 35 Scotland 12 (Cardiff)	France	1	0	3	61	66
England 12 Ireland 16 (Twickenham)	England	0	0	4	36	88
France 37 England 12 (Paris)						
Scotland 23 England 9 (Murrayfield)						
Wales 20 France 6 (Cardiff)						

Wales and Scotland refused to play Ireland because of terrorist activities

1972/73		W	D	L	For	Ag
France 16 Scotland 13 (Paris)	Scotland	2	0	2	55	59
Wales 25 England 9 (Cardiff)	Wales	2	0	2	53	43
Scotland 10 Wales 9 (Murrayfield)	England	2	0	2	52	62
Ireland 18 England 9 (Dublin)	Ireland	2	0	2	50	48
England 14 France 6 (Twickenham)	France	2	0	2	38	36
Scotland 19 Ireland 14 (Murrayfield)						
Wales 16 Ireland 12 (Cardiff)						
England 20 Scotland 13 (Twickenham)						
France 12 Wales 3 (Paris)						
Ireland 6 France 4 (Dublin)						

1973/74		W	D	L	For	Ag
France 9 Ireland 6 (Paris)	Ireland	2	1	1	50	45
Wales 6 Scotland 0 (Cardiff)	Wales	1	2	1	43	41
Ireland 9 Wales 9 (Dublin)	France	1	2	1	43	53
Scotland 16 England 14 (Murrayfield)	Scotland	2	0	2	41	35
England 21 Ireland 26 (Twickenham)	England	1	1	2	63	66
Wales 16 France 16 (Cardiff)						
France 12 England 12 (Paris)						
Ireland 9 Scotland 6 (Dublin)						
England 16 Wales 12 (Twickenham)						
Scotland 19 France 6 (Murrayfield)						

1974/75		W	D	L	For	Ag
France 10 Wales 25 (Paris)	Wales	3	0	1	87	30
Ireland 12 England 9 (Dublin)	Ireland	2	0	2	54	67
England 20 France 27 (Twickenham)	France	2	0	2	53	79
Scotland 20 Ireland 13 (Murrayfield)	Scotland	2	0	2	47	40
France 10 Scotland 9 (Paris)	England	1	0	3	40	65
Wales 20 England 4 (Cardiff)						
Ireland 25 France 6 (Dublin)						
Scotland 12 Wales 10 (Murrayfield)						
England 7 Scotland 6 (Twickenham)						
Wales 32 Ireland 4 (Cardiff)						

1975/76		W	D	L	For	Ag

Scotland 6 France 13 (Murrayfield)

		W	D	L	For	Ag
	Wales	4	0	0	102	37
	France	3	0	1	82	37
	Scotland	2	0	2	49	59
	Ireland	1	0	3	31	87
	England	0	0	4	42	86

England 9 Wales 21 (Twickenham)
France 26 Ireland 3 (Paris)
Wales 28 Scotland 6 (Cardiff)
Ireland 9 Wales 34 (Dublin)
Scotland 22 England 12 (Murrayfield)
England 12 Ireland 13 (Twickenham)
Wales 19 France 13 (Cardiff)
France 30 England 9 (Paris)
Ireland 6 Scotland 15 (Dublin)

1976/77		W	D	L	For	Ag

England 26 Scotland 6 (Twickenham)

		W	D	L	For	Ag
	France	4	0	0	58	21
	Wales	3	0	1	66	43
	England	2	0	2	42	24
	Scotland	1	0	3	39	85
	Ireland	0	0	4	33	65

Wales 25 Ireland 9 (Cardiff)
France 16 Wales 9 (Paris)
Ireland 0 England 4 (Dublin)
England 3 France 4 (Twickenham)
Scotland 21 Ireland 18 (Murrayfield)
France 23 Scotland 3 (Paris)
Wales 14 England 9 (Cardiff)
Ireland 6 France 15 (Dublin)
Scotland 9 Wales 18 (Murrayfield)

1977/78		W	D	L	For	Ag

France 15 England 6 (Paris)

		W	D	L	For	Ag
	Wales	4	0	0	67	43
	France	3	0	1	51	47
	England	2	0	2	42	33
	Ireland	1	0	3	46	54
	Scotland	0	0	4	39	68

Ireland 12 Scotland 9 (Dublin)
England 6 Wales 9 (Twickenham)
Scotland 16 France 19 (Murrayfield)
France 10 Ireland 9 (Paris)
Wales 22 Scotland 14 (Cardiff)
Ireland 16 Wales 20 (Dublin)
Scotland 0 England 15 (Murrayfield)
England 15 Ireland 9 (Twickenham)
Wales 16 France 7 (Cardiff)

1978/79		W	D	L	For	Ag

Ireland 9 France 9 (Dublin)

		W	D	L	For	Ag
	Wales	3	0	1	83	51
	France	2	1	1	50	46
	Ireland	1	2	1	53	51
	England	1	1	2	24	52
	Scotland	0	2	2	48	58

Scotland 13 Wales 19 (Murrayfield)
England 7 Scotland 7 (Twickenham)
Wales 24 Ireland 21 (Cardiff)
France 14 Wales 13 (Paris)
Ireland 12 England 7 (Dublin)
England 7 France 6 (Twickenham)
Scotland 11 Ireland 11 (Murrayfield)
France 21 Scotland 17 (Paris)
Wales 27 England 3 (Cardiff)

1979/80

			W	D	L	For	Ag
England 24 Ireland 9 (Twickenham)	England		4	0	0	80	48
Wales 18 France 9 (Cardiff)	Ireland		2	0	2	70	65
France 13 England 17 (Paris)	Wales		2	0	2	50	45
Ireland 22 Scotland 15 (Dublin)	Scotland		1	0	3	61	83
England 9 Wales 8 (Twickenham)	France		1	0	3	55	75
Scotland 22 France 14 (Murrayfield)							
France 19 Ireland 18 (Paris)							
Wales 17 Scotland 6 (Cardiff)							
Ireland 21 Wales 7 (Dublin)							
Scotland 18 England 30 (Murrayfield)							

1980/81

			W	D	L	For	Ag
France 16 Scotland 9 (Paris)	France		4	0	0	70	49
Wales 21 England 19 (Cardiff)	England		2	0	2	64	60
Ireland 13 France 19 (Dublin)	Scotland		2	0	2	51	54
Scotland 15 Wales 6 (Murrayfield)	Wales		2	0	2	51	61
England 23 Scotland 17 (Twickenham)	Ireland		0	0	4	36	48
Wales 9 Ireland 8 (Cardiff)							
France 19 Wales 15 (Paris)							
Ireland 6 England 10 (Dublin)							
England 12 France 16 (Twickenham)							
Scotland 10 Ireland 9 (Murrayfield)							

1981/82

			W	D	L	For	Ag
Scotland 9 England 9 (Murrayfield)	Ireland		3	0	1	66	61
Ireland 20 Wales 12 (Dublin)	Scotland		2	1	1	71	55
England 15 Ireland 16 (Twickenham)	England		2	1	1	68	47
Wales 22 France 12 (Cardiff)	Wales		1	0	3	59	83
France 15 England 27 (Paris)	France		1	0	3	56	74
Ireland 21 Scotland 12 (Dublin)							
England 17 Wales 7 (Twickenham)							
Scotland 16 France 7 (Murrayfield)							
France 22 Ireland 9 (Paris)							
Wales 18 Scotland 34 (Cardiff)							

1982/83

			W	D	L	For	Ag
England 15 France 19 (Twickenham)	Ireland		3	0	1	71	67
Scotland 13 Ireland 15 (Murrayfield)	France		3	0	1	70	61
France 19 Scotland 15 (Paris)	Wales		2	1	1	64	53
Wales 13 England 13 (Cardiff)	Scotland		1	0	3	65	65
Ireland 22 France 16 (Dublin)	England		0	1	3	55	79
Scotland 15 Wales 19 (Murrayfield)							
England 12 Scotland 22 (Twickenham)							
Wales 23 Ireland 9 (Cardiff)							
France 16 Wales 9 (Paris)							
Ireland 25 England 15 (Dublin)							

1983/84

		W	D	L	For	Ag
France 25 Ireland 12 (Paris)	Scotland	4	0	0	86	36
Wales 9 Scotland 15 (Cardiff)	France	3	0	1	90	67
Scotland 18 England 6 (Murrayfield)	Wales	2	0	2	67	60
Ireland 9 Wales 18 (Dublin)	England	1	0	3	51	83
England 12 Ireland 9 (Twickenham)	Ireland	0	0	4	39	87
Wales 16 France 21 (Cardiff)						
France 32 England 18 (Paris)						
Ireland 9 Scotland 32 (Dublin)						
Scotland 21 France 12 (Murrayfield)						
England 15 Wales 24 (Twickenham)						

1984/85

		W	D	L	For	Ag
England 9 France 9 (Twickenham)	Ireland	3	1	0	67	49
Scotland 15 Ireland 18 (Murrayfield)	France	2	2	0	49	30
France 11 Scotland 3 (Paris)	Wales	2	0	2	61	71
Ireland 15 France 15 (Dublin)	England	1	1	2	44	53
Scotland 21 Wales 25 (Murrayfield)	Scotland	0	0	4	46	64
England 10 Scotland 7 (Twickenham)						
Wales 9 Ireland 21 (Cardiff)						
Ireland 13 England 10 (Dublin)						
France 14 Wales 3 (Paris)						
Wales 24 England 15 (Cardiff)						

1985/86

		W	D	L	For	Ag
England 21 Wales 18 (Twickenham)	France	3	0	1	98	52
Scotland 18 France 17 (Murrayfield)	Scotland	3	0	1	76	54
Wales 22 Scotland 15 (Cardiff)	Wales	2	0	2	74	71
France 29 Ireland 9 (Paris)	England	2	0	2	62	100
Scotland 33 England 6 (Murrayfield)	Ireland	0	0	4	50	83
Ireland 12 Wales 19 (Dublin)						
England 25 Ireland 20 (Twickenham)						
Wales 15 France 23 (Cardiff)						
France 29 England 10 (Paris)						
Ireland 9 Scotland 10 (Dublin)						

1986/87

		W	D	L	For	Ag
Ireland 17 England 0 (Dublin)	France	4	0	0	82	59
France 16 Wales 9 (Paris)	Ireland	2	0	2	57	46
Scotland 16 Ireland 12 (Murrayfield)	Scotland	2	0	2	71	76
England 15 France 19 (Twickenham)	Wales	1	0	3	54	64
France 28 Scotland 22 (Paris)	England	1	0	3	48	67
Wales 19 England 12 (Cardiff)						
Scotland 21 Wales 15 (Murrayfield)						
Ireland 13 France 19 (Dublin)						
England 21 Scotland 12 (Twickenham)						
Wales 11 Ireland 15 (Cardiff)						

1987/88		**W**	**D**	**L**	**For**	**Ag**
France 10 England 9 (Paris)	Wales	3	0	1	57	42
Ireland 22 Scotland 18 (Dublin)	France	3	0	1	57	47
England 3 Wales 11 (Twickenham)	England	2	0	2	56	30
Scotland 23 France 12 (Murrayfield)	Scotland	1	0	3	67	68
France 25 Ireland 6 (Paris)	Ireland	1	0	3	40	90
Wales 25 Scotland 20 (Cardiff)						
Ireland 9 Wales 12 (Dublin)						
Scotland 6 England 9 (Murrayfield)						
Wales 9 France 10 (Cardiff)						
England 35 Ireland 3 (Twickenham)						

1988/89		**W**	**D**	**L**	**For**	**Ag**
Scotland 23 Wales 7 (Murrayfield)	France	3	0	1	76	47
Ireland 21 France 26 (Dublin)	England	2	1	1	48	27
Wales 13 Ireland 19 (Cardiff)	Scotland	2	1	1	75	59
England 12 Scotland 12 (Twickenham)	Ireland	1	0	3	64	92
France 31 Wales 12 (Paris)	Wales	1	0	3	44	82
Ireland 3 England 16 (Dublin)						
England 11 France 0 (Twickenham)						
Scotland 37 Ireland 21 (Murrayfield)						
France 19 Scotland 3 (Paris)						
Wales 12 England 9 (Cardiff)						

1989/90		**W**	**D**	**L**	**For**	**Ag**
England 23 Ireland 0 (Twickenham)	Scotland	4	0	0	60	26
Wales 19 France 29 (Cardiff)	England	3	0	1	90	26
France 7 England 26 (Paris)	France	2	0	2	61	78
Ireland 10 Scotland 13 (Dublin)	Ireland	1	0	3	36	75
England 34 Wales 6 (Twickenham)	Wales	0	0	4	42	84
Scotland 21 France 0 (Murrayfield)						
Wales 9 Scotland 13 (Cardiff)						
France 31 Ireland 12 (Paris)						
Scotland 13 England 7 (Murrayfield)						
Ireland 14 Wales 8 (Dublin)						

1990/91		**W**	**D**	**L**	**For**	**Ag**
France 15 Scotland 9 (Paris)	England	4	0	0	83	44
Wales 6 England 25 (Cardiff)	France	3	0	1	91	46
Scotland 32 Wales 12 (Murrayfield)	Scotland	2	0	2	81	73
Ireland 13 France 21 (Dublin)	Ireland	0	1	3	66	86
England 21 Scotland 12 (Twickenham)	Wales	0	1	3	42	114
Wales 21 Ireland 21 (Cardiff)						
Ireland 7 England 16 (Dublin)						
France 36 Wales 3 (Paris)						
England 21 France 19 (Twickenham)						
Scotland 28 Ireland 25 (Murrayfield)						

1991/92

	W	D	L	For	Ag
Ireland 15 Wales 16 (Dublin)	England	4	0	0	118	29
Scotland 7 England 25 (Murrayfield)	France	2	0	2	75	62
England 38 Ireland 9 (Twickenham)	Scotland	2	0	2	47	56
Wales 9 France 12 (Cardiff)	Wales	2	0	2	40	63
France 13 England 31 (Paris)	Ireland	0	0	4	46	116
Ireland 10 Scotland 18 (Dublin)						
England 24 Wales 0 (Twickenham)						
Scotland 10 France 6 (Murrayfield)						
Wales 15 Scotland 12 (Cardiff)						
France 44 Ireland 12 (Paris)						

1992/93

	W	D	L	For	Ag
Scotland 15 Ireland 3 (Murrayfield)	France	3	0	1	73	35
England 16 France 15 (Twickenham)	Scotland	2	0	2	50	40
Wales 10 England 9 (Cardiff)	England	2	0	2	54	54
France 11 Scotland 3 (Paris)	Ireland	2	0	2	45	53
Ireland 6 France 21 (Dublin)	Wales	1	0	3	34	74
Scotland 20 Wales 0 (Murrayfield)						
Wales 14 Ireland 19 (Cardiff)						
England 26 Scotland 12 (Twickenham)						
Ireland 17 England 3 (Dublin)						
France 26 Wales 10 (Paris)						

1993/94

	W	D	L	For	Ag
Wales 29 Scotland 6 (Cardiff)	Wales	3	0	1	78	51
France 35 Ireland 15 (Paris)	England	3	0	1	60	49
Scotland 14 England 15 (Murrayfield)	France	2	0	2	84	69
Ireland 15 Wales 17 (Dublin)	Ireland	1	1	2	49	70
England 12 Ireland 13 (Twickenham)	Scotland	0	1	3	38	70
Wales 24 France 15 (Cardiff)						
France 14 England 18 (Paris)						
Ireland 6 Scotland 6 (Dublin)						
England 15 Wales 8 (Twickenham)						
Scotland 12 France 20 (Murrayfield)						

1994/95

	W	D	L	For	Ag
Ireland 8 England 20 (Dublin)	England	4	0	0	98	39
France 21 Wales 9 (Paris)	Scotland	3	0	1	87	71
Scotland 26 Ireland 13 (Murrayfield)	France	2	0	2	77	70
England 31 France 10 (Twickenham)	Ireland	1	0	3	44	83
Wales 9 England 23 (Cardiff)	Wales	0	0	4	43	86
France 21 Scotland 23 (Paris)						
Scotland 26 Wales 13 (Murrayfield)						
Ireland 7 France 25 (Dublin)						
Wales 12 Ireland 16 (Cardiff)						
England 24 Scotland 12 (Twickenham)						

1995/96		**W**	**D**	**L**	**For**	**Ag**
Ireland 10 Scotland 16 (Dublin)	England	3	0	1	79	54
France 15 England 12 (Paris)	Scotland	3	0	1	60	56
Scotland 19 France 14 (Murrayfield)	France	2	0	2	89	57
England 21 Wales 15 (Twickenham)	Wales	1	0	3	62	82
France 45 Ireland 10 (Paris)	Ireland	1	0	3	65	106
Wales 14 Scotland 16 (Cardiff)						
Ireland 30 Wales 17 (Dublin)						
Scotland 9 England 18 (Murrayfield)						
Wales 16 France 15 (Cardiff)						
England 28 Ireland 15 (Twickenham)						

1996/97		**W**	**D**	**L**	**For**	**Ag**
Scotland 19 Wales 34 (Mrrayfield)	France	4	0	0	129	77
Ireland 15 France 32 (Dublin)	England	3	0	1	141	55
England 41 Scotland 13 (Twickenham)	Wales	1	0	3	94	106
Wales 25 Ireland 26 (Cardiff)	Scotland	1	0	3	90	132
Ireland 6 England 46 (Dublin)	Ireland	1	0	3	57	141
France 27 Wales 22 (Paris)						
Scotland 38 Ireland 10 (Murrayfield)						
England 20 France 23 (Twickenham)						
France 47 Scotland 20 (Paris)						
Wales 13 England 34 (Cardiff)						

1997/98		**W**	**D**	**L**	**For**	**Ag**
Ireland 16 Scotland 17 (Dublin)	France	4	0	0	144	49
France 24 England 17 (Paris)	England	3	0	1	146	87
England 60 Wales 26 (Twickenham)	Wales	2	0	2	75	145
Scotland 16 France 51 (Murrayfield)	Scotland	1	0	3	66	120
France 18 Ireland 16 (Paris)	Ireland	0	0	4	70	100
Wales 19 Scotland 13 (Wembley)						
Ireland 21 Wales 30 (Dublin)						
Scotland 20 England 34 (Murrayfield)						
England 35 Ireland 17 (Twickenham)						
Wales 0 France 51 (Wembley)						

1998/99		**W**	**D**	**L**	**For**	**Ag**
Ireland 9 France 10 (Dublin)	Scotland	3	0	1	120	79
Scotland 33 Wales 20 (Murrayfield)	England	3	0	1	103	78
England 24 Scotland 21 (Twickenham)	Wales	2	0	2	109	126
Wales 23 Ireland 29 (Wembley)	Ireland	1	0	3	66	90
France 33 Wales 34 (Paris)	France	1	0	3	75	100
Ireland 15 England 27 (Dublin)						
England 21 France 10 (Twickenham)						
Scotland 30 Ireland 13 (Murrayfield)						
France 22 Scotland 36 (Paris)						
Wales 32 England 31 (Wembley)						